# YEARBOOK

## ON

# HUMAN RIGHTS

## FOR 1982

**UNITED NATIONS**
New York, 1989

## NOTE

The designations employed and the presentation of the material in this publication do not imply the expression of any opinion whatsoever on the part of the Secretariat of the United Nations concerning the legal status of any country, territory, city or area, or of its authorities, or concerning the delimitation of its frontiers or boundaries.

UNITED NATIONS PUBLICATION

*Sales No.* E.88.XIV.6

ISBN 92-1-154071-2
ISSN 0251-6519

03000P

# CONTENTS

## Section B. Trust and Non-Self-Governing Territories

# PART II

# ACTIVITIES OF THE SUPERVISORY BODIES

## Section A. Practice of the supervisory bodies

### Section B. Relevant decisions, general recommendations, comments and observations of the supervisory bodies

PART III

## INTERNATIONAL DEVELOPMENTS

### Section A. United Nations organs

## Section B. Specialized agencies

### *ANNEX*

## INDEX

# INTRODUCTION

The *Yearbook on Human Rights for 1982* has been prepared in accordance with the "Guidelines for the contents and format of the Yearbook on Human Rights" annexed to Economic and Social Council resolution 1979/37 adopted on 10 May 1979.

The present volume consists of three parts. Part I covers national developments; part II provides information on activities of the supervisory bodies; part III relates to international developments in the field of human rights.

PART I contains two sections:

*Section A* consists of a selection of material reflecting legislative, administrative, judicial and other national measures and court decisions, taken from government reports submitted under the international human rights instruments, and from contributions submitted by States intended specifically for the *Yearbook* and covering the year 1982.

Extracts from reports made by the following States under relevant international instruments in the field of human rights are reflected in the 1982 *Yearbook*: Algeria, Argentina, Australia, Belgium, Bolivia, Brazil, Bulgaria, Byelorussian Soviet Socialist Republic, Canada, Cape Verde, Chile, China, Cuba, Cyprus, Denmark, Dominican Republic, Egypt, El Salvador, Ethiopia, Finland, France, German Democratic Republic, Germany, Federal Republic of, Haiti, Holy See, Hungary, Iceland, India, Iraq, Israel, Italy, Japan, Kuwait, Lao People's Democratic Republic, Lesotho, Luxembourg, Madagascar, Malta, Mauritius, Mexico, Mongolia, Netherlands, New Zealand, Nicaragua, Niger, Nigeria, Norway, Peru, Philippines, Portugal, Republic of Korea, Rwanda, Seychelles, Solomon Islands, Spain, Sri Lanka, Sweden, Switzerland, Uganda, Ukrainian Soviet Socialist Republic, Union of Soviet Socialist Republics, United Kingdom of Great Britain and Northern Ireland, United Republic of Tanzania, Venezuela and Yugoslavia.

Lesotho, Philippines and Switzerland provided contributions specifically intended for the *Yearbook on Human Rights*.

The material used in part I, section A, has been arranged under country-headings with subject subheadings relating to the pertinent articles of the Universal Declaration of Human Rights as well as to relevant articles of the international instruments under which the State reports used as source of information have been submitted.

*Section B* contains information relating to the exercise, in certain Trust and Non-Self-Governing Territories, of the right to self-determination. It provides a brief account of developments in Trust and Non-Self Governing Territories. Information contained in this section is essentially based on the Report of the Special Committee on the Situation with regard to the Implementation of the Declaration on

xvii

the Granting of Independence to Colonial Countries and Peoples,[1] and on working papers prepared by the Secretariat containing information on developments concerning the Territories.

PART II consists of two sections:

Section A, which deals with the practice of the supervisory bodies concerning the examination of government reports and other tasks entrusted to these bodies under the relevant international instruments consists of extracts of the following reports of the supervisory bodies to the respective parent organs:

Report of the Committee on the Elimination of Racial Discrimination, *Official Records of the General Assembly, Thirty-seventh Session, Supplement No. 18* (A/37/18);

Report of the Human Rights Committee, *Official Records of the General Assembly, Thirty-seventh Session, Supplement No. 40* (A/37/40);

Report of the Human Rights Committee, *Official Records of the General Assembly, Thirty-eighth Session, Supplement No. 40* (A/38/40);

Report of the Sessional Working Group on the Implementation of the International Covenant on Economic, Social and Cultural Rights (E/1982/56);

Report of the Group of Three Established under the Convention on the Suppression and Punishment of the Crime of *Apartheid* (E/CN.4/1507).

Section B reflects relevant decisions, general recommendations, comments and observations made by the supervisory bodies in connection with the examination of reports submitted and other tasks entrusted to them under the relevant international instruments. Relevant decisions and resolutions of parent bodies, namely, the Commission on Human Rights, the Economic and Social Council and the General Assembly have also been included in this section.

PART III also contains two sections:

Section A provides a brief account of activities in the field of human rights in the relevant United Nations organs, namely the General Assembly, the Economic and Social Council, the Commission on Human Rights and the Sub-Commission on Prevention of Discrimination and Protection of Minorities.

Section B reflects major developments on human rights questions in specialized agencies.

The text of additional guidelines for the implementation of article 7 of the International Convention on the Elimination of All Forms of Racial Discrimination has been included in an annex to the present volume.

---

[1] *Official Records of the General Assembly, Thirty-seventh Session, Supplement No. 23* (A/37/23/Rev.1).

# PART I

# NATIONAL DEVELOPMENTS

# Section A. States

# ALGERIA

## A. Promotion of understanding, tolerance and friendship among all nations, racial and ethnic groups

*(article 26 (2) of the Universal Declaration;*
*article 7 of the International Convention on the Elimination*
*of All Forms of Racial Discrimination)*[1]

One of the tasks of the Algerian cultural revolution in the fields of teaching, education, culture and information, is, according to the National Charter, "to combat prejudices based on race, class, sex, or occupation, as well as anti-social violence, chauvinism and sectarian ideas. This cultural dimension will further solidarity with oppressed peoples who are subjected to segregation or racial contempt and peoples who are still being exploited or who were formerly colonized, with a view to enhancing understanding of their history, their liberation struggles and their nation-building problems, as well as respect for cultures and civilizations different from our own."

Where teaching is concerned, civic and moral education courses given in all educational and technical institutions in Algeria are based directly on the principles embodied in the National Charter.

In addition, Human Rights Day has always been celebrated in Algerian schools in a ceremony at which the teacher reads and explains to the students the principles of the Universal Declaration of Human Rights.

With regard to culture and information, the Algerian film library, the radio, the television and the press as a whole are doing their share in various ways (film shows, press articles) to increase understanding of the basic principles of human rights and, in particular, of action to combat all forms of racial discrimination.

## B. Right to a social and international order in which human rights can be realized

*(article 28 of the Universal Declaration)*[2]

Algeria has ratified the International Convention on the Suppression and Punishment of the Crime of *Apartheid*, which came into force in Algeria on 25 June 1982.

---

[1] Report submitted by State (CERD/C/106/Add.4).
[2] *Ibid.* (CERD/C/106/Add.4).

3

# ARGENTINA

## A. Elimination of racial discrimination; development and protection of certain racial groups or individuals belonging to them

*(articles 2 and 7 of the Universal Declaration;*
*article 2 (2) of the International Convention on the Elimination*
*of All Forms of Racial Discrimination)*[1]

In December 1982 the Indigenous Policy Commission was formally set up and approved by Ministerial Decision No. 438/82 of the Ministry for Social Activities, to review the present indigenous situation and the feasibility of putting into effect any proposals made on topics of major importance such as land, health, education, housing, social security, etc.

National and provincial bodies are represented on this Commission, the functions of the executive secretariat being performed by the Directorate for Social Promotion and Welfare.

## B. Promotion of understanding, tolerance and friendship among all nations, racial and ethnic groups

*(article 26 (2) of the Universal Declaration;*
*article 7 of the International Convention on the Elimination*
*of All Forms of Racial Discrimination)*[2]

By Decision No. 1075 of 13 August 1982, the Ministry of Culture and Education will participate in the Indigenous Policy Commission which functions within the Ministry for Social Activities. The Ministry has announced its intention of extending the measures designed to protect the aboriginal community.

All the measures and activities in the education plan are directed towards making it easier for members of the aboriginal communities to express their identity and to pursue their cultural or religious practices freely.

The members of these communities are instructed on the rights and duties guaranteed by the National Constitution and United Nations recommendations.

In the course of 1982 and as part of the programme on the world-wide experiment on the study of world problems organized by UNESCO, the Higher National Institute of Modern Language Teachers "Juan Ramón Fernández" worked from August to November of that year on the topic of disarmament

---

[1] Report submitted by State (CERD/C/118/Add.1).

[2] *Ibid.* (CERD/C/118/Add.1).

The "Madre de los Emigrantes", a school at La Boca, Buenos Aires, considered the topic of the New International Economic Order and Trade School No. 30 of the federal capital dealt with the subject of human rights.

From 24 to 28 November 1982, two secondary school teachers of social sciences and history, and co-ordinators in associated schools took part in a study seminar organized by UNESCO in the town of Valdivia, Chile, on the problems of implementing the Associated Schools Project.

# AUSTRALIA

## Introduction: general legal framework[1]

The most significant development has been the establishment of the Human Rights Commission. The Human Rights Commission Act was proclaimed on 10 December 1981 when the Commission began operations. The Act is intended to ensure that Commonwealth laws, acts and practices conform with the International Covenant on Civil and Political Rights, the Declaration on the Rights of the Child, the Declaration on the Rights of Mentally Retarded Persons and the Declaration on the Rights of Disabled Persons. The Act also applies to all laws of the Australian Capital Territory and Australia's external territories.

Under the legislation, persons who consider their rights have been violated are able to take their complaints to the Commission to seek redress. When it is unable to effect a settlement of the matter, the Commission is required to report to the Minister. Its reports must also be tabled in both Houses of Parliament. The Commission has the power to call for persons and papers and to report on laws and practices which may be inconsistent with the International Covenant and the Declarations, on laws that should be passed and any other action that should be taken by the Commonwealth in relation to human rights. The Commission is also empowered to enter into arrangements with any state for the co-operative administration (Commonwealth/state) of human rights matters in that state.

The Human Rights Commission has also assumed the educative and research functions of the Commissioner for Community Relations through two amendments to the Racial Discrimination Act 1975. However, the Commissioner retains the function of investigating and attempting to settle complaints of racial discrimination. In this context, it is appropriate to mention that a new Commissioner for Community Relations has recently been appointed on the expiration of the term of the previous Commissioner, Mr. A. J. Grassby. The new Commissioner is Mr. Jeremy Long, formerly a senior civil servant with extensive experience in the field of Aboriginal affairs.

Further significant functions of the Human Rights Commission are to promote understanding and acceptance of human rights in Australia and to undertake research and educational programmes. As has been emphasized in previous reports to the Committee, the Australian Government sees these activities aimed at raising community awareness of human rights issues such as racial discrimination as being of particular importance.

There is now in force in South Australia legislation entitled the South Australian Ethnic Affairs Commission Act 1980-1982 which establishes an Ethnic Affairs Commission.

---

[1] Report submitted by State (CERD/C/88/Add.3).

A discussion of the legislative framework within which measures to combat racial discrimination operate in Australia would not be complete without reference being made to a recent court decision. The validity of the Racial Discrimination Act 1975 was upheld in a decision of the High Court of Australia handed down in May 1982 in the cases *Koowarta* v. *Bjelke-Petersen and Ors*; and *State of Queensland* v. *Commonwealth of Australia* (1982).

The former case arose out of a refusal by the Queensland Government to permit the transfer of leasehold land to the Aboriginal Land Fund Commission which was acting at the request of the Winychanam Group of Aboriginals of which Mr. Koowarta was a member. The latter action arose when the State of Queensland brought an action against the Commonwealth in the High Court seeking a declaration that the Racial Discrimination Act was invalid under the Constitution.

The High Court, by a majority (4 to 3) upheld the relevant provisions of the Commonwealth Racial Discrimination Act 1975 as within the "external affairs" power in s. 51 (xxix) of the Constitution. Stephen J. upheld the Act as giving effect to a treaty on a subject of international concern. Mason, Murphy and Brennan JJ. upheld it on the basis simply that it was giving effect to a genuine treaty.

## A. Elimination of racial discrimination
*(article 2 of the Universal Declaration;*
*article 2 (1) (e) of the International Convention on the Elimination*
*of All Forms of Racial Discrimination)*[2]

The Australian Government has received the report of the Australian Institute of Multicultural Affairs (AIMA) on its Evaluation of the Objectives and Implementation of the Report of the Review of Post-Arrival Programmes and Services to Migrants, more commonly referred to as the Galbally Report. The Evaluation found an impressive record of implementation of the Galbally Report and that the package of measures recommended by that Report has made "a crucial contribution to the well-being of migrants and to the commitment to a multicultural nation". The Evaluation did note some shortcomings in implementation and recommended some major new directions.

In accepting the recommendations and proposals of the Evaluation Report almost without exception the Australian Government has demonstrated a continuing commitment to the support and development of programmes and services for migrants, the encouragement of multiculturalism and most particularly, equality before the law.

In the area of the law, the Australian Government has committed itself to a substantial programme of legal reform aimed at putting all migrants on an equal legal footing. It has already amended the Commonwealth Electoral Act to make Australian citizenship rather than British subject status the nationality requirement for enrolment to vote and to nominate for Parliament. This amendment is awaiting proclamation. The Government will also amend all Commonwealth Acts which have a nationality requirement for Commonwealth employment so that Australian citizenship is the only requirement for eligibility. Beyond this, the Attorney-

---

[2] *Ibid.* (CERD/C/88/Add.3).

General's Department will prepare a report on all other legislation discriminating between migrants from different countries, and suggest amendments necessary to remedy the situation.

## B.  Elimination of racial discrimination; development and protection of certain racial groups or individuals belonging to them

*(article 2 of the Universal Declaration;*
*article 2 (2) of the International Convention on the Elimination*
*of All Forms of Racial Discrimination)*[3]

The Australian Government's present policies are based on the right of Aboriginals to determine and manage their future. These policies allow for the preservation and promotion of traditional culture and for Aboriginals to be integrated into the wider Australian society, if they so wish.

The Australian Government seeks to enable Aboriginals access to services available to the wider community, together with additional assistance appropriate to their state of disadvantage. Commonwealth programmes recognize the past dispossession and dispersal of the Aboriginal people, by providing certain special benefits. The Australian Government acknowledges that the needs of Aboriginal people will continue to require priority attention until at least their general position is enhanced to match that of the community in general.

The New South Wales Government established a Ministry of Aboriginal Affairs in January 1982. The Ministry was created as a direct result of a New South Wales Parliamentary Select Committee's Report on Aborigines. The Ministry's priorities lie with securing land rights for Aboriginals but it has an equally important task in the areas of health, housing, employment and education.

The Land Act in Queensland was amended in April 1982 to enable persons living on reserves to become trustees over them. The title given is not subject to any time limitation, and guarantees occupational security for the present residents and their successors. Provision is also made for the trustees to allow leases of land to individuals.

## C.  Freedom of movement and residence

*(article 13 of the Universal Declaration;*
*article 5 of the International Convention on the Elimination*
*of All Forms of Racial Discrimination)*[4]

A new Migrant Selection System came into effect on 19 April 1982. This system continues the Australian Government's universal immigration policy which does not discriminate on racial grounds. In the assessment of applicants, the emphasis is upon family connections and the skills, occupational and social, required for successful settlement. Concessions are available to refugees and to others with special humanitarian claims.

---

[3] *Ibid.* (CERD/C/88/Add.3).
[4] *Ibid.* (CERD/C/88/Add.3).

## D. Right to social security; right to health
*(articles 22 and 25 (1) of the Universal Declaration;
article 9 of the International Covenant on Economic,
Social and Cultural Rights)*[5]

In October 1982, at its 94th Session, the National Health and Medical Research Council adopted the first report of the working party it had set up on ethics in medical research.

Arising from this report, the Council recommended that it establish a national Medical Research Ethics Committee and that the Committee report directly to the Council and thence, through the Chairman of the Council, to the Federal Minister for Health and the State Ministers of Health and, through the Secretary of the Council, to the heads of state health authrorities.

## E. Right to work; right to equal opportunity to gain one's living by work
*(article 23 of the Universal Declaration;
article 6 of the International Covenant on Economic,
Social and Cultural Rights)*[6]

STATES LEGISLATION

### New South Wales

The New South Wales Anti-Discrimination Act 1977 which prohibits, *inter alia*, discrimination on the grounds of race, sex, marital status and physical impairment in employment has been subject to several noteworthy amendments.

In 1982, the Office of the Counsellor for Equal Opportunity (which originally had investigative and conciliatory functions) was abolished and the Anti-Discrimination Board took over its complaint-handling functions. The Act is now administered by the President of the Anti-Discrimination Board whose functions are: investigation and conciliation of complaints, education and research, and the hearing of exemption applications. Unresolved complaints are referred to the Equal Opportunity Tribunal for determination. Further amendments in 1982 added advertising to the areas covered, and intellectual impairment and homosexuality to the grounds of discrimination.

### Victoria

The Equal Opportunity Act 1977 came into force on 24 May 1977 and was subsequently amended in December 1982. The Act, as amended, makes unlawful discrimination on the grounds of sex, marital status or physical or intellectual impairment in a number of areas, including employment. The Act establishes a Commissioner for Equal Opportunity with responsibility for making all reasonable

---

[5] *Ibid.* (E/1984/7/Add.22).
[6] *Ibid.* (E/1984/7/Add.22).

endeavours to resolve complaints by conciliation. Where matters cannot be resolved by conciliation, the Commission is to refer matters to the Equal Opportunity Board.

The Ethnic Affairs Commission of Victoria has been established pursuant to legislation which came into operation in November 1982 with the objective of, *inter alia*, combating discrimination in employment on the basis of ethnic origin.

### Vocational training programmes

The Labour Adjustment Training Arrangements (LATA) were introduced in November 1982 in recognition of the special employment problems faced by retrenched workers in obtaining alternative employment in other industries or areas. The broad objectives are:

(*a*) To assist the process of adjustment for eligible redundant workers from retrenchment to stable and satisfying employment in other firms or industries by upgrading, refreshing, updating or broadening their skills base;

(*b*) To reduce the impact of large-scale retrenchments on regions and industries already suffering from a high rate of unemployment;

(*c*) In recognition of the changing industry base of the Australian economy, to improve the level of technical skill and expertise in the Australian work-force, looking towards economic recovery.

## F.  Right to just and favourable conditions of work
*(article 23 of the Universal Declaration;*
*article 7 of the International Covenant on Economic,*
*Social and Cultural Rights)*[7]

There have been several important changes in the activities of the National Health and Medical Research Council.

The Council is assisted in its work by a number of expert advisory committees. The Occupational Health (Standing) Committee, established to advise the Council on all matters relating to industrial hygiene and occupational health, has drawn up an Occupational Health Guide, *Occupational Health Services*. The guide, adopted by the Council in June 1982, discusses the nature, benefits, organization and role of an occupational health and safety programme and provides specific details for establishing such a programme. This guide replaces the previous publication, *Recommended Practice for Occupational Health Services in Australia*.

The Council also published in 1982 a comprehensive document, *Report on the Health Hazards of Asbestos*. The report is the result of an extensive inquiry by a specialist tripartite sub-committee appointed by the Council to investigate the production, use, handling and disposal of asbestos; to report on hygiene standards for occupational exposure to asbestos; and to review and report on the medical evidence of exposure to asbestos.

---

[7] *Ibid.* (E/1984/7/Add.22).

## G. Right to education

*(article 26 of the Universal Declaration;*
*article 13 of the International Covenant on Economic,*
*Social and Cultural Rights)*[8]

Regarding the right to primary education, under the Commonwealth Schools Commission's Disadvantaged Schools Programme, which began in 1974, funds additional to those normally available are provided to selected schools with enrolments from areas which are relatively deprived in socio-economic terms. The Programme has three main objectives:

(*a*) That schools should provide greater equality of opportunity, that is, that all children should be assisted to gain the fundamental skills necessary to participate fully and equally in society;

(*b*) That schooling should be relevant, enjoyable and fruitful in itself, not merely preparation for later life; and

(*c*) That schools might evolve through successful interaction with their communities into institutions less alienated from their communities than was generally the case in disadvantaged areas.

In 1982 this Programme will be retitled the Country Areas Programme to reflect the approved new criteria for allocation of funds in terms of relative isolation and size of settlements. State authorities will have greater freedom to allocate resources and total funding will be increased.

Concerning the improvement of the material conditions of teaching staff, teacher organizations have sought (and obtained) a range of improvements in salaries and conditions through the established machinery. During 1979 and 1980, most teachers in Australia sought and obtained a general salary increase based on changes in the value of work performed by teachers (curriculum changes, greater decentralization of administrative matters to local schools etc.). The vast majority of Australian teachers have also received regular salary increases derived from the operation of a centralized system of wage fixation based on indexation. Under this system, most teachers (and most other Austalian workers) received wage adjustments, initially each quarter and subsequently each half-year, broadly in line with increases in the consumer price index.

Although the centralized wage indexation system has now been discontinued, national wage hearings are to continue in the Commonwealth Conciliation and Arbitration Commission, and most teachers would receive any general increase awarded on economic grounds. The next such hearing is scheduled for February 1982. In the mean time, teacher organizations are, of course, free to seek improved salaries and conditions through the established tribunal or Commission mechanisms and a number of such claims are currently being processed.

---

[8] *Ibid.* (E/1982/3/Add.9).

# BELGIUM

## A. Right to an effective remedy

*(article 8 of the Universal Declaration;*
*article 6 of the International Convention on the Elimination*
*of All Forms of Racial Discrimination)*[1]

Since the adoption of the Act of 30 July 1981, the prosecutors' offices have provided the following information:

*Prosecutor's Office, Brussels Court of Appeal (as at 19 August 1982)*

As at the above date, no judgement had been delivered under the Act of 30 July 1981. Of the 34 files opened in connection with offences charged under the Act, action has either been discontinued or the matter is before the examining magistrate. During 1981, 17 files were opened; on 14, action has been discontinued and 3 have still not been closed. Since the beginning of 1982, 17 new files have been opened; of these, action has been discontinued on 9 and 8 are still before the examining magistrate.

*Prosecutor's Office, Mons Court of Appeal (as at 22 July 1982)*

Under this Office's jurisdiction, only one judgement was delivered in connection with an offence charged under the Act of 30 July 1981. This was handed down by the Mons Correctional Court.

*Prosecutor's Office, Ghent Court of Appeal (as at 24 August 1982)*

No judgement has been delivered pursuant to the Act of 30 July 1981. Some enquiries have been held; certain have been disposed of without any action being taken, but others are still pending.

*Prosecutor's Office, Antwerp Court of Appeal (as at 20 August 1982)*

Five cases coming within the jurisdiction of this Office were filed without any action being taken. Two persons were summoned to appear; two cases are at the preliminary enquiry stage; another is before the examining magistrate and yet another (at Malines) is to be brought before the court (but the case has not yet been entered on the cause list).

---

[1] Report submitted by State (CERD/C/88/Add.5).

12

## B. Political rights
*(article 21 of the Universal Declaration;*
*article 5 of the International Convention on the Elimination*
*of All Forms of Racial Discrimination)*[2]

A Higher Flemish Council for Migrants for the Flemish Community was set up by an order of the Flemish Executive dated 3 March 1982.

## C. Promotion of understanding, tolerance and friendship among all nations, racial and ethnic groups
*(article 26 (2) of the Universal Declaration;*
*article 7 of the International Convention on the Elimination*
*of All Forms of Racial Discrimination)*[3]

At the primary and secondary levels, instruction in human rights is largely a question of the implementation of ministerial circulars which are issued in particular on the occasion of Human Rights Day. These circulars, however, stress that human rights concepts must be observed throughout the academic year and not just on the anniversary of the Universal Declaration. Human rights form the subject of lessons given as part of courses on the humanities at certain stages of secondary education.

There is no special education so far as racism is concerned. The problem is discussed, as and when the opportunity arises, in various courses, but more particularly in courses on ethics, religion and the human and social sciences, and at the higher level in the context of several faculties. In non-university higher education, this type of education is given mainly in courses such as sociology, philosophy, psychology.

The Ministries of the French Community and the Flemish Community encourage association in everyday life between the various ethnic communities and groups combating racial discrimination in the cultural field.

Each year the Government seizes the opportunities afforded by the International Day for the Elimination of Racial Discrimination and the anniversary of the Universal Declaration of Human Rights to circulate communiqués which are widely reported in the press and in radio/televised statements by the Minister for Foreign Affairs with a view to alerting public opinion even more to the problems raised by respect for human rights and the struggle against racism and *apartheid*.

---

[2] *Ibid.* (CERD/C/88/Add.5).
[3] *Ibid.* (CERD/C/88/Add.5).

# BOLIVIA

### Elimination of racial discrimination; development and protection of certain racial groups or individuals belonging to them

*(articles 2 and 7 of the Universal Declaration;*
*article 2 (2) of the International Convention on the Elimination*
*of All Forms of Racial Discrimination)*[1]

The Bolivian Indian Institute was originally created by Decree-law No. 0684 of 10 May 1941 as the Department of Indian Affairs responsible to the Ministry of Education.

It became, under the terms of Supreme Decree No. 01666, the Bolivian Indian Institute, with specific functions limited to carrying out "scientific studies of a pedagogic, historic, economic, legal and cultural nature among traditional peoples, including forest-dwelling groups".

In 1965, the Institute was subordinated to the newly created Ministry of Rural Affairs, pursuant to Supreme Decree No. 07443. The period from 1966 to 1981 is noteworthy for a series of changes in its organizational structure, its functions and, above all, in the fact that the limitations on its human and material resources jeopardized the normal performance of its tasks.

From 1981 onwards, thanks in particular to the dedication of its management and operational staff, the first steps were taken to reactivate the Institute and, in January 1982, two specific fields of activity were agreed upon:

(*a*) To study and investigate the socio-economic and cultural situation of the indigenous communities in Bolivia with a view to outlining national and/or multinational policies in their regard and as support in the tasks being carried out by the various institutions engaged in the promotion of rural development in Bolivia.

(*b*) To centralize and disseminate information regarding the Bolivian Indians, whether resulting from its own research or from that of other national and/or foreign bodies, preferably on anthropological, economic, cultural and linguistic subjects.

---

[1] Report submitted by State (CERD/C/107/Add.1).

# BRAZIL

### A. Condemnation of racial segregation and *apartheid*
(*articles 1 and 2 of the Universal Declaration;
article 3 of the International Convention on the Elimination
of All Forms of Racial Discrimination*)[1]

Consistently with the positions adopted by the Brazilian Government with regard to the policy of *apartheid*, approaches have been made to private sports bodies with a view to discouraging contacts between Brazilian athletes or players and those of South Africa. This endeavour is the subject of an instruction from the Ministry of Education and Culture, which is the responsible authority in the matter. Permission for participants in sports to enter the country and for the holding of the Capetown-Rio de Janeiro yacht race has been withheld. At the same time Brazil is following with interest the initial work on drafting the International Convention against *Apartheid* in Sports, and shall endeavour to share in this task.

Bilateral relations with South Africa outside the area of direct Government action have reflected current priorities and aims. To take the most noteworthy example, trade relations between the two countries have declined in scope by comparison with the trade carried on with other areas, and in particular with other African countries. Whether because it is small in volume, in both relative and absolute terms, or because of its nature, the maintenance of such trade has in no way influenced the priority aims of the Brazilian Government. There are no Brazilian investments in South Africa.

Brazil endeavours to ensure consistency between these measures adopted at the bilateral level and the positions it takes in the United Nations and other multilateral forums where the situation in southern Africa comes up for consideration. The Brazilian representatives have taken every opportunity to place our views on record and have striven to make our positions consistent with the growing international consensus that assures the resolutions adopted in the United Nations of an ample majority.

Consistently with these positions, Brazil regularly contributes about $US 60,000 to the various funds in existence: the United Nations Trust Fund for South Africa, the Trust Fund for Publicity against *Apartheid*, the Educational and Training Programme for southern Africa, the United Nations Fund for Namibia, the United Nations Institute for Namibia and the Nationhood Programme for Namibia.

---

[1] Report submitted by State (CERD/C/91/Add.25).

15

## B. Elimination of racial discrimination; development and protection of certain racial groups or individuals belonging to them

*(article 2 of the Universal Declaration;*
*article 2 (2) of the International Convention on the Elimination*
*of All Forms of Racial Discrimination)*[2]

In 1982 an Indigenous Communities Development Programme is in process of execution. This Programme is designed to create conditions in which, through effective participation at various levels, the indigenous communites will be able to rule their own destinies, organizing their resources and managing their estates so that, on a self-supporting basis, they may interact on a more equal footing with the surrounding national society.

It is hoped that this Programme will succeed in increasing the effectiveness of the economic projects directed by FUNAI, which will involve some $US 20 million in the next three years.

A decision was taken on 9 March 1982 prohibiting access to a continuous area of 7.7 million hectares intended for the Ianomamis. Work began immediately to withdraw two groups of prospectors located in the area.

## C. Promotion of understanding, tolerance and friendship among all nations, racial and ethnic groups

*(article 26 (2) of the Universal Declaration;*
*article 7 of the International Convention on the Elimination*
*of All Forms of Racial Discrimination)*[3]

Education, viewed from the standpoint of present-day social policy, is committed to collaboration in reducing social inequalities; it strives to be a partner in the national effort to redistribute the benefits of economic growth and to foster participation by bringing new segments of the population into the political development process.

The elimination of social inequalities, allied with a non-discriminatory tradition, has contributed to the collective involvement of all citizens in the political and social process, reducing the likelihood of situations arising that might make for the spread of prejudiced attitudes connected with ethnic characteristics.

All governmental action in the cultural field is based on a broad conception of culture as meaning any interdependent and ordered system of human activities. This conception comprises, in addition to movable and immovable property of great historical and artistic value, a whole range of behaviour patterns, habits and forms of perception observed in daily life.

The fundamental objective is cultural development conceived as one of the essential dimensions of Brazilian life and aimed essentially at the less-privileged sectors of the population, egalitarian in outlook and committed to the identification,

---

[2] *Ibid.* (CERD/C/91/Add.25).
[3] *Ibid.* (CERD/C/91/Add.25).

preservation and, above all, full development of the basic cultural and ethnically diversified characteristics of the Brazilian people.

In the last analysis, it is a matter of bringing to fruition the most representative cultural manifestations, which have been saturated with the influence of the black and indigenous populations in our midst since the national society began to take shape.

The aims of the Brazilian Government's educational and cultural policy have led to countless useful activities of technical co-operation through the execution of various exchange programmes with countries of the most diverse ethnic and racial characteristics.

Programmes are at present being carried out with Canada, the Federal Republic of Germany, France and Japan, and with countries in Latin America and Africa.

Special emphasis is being placed on mutual co-operation agreements with developing countries, especially in Latin America and Africa, to promote the economic and social development of their peoples and to strengthen their ties of solidarity.

Beginning in 1983 the Brazilian Government will carry out a programme for postgraduate students, which arises out of the cultural agreements signed by Brazil with other developing countries in Africa and Latin America and which provides for the grant of fellowships and payment of the students' return air fares to their countries of origin.

# BULGARIA

## A. Condemnation of racial segregation and *apartheid*
### *(articles 1 and 2 of the Universal Declaration;*
### *articles IV and VI of the International Convention on the Suppression*
### *and Punishment of the Crime of* Apartheid)[1]

The mass media in the People's Republic of Bulgaria devote particular attention to the struggle to eliminate racism, racial discrimination and *apartheid*. Each year public opinion in Bulgaria marks the International Day for the Elimination of Racial Discrimination, the Day of Solidarity with South African Political Prisoners, the Africa Liberation Day, the International Day of Solidarity with the Struggling People of South Africa, and others. The press, radio and television media regularly inform the Bulgarian people about United Nations activities aimed at carrying out the Programme for the Decade for Action to Combat Racism and Racial Discrimination. An important role for instilling an intransigent attitude towards racial prejudices and manifestations and for educating young people in a spirit of respect for the dignity of the human person is played by the system of education.

## B. Right to take part in the cultural life of the community
### *(article 27 of the Universal Declaration;*
### *article 15 of the International Covenant on Economic,*
### *Social and Cultural Rights)[2]*

In May 1982, a World Theatrical Festival was organized, under the auspices of UNESCO, as well as a World Festival of Cartoons and a World Festival of Films of the Red Cross; every other year, an international competition is held in Sofia for young opera singers, as well as an international ballet competition, and many other similar events.

---

[1] Report submitted by State (E/CN.4/1983/24/Add.8).

[2] *Ibid.* (E/1982/3/Add.23).

# BYELORUSSIAN SOVIET SOCIALIST REPUBLIC

## A. Treatment of offenders
*(article 5 of the Universal Declaration;*
*article 10 of the International Covenant on Civil and Political Rights)*[1]

The Decree of the Presidium of the Supreme Soviet of the Byelorussian SSR dated 16 December 1982 introduced a number of amendments and additions to the penal, criminal procedure and corrective-labour legislation in force with a view to ensuring that the law has optimum effects on offenders and on their rehabilitation and reform.

New types of penalty unconnected with deprivation of liberty have been introduced; they include suspending execution of custodial sentences for first offenders sentenced to a term of up to three years if there is a possibility of their reform and rehabilitation without isolation from society; for many offences the punishment provided for by law takes the form of a fine, and extensive use is made of penalties such as suspended custodial sentences and suspended sentences with a compulsory work assignment, corrective labour at the offender's place of work, dismissal of the offender from his post, and public censure.

The Decrees of the Presidium of the Supreme Soviet of the Byelorussian SSR dated 29 March 1977 and 16 December 1982 introduced substantial amendments to articles 48 and 48-1 of the Byelorussian Penal Code; these amendments provide for the exemption from criminal responsibility and punishment, in certain circumstances, of persons who have committed an offence which does not constitute a serious danger to society if the person concerned can be reformed and re-educated without resort to punishment under the criminal law. Administrative measures may be taken concerning them, or information on them may be sent to social organizations.

## B. Protection against arbitrary interference with privacy
*(article 12 of the Universal Declaration;*
*article 17 of the International Covenant on Civil and Political Rights)*[2]

The Decree of the Supreme Soviet of the Byelorussian SSR dated 16 December 1982 concerning the introduction of amendments and additions to the Byelorussian Penal Code makes the violation of the privacy not only of correspondence but also of telephone conversations and telegraphic communications a criminal offence (article 135 of the Byelorussian Penal Code).

---

[1] Report submitted by State (CCPR/C/28/Add.4).
[2] *Ibid.* (CCPR/C/28/Add.4).

## C.  Freedom of association

*(article 20 of the Universal Declaration;*
*article 22 of the International Covenant on Civil and Political Rights)[3]*

Various changes were made to the existing USSR trade union statutes at the seventeenth Congress of USSR trade unions in 1982, aimed at extending the competence of trade unions in deciding matters relating to the utilization of labour and material resources, the protection of mothers and childen, the provision of healthy and safe working conditions, the increased production and fair distribution of consumer goods, the control of their utilization, etc.

## D.  Right to take part in the conduct of public affairs

*(article 21 of the Universal Declaration;*
*article 25 of the International Covenant on Civil and Political Rights)[4]*

On 11 February 1982 the Presidium of the Supreme Soviet of the Byelorussian SSR adopted a Decree entitled "On the organization of work with regard to the instructions from electors". Activities undertaken in implementation of instructions from electors are given extensive publicity. Soviets of people's deputies and their organs inform the population about progress in the implementation of instructions from electors. The work of state organs, enterprises, institutions, organizations and deputies in connection with instructions from electors is covered in the press, on the radio, television and in other mass media.

---

[3] *Ibid.* (CCPR/C/28/Add.4).
[4] *Ibid.* (CCPR/C/28/Add.4).

# CANADA

## Introduction: general legal framework[1]

### New constitutional provisions

At the request of Canada, the Parliament of the United Kingdom enacted the Canada Act, 1982. Appended to this Act is the Constitution Act, 1982, which came into force on 17 April 1982.

The Constitution Act, 1982, contains a charter of rights and freedoms (the Canadian Charter of Rights and Freedoms) and additional provisions which contribute to the protection and implementation of the rights enunciated in the International Convention on the Elimination of All Forms of Racial Discrimination.

### Canadian Charter of Rights and Freedoms

The Canadian Charter of Rights and Freedoms provides protection of the following: fundamental freedoms; democratic rights; mobility rights; legal rights; equality rights for all individuals; official languages of Canada; minority language education rights; Canada's multicultural heritage; aboriginal rights and freedoms.

### Ontario

The most recent Ontario Human Rights Code, which came into force on 15 June 1982, brings Ontario's legislation up to the highest international standards, and marks a fitting culmination of legislative activity over the past four decades.

### Manitoba

One important development on the legislative front took place just at the end of the period under review. A number of amendments to the Human Rights Act were passed by the Manitoba Legislature in July 1982, including a substantial expansion of the "accommodation" provision of the Act.

### Quebec

The Quebec Government recently took advantage of its right in section 33 of the Charter, to incorporate an opting-out clause into all provincial Acts in force as of 17 April 1982 (An Act concerning the Constitution Act, 1982, sanctioned on 23 June 1982). The provincial Government also indicated that such an opting-out clause will be incorporated into all Acts adopted after the coming into force of the Charter. As

---

[1] Reports submitted by State (CERD/C/76/Add.6; CCPR/C/1/Add.62).

a result, Charter provisions concerning fundamental freedoms, legal rights and equality rights do not apply to Acts adopted by the province in exercising its jurisdictions. This result, however, does not mean that Quebec residents are without these protections. They may rely upon the Quebec Charter of Human Rights and Freedoms, R.S.Q., c. C-12, which binds the provincial Crown.

The Quebec Government has recently amended the Charter of Human Rights and Freedoms to better meet the needs of Quebec society (An Act to amend the Charter of Human Rights and Freedoms, Bill 86, sanctioned on 18 December 1982). Once put into force, the new Quebec Charter will provide protection similar to that in the entrenched Charter with respect to human rights and fundamental freedoms.

### A. Condemnation of racial segregation and *apartheid*

*(articles 1 and 2 of the Universal Declaration;*
*article 3 of the International Convention on the Elimination*
*of All Forms of Racial Discrimination)*[2]

In February 1982, further financial measures were introduced to restrain competition between Canadian and South African athletes in third countries.

### B. Elimination of discrimination on grounds of sex

*(article 2 of the Universal Declaration;*
*article 3 of the International Covenant on Civil and Political Rights)*[3]

In Quebec, Bill 86 (An Act to amend the Charter of Human Rights and Freedoms), sanctioned on 18 December 1982, empowers the human rights commission to approve such measures submitted to it, to suggest the adoption of such programmes when it finds a systematic discrimination, and to recommend to the tribunal to impose such programmes when its own recommendations are not followed. The Act also provides that the Government must require from its ministries and agencies that they implement such programmes.

The Federal Government has undertaken to make certain changes between now and 1985 in areas of policy, research and programmes.

### C. Elimination of racial discrimination

*(article 2 of the Universal Declaration;*
*article 2 (1) of the International Convention on the Elimination*
*of All Forms of Racial Discrimination)*[4]

During the summer of 1982, in order to continue the efforts undertaken to deal with the problems of racism, the Minister of State for Multiculturalism created a Race Relations Unit within the Multiculturalism Directorate. Earlier programmes in

---

[2] *Ibid.* (CERD/C/76/Add.6; CCPR/C/1/Add.62).

[3] *Ibid.* (CCPR/C/1/Add.62).

[4] *Ibid.* (CERD/C/76/Add.6).

this area included new funding for the development of educational material and a communications plan to stimulate public awareness of the issues. The new section will conduct research into such areas as the influence of economic factors on social tensions and the causes and implications of the recent resurgence of extreme right wing organizations. The findings of such research will assist the Multiculturalism Directorate in designing new programmes.

## D. Elimination of racial discrimination; development and protection of certain racial groups or individuals belonging to them

*(article 2 of the Universal Declaration;*
*article 2 (2) of the International Convention on the Elimination*
*of All Forms of Racial Discrimination;*
*article 27 of the International Covenant on Civil and Political Rights)*[5]

In addition to the Canadian Charter of Rights and Freedoms, Canada undertook to protect the rights of aboriginal peoples in its Constitution, as of 17 April 1982, the date when the Constitution Act, 1982, c. 11 (UK), took effect. Pursuant to section 35 of the Constitution Act, 1982, the existing aboriginal and treaty rights of the Indian, Inuit and Métis people of Canada are recognized and confirmed. Any law that is inconsistent with this provision is of no force or effect (sect. 52). Before 17 April 1983 the Federal Government must convene a constitutional conference with the participation of the native representatives, at which the rights of aboriginal peoples shall be discussed (sect. 37). If the various governments in Canada are unable to agree on the identification and definition of the rights of aboriginal peoples, the courts reserve the right which they already possess to define these rights.

The Government's policy on the Indian and aboriginal peoples may be summed up in a few words: to end a state of dependency, resulting from a much too paternalistic policy, by encouraging a feeling of community belonging and autonomy from the Government. An example of the application of this policy may be found in the medical and hospital field. The Department of National Health and Welfare intends to have the native community take a much larger part in the local administration of health programmes.

### Ontario

On 15 June 1982 the Human Rights Code, 1981 (Statutes of Ontario, 1981, chapter 53), was proclaimed as law. This represents the first comprehensive review of the Human Rights Code since its passage in 1962.

The new Code contains many additional provisions that protect the rights of racial minorities.

### Saskatchewan

In 1982 Canada's Constitution was amended and it now contains protection for aboriginal peoples' rights in the country. The Government of Saskatchewan played a key role in securing these reforms.

---

[5] *Ibid.* (CERD/C/76/Add.6; CCPR/C/1/Add.62).

The most recent initiative (March 1982) in the field of human justice is the Indian and Native Institutional Liaison Programme. This programme will provide pre-release and post-release counselling for native inmates of correctional centres.

In 1982, the Government contributed $Can 75,000 to the World Assembly of First Nations, an international gathering of indigenous peoples from around the world.

## E. Right to life, liberty and security of person; right not to be subjected to arbitrary arrest or detention

*(articles 3 and 9 of the Universal Declaration; article 9 of the International Covenant on Civil and Political Rights)*[6]

In Canada, section 7 of the Canadian Charter of Rights and Freedoms recognizes the right of everyone to life, liberty and security of the person and the right not to be deprived thereof except in accordance with the principles of fundamental justice. Section 9 of the Charter recognizes the right of everyone not to be arbitrarily detained or imprisoned, even if the imprisonment is authorized under an Act. Section 10 guarantees to everyone the right on arrest or detention to have the validity of the detention determined by way of *habeas corpus* and to be released if the detention is not lawful. Within the jurisdiction of Quebec, sections 24 and 30 of the Charter of Human Rights and Freedoms recognize, "No one may be deprived of his liberty or of his rights except on grounds provided by law and in accordance with prescribed procedure", and that everyone deprived of his or her freedom has the right to the remedy of *habeas corpus.*

The Criminal Code provides for arrest with or without a warrant. The provisions of the Code setting out the powers of arrest may not be arbitrary, nor arbitrarily applied. These provisions are subject to section 9 of the Canadian Charter of Rights and Freedoms, by virtue of which everyone has the right not to be arbitrarily detained or imprisoned.

As a general rule, the police officer or any citizen who arrests a person must advise that person of the reasons for the arrest. To this end, subsection 10 (*a*) of the Canadian Charter of Rights and Freedoms is clear: "Everyone has the right on arrest or detention to be informed promptly of the reasons therefor."

Under subsection 24 (1) of the Canadian Charter of Rights and Freedoms a court of competent jurisdiction may grant anyone whose rights or freedoms, as guaranteed by the Charter, have been infringed or denied, such remedy as the court considers appropriate and just in the circumstances. Such a remedy, may be in the nature of monetary compensation.

In Quebec, section 28.1 of Bill 86 (An Act to amend the Charter of Human Rights and Freedoms), sanctioned on 18 December 1982, recognizes the right of all accused persons to be informed promptly of the charges against them.

---

[6] *Ibid.* (CCPR/C/1/Add.62).

## F. Right to equal protection of the law

*(article 7 of the Universal Declaration;*
*article 26 of the International Covenant on Civil and Political Rights)*[7]

As of 17 April 1985, all federal, provincial and territorial laws will be subject to subsection 15 (1) of the Canadian Charter of Rights and Freedoms, unless they have been declared to apply notwithstanding the Charter, in accordance with section 33. This provision sets out, "Every individual is equal before and under the law and has the right to the equal protection and equal benefit of the law without discrimination and, in particular, without discrimination based on race, national or ethnic origin, colour, religion, sex, age or mental or physical disability." This provision, however, does not preclude any law, programme or activity that has as its object the amelioration of conditions of disadvantaged individuals or groups (subsect. 15 (2)). The equality rights recognized by the Charter do contain certain limits. In the first place, a government may incorporate a notwithstanding clause into its laws which has effect for no more than five years, but which is renewable indefinitely. The Charter also recognizes that a right may be restricted by reasonable limits prescribed by law, if they can be justified in a free and democratic society (sects. 1 and 33).

## G. Right to an effective remedy

*(article 8 of the Universal Declaration;*
*article 6 of the International Convention on the Elimination*
*of All Forms of Racial Discrimination)*[8]

In August 1982 the Canadian Human Rights Commission announced its policy regarding harassment. The policy states the following principles: no person shall harass any other person; protection against acts of harassment extends to incidents occurring at or away from the workplace, during or outside normal working hours provided such acts are committed within the context of employment, or in the provision of goods, services, facilities or accommodation; harassment may be related to any of the discriminatory grounds contained in the Canadian Human Rights Act.

*Ontario*

### F. W. Woolworth Co. Ltd. and Dhillon (1982)

A board of inquiry heard the complaint of Mr. Dhillon, a Canadian immigrant from India, who alleged discriminatory terms and conditions in, and dismissal from, employment because of his race, colour and nationality. The board found that the company's non-white warehouse employees experienced a severe problem of verbal racial abuse from the white workers, and that the management, which had been made aware of the growing problem, had neglected their duty to provide a working atmosphere free from such abuse. By way of remedy, the board ordered that the man be awarded monetary compensation for insult to his dignity and that a committee be

---

[7] *Ibid.* (CCPR/C/1/Add.62).
[8] *Ibid.* (CERD/C/76/Add.6).

formed to include company management, employees and a member of the Commission's staff, to assess and make recommendations on how to improve race relations at the workplace. The board retained jurisdiction over the case for a six-month period following the decision to give the employer and the Commission an opportunity to redress racial tension in the company.

## H. Right to a public trial
### (article 10 of the Universal Declaration; article 14 of the International Covenant on Civil and Political Rights)[9]

In criminal matters, the principle of public trial has received constitutional sanction. In effect, subsection 11 (*d*) of the Canadian Charter of Rights and Freedoms recognizes that any person charged with an offence has the right to a public hearing. Any such person whose right has been infringed or denied may apply to a court of competent jurisdiction to obtain such remedy as the court considers appropriate and just in the circumstances. This provision does not apply in Quebec where the Government relied on Charter section 33 (the notwithstanding clause). The Quebec Charter of Human Rights and Freedoms, however, recognizes the right to a public hearing before administrative, civil and criminal tribunals in matters coming within provincial jurisdiction (Charter, sect. 23).

In re section 12 of the Juvenile Delinquents Act (1982), 8 W.C.B. 206, Judge Smith of the Ontario High Court declared subsection 12 (1) of the Juvenile Delinquents Act, which requires *in camera* hearings in certain circumstances, to be inoperative. This section was found to be contrary to the freedom of expression and the press and the right to a public hearing in criminal matters, as recognized in subsections 2 (*b*) and 11 (*d*) of the Canadian Charter of Rights and Freedoms. According to Judge Smith, it is for the courts to decide, based on principles of common law or on standards adopted by Parliament, whether a closed hearing is justified in a given case. As an example, he referred to the new Young Offenders Act, S.C. 1980-1981-1982, c. 110. This Act, not yet proclaimed in force, authorizes a judge to exclude from the court-room any person, except those required by law, where necessary in the interest of public morals, the maintenance of order or the proper administration of justice or where any evidence or information presented to the court would be seriously injurious or prejudicial to a child or young person (sect. 39).

## I. Presumption of innocence; non-retroactivity of criminal law; right to all the guarantees necessary for defence
### (article 11 of the Universal Declaration; articles 14 and 15 of the International Covenant on Civil and Political Rights)[10]

In Canadian law, a person accused of a criminal offence is presumed to be innocent (Canadian Charter of Rights and Freedoms, subsect. 11 (*d*); Quebec Charter of Rights and Freedoms, sect. 33).

---

[9] *Ibid.* (CCPR/C/1/Add.62).
[10] *Ibid.* (CCPR/C/1/Add.62).

The Canadian Charter of Rights and Freedoms protects Canadians against retroactive penal legislation.

In Quebec, an equivalent provision (s. 37.2) was inserted into the Charter of Human Rights and Freedoms through the adoption of Bill 86 (An Act to amend the Charter of Human Rights and Freedoms), sanctioned on 18 December 1982.

In Quebec, the National Assembly has enacted one retroactive law, an Act respecting the Constitution Act, 1982, S.Q. 1982, c. 62.

In Quebec, where section 14 does not apply to provincial laws, section 36 of the Charter of Human Rights and Freedoms recognizes the right of every accused person to be assisted free of charge by an interpreter if he or she does not understand the language used at the hearing. Furthermore, Bill 86 (An Act to amend the Charter of Human Rights and Freedoms, sanctioned on 18 December 1982), extends this right to the deaf.

In *Grant* v. *Director of Public Prosecutions* (1982), A.C. 190, at p. 200, the Judicial Committee of the Privy Council interpreted a provision of the Jamaican Constitution similar to subsection 11 (6) of the Charter. The Court concluded that a delay of three and a half years from the time of the offence to the beginning of the trial would not have given rise to an impartial hearing, except for the fact that the accused were responsible for two thirds of this delay by their legal manœuvring. If this decision is followed in Canada, *Rourke* will have no probative value.

In criminal matters, the Canadian Charter of Rights and Freedoms recognizes the right of any person charged with an offence to a fair and public hearing (sect. 11 (*d*)).

Subsection 11 (*h*) of the Canadian Charter of Rights and Freedoms set out that any person charged with an offence has the right if finally acquitted of the offence, not to be tried again and, if finally found guilty and punished for the offence, not to be tried or punished for it again.

Parliament recently adopted the Young Offenders Act, S.C. 1980-1981-1982, c. 110. Once proclaimed, this Act will abolish the Juvenile Delinquents Act (sect. 80). In the Young Offenders Act, however, the legislation recognizes that where a young person has wilfully contravened a disposition made pursuant to the Act, the youth court may vary the disposition (sect. 33). In this regard, the Young Offenders Act, even though less severe than the Juvenile Delinquents Act, follows the same principle: the sentence imposed on a youth is conditional and, if its terms are not respected, the punishment is subject to review.

## J. Freedom of opinion and expression

*(article 19 of the Universal Declaration;*
*articles 19 and 20 of the International Covenant on Civil and Political Rights)*[11]

In Canada, the Canadian Charter of Rights and Freedoms renders inoperative all laws which result in discrimination against an individual because of his or her political views and opinions, as long as such laws are neither reasonable nor

---

[11] *Ibid.* (CCPR/C/1/Add.62).

justifiable in a free and democratic society. Section 2 of the Charter recognizes the right of everyone to freedom of thought, opinion, expression and association. Furthermore, section 15, which will come into force on 17 April 1983, states "Every in dividual is equal before and under the law and has the right to the equal protection and equal benefit of the law without exception."

## K.  Freedom of peaceful assembly

*(article 20 of the Universal Declaration;*
*article 21 of the International Covenant on Civil and Political Rights)*[12]

In Canada, freedom of assembly cannot be dissociated from freedom of speech, of the press and of association. These freedoms, which are often referred to as fundamental freedoms, are complementary. The proper functioning of the Canadian political system is founded on the existence of these freedoms.

Implicitly recognized in the Anglo-Canadian judicial tradition, these freedoms (as well as the freedom of religion) are expressly guaranteed in the Canadian Charter of Rights and Freedoms (sect. 2). In the same way, these freedoms are recognized in Quebec under section 3 of the Charter of Human Rights and Freedoms, R.S.Q., c. C-12.

In Canadian law, a distinction must be made between the right of peaceful assembly and the right to use public property. There is no doubt that in Canada there is a right of peaceful assembly (Canadian Charter of Rights and Freedoms, sect. 2; Charter of Human Rights and Freedoms, sect. 3).

## L.  Political rights

*(article 21 of the Universal Declaration;*
*article 5 of the International Convention on the Elimination*
*of All Forms of Racial Discrimination)*[13]

*Quebec*

In its Plan of Action for Cultural Communities, the Quebec Government announced specific measures to correct these communities' under-representation in the public service (a programme of information about the public service, and publication of job advertisements in various languages in the media of the cultural communities).

## M.  Right to an adequate standard of living

*(article 25 (1) of the Universal Declaration;*
*article 11 of the International Covenant on Economic,*
*Social and Cultural Rights)*[14]

The Government of Canada's economic departments and Cabinet's decision-making process were reorganized in 1982 in order to involve the entire Government

---

[12] *Ibid.* (CCPR/C/1/Add.62).

[13] *Ibid.* (CERD/C/76/Add.6).

[14] *Ibid.* (E/1980/6/Add.32).

in regional economic development. Prior to this reorganization, the Department of Regional Economic Expansion was the only department with the specific mandate of assisting and encouraging each region in Canada to realize its potential. Henceforth, all departments working in economic development will be more directly involved at the regional level as a result of an increase in manpower and programmes in the regions. The regional activities of these departments are co-ordinated by the Ministry of State of Economic and Regional Development, which is also responsible for regional economic planning in general.

The creation of the Department of Regional Industrial Expansion was also announced in 1982. This new department groups the services administering regional programmes within the Department of Regional Economic Expansion and those dealing with industry, small business and tourism within the Department of Industry, Trade and Commerce. This reorganization is aimed at promoting the development of industrial programmes and policies adapted to the needs of the country as a whole as well as those of the various regions and at improving the administration of industrial programmes in each region.

*Prince Edward Island*

The 1982 Prince Edward Island Lands Protection Act puts a limit on the amount of land individuals and corporations can hold. An individual person is not allowed to acquire an aggregate land holding in excess of 1,000 acres, and a corporation in excess of 3,000 acres. However, special permits to hold more can be granted by the Lieutenant Governor in Council if this is considered in the public interest; the particulars of such special permits must then be submitted to the Legislative Assembly.

The Government has undertaken an extensive review of all aspects of occupational health and safety. As a result of that study, in May 1982 the Legislative Assembly adopted the Occupational Health and Safety Council Act, S.P.E.I. 1982, c. 21, which creates a corporation known as the Occupational Health and Safety Council.

The Council is composed of not less than six members, one of whom must be a person nominated by the Workers' Compensation Board of Prince Edward Island, appointed by the Lieutenant Governor in Council who, in his opinion, are representative of management, labour and technical or professional persons and the public, and who are concerned with and have knowledge of occupational health and safety.

The objective of the Council is to prevent accidents and injury to health and well-being arising in the course of work and to eliminate or minimize hazards inherent in the working environment and working practices.

## N. Promotion of understanding, tolerance and friendship among all nations, racial and ethnic groups

*(article 26 (2) of the Universal Declaration;*
*article 7 of the International Convention on the Elimination*
*of All Forms of Racial Discrimination)*[15]

*Ontario*

In 1982, the Multiculturalism and Citizenship Division in the Ministry of Citizenship and Culture undertook a joint project with the Urban Alliance on Race Relations, which suggested the production of two handbooks. One, the *Guide to Race Relations Organizations in Metro Toronto*, is designed to acquaint the print and broadcast media with the various Metro and area organizations involved in the area of race relations. The second, the *Guide to the Use of the Media*, is intended for use by community organizations to identify appropriate media contacts. It also gives information on how best to utilize the media.

*Quebec*

In March 1982 the Ministry of Education issued a revised edition of the document entitled *Grille d'analyse des stéréotypes discriminatoires dans le matériel didactique imprimé* (Analytical Grid of Discriminatory Stereotypes in Printed Teaching Materials), which has been in force since October 1981. Thus, any textbook forwarded by a publisher has to comply adequately with all criteria set forth in the grid. According to this document, there are three textbook categories: those requiring correction; those that cannot be corrected, since they must be written all over again; and those that are accepted without corrections.

---

[15] *Ibid.* (CERD/C/76/Add.6).

# CAPE VERDE

## Condemnation of racial segregation and *apartheid*
### (*articles 1 and 2 of the Universal Declaration;*
### *article IV of the International Convention on the Suppression*
### *and Punishment of the Crime of* Apartheid)[1]

The National Assembly of the People, Cape Verde's supreme sovereign body, at its latest session in December 1982 approved a motion reiterating its solidarity with the struggle of the South African peoples against *apartheid* and the oppressive régime in South Africa and calling upon the international community to take all possible steps to suspend the application of the death penalty to nationalist combatants of the African National Congress.

---

[1] Report submitted by State (E/CN.4/1984/36/Add.4).

# CHILE

## A. Prohibition of torture or cruel, inhuman or degrading treatment or punishment

### (*article 5 of the Universal Declaration; article 7 of the International Covenant on Civil and Political Rights*)[1]

Article 150 of the Penal Code states:

"The penalties of medium-term rigorous imprisonment or ordinary imprisonment and suspension in any degree shall be applied to:

"Anyone who orders a prisoner to be held incommunicado for an unduly long period or ensures that he is so held, or subjects him to torture or to unnecessarily harsh treatment. If the administration of torture or of unnecessarily harsh treatment injures or results in the death of the subject, the person responsible shall incur the penalties prescribed for those offences in their maximum degrees."

There is a recent instance of the implementation of this provision in the case of two former Security Services officials who, in 1982, made improper use of their authority and tortured and killed two persons. Both were sentenced to death by civil courts, and the sentence was carried out after the presidential pardon had been denied in view of the seriousness of the offence committed.

## B. Right to an effective remedy

### (*article 8 of the Universal Declaration; article 6 of the International Convention on the Elimination of All Forms of Racial Discrimination*)[2]

The Political Constitution which is now in force, and which the people of Chile in the exercise of its sovereignty has freely approved, prescribes these exceptional measures of a transitional nature in transitional article 24.

Transitional article 24 is a rule of an exceptional nature to be applied only in specific cases to be determined by the President of the Republic.

There are various types of recourse against decisions taken by the President of the Republic in the exercise of this constitutional power. In the first place, there is the administrative recourse, a request for review. Next, if it is claimed that these measures are being applied beyond the limits established by the Constitution or in a manner contrary to its provisions, possible remedies include applications for protec-

---

[1] Report submitted by State (CCPR/C/32/Add.1).

[2] *Ibid.* (CERD/C/90/Add.4).

tion and *amparo* (enforcement of constitutional rights) which are heard by the courts of justice.

In this respect it should be mentioned that the Supreme Court of Justice, the highest court in Chile, issued a ruling on 4 May 1982 stating in brief that, in the cases referred to in transitional article 24 of the Constitution, the security agencies must strictly fulfil their constitutional legal obligation to comply with the decisions of the ordinary courts of justice in all matters relating to applications for *habeas corpus*. The Executive Power has expressly complied with this ruling, and has circulated appropriate instructions to the agencies in question.

# CHINA

## A. Protection of human rights and freedoms

*(article 2 of the Universal Declaration;*
*article 5 of the International Convention on the Elimination*
*of All Forms of Racial Discrimination)*[1]

Provisions are made in articles 13, 35-40, 42, 43, 45-47 and 49 of the Constitution of the People's Republic of China with respect to freedom of religious belief, the inviolability of freedom of the person, the inviolability of personal dignity, the inviolability of citizens' homes, freedom of correspondence, right to work, to rest, to health service and social relief, the right to receive education, the freedom to engage in scientific research, literary and artistic creation and other cultural pursuits, the freedom of marriage and protection by the State of the right to own or to inherit private property.

## B. Elimination of racial discrimination; development and protection of certain racial groups or individuals belonging to them

*(article 2 of the Universal Declaration;*
*article 2 (2) of the International Convention on the Elimination*
*of All Forms of Racial Discrimination)*[2]

Regarding the question of nationality, the Constitution of 1982 summarizes experience in this field since the founding of the People's Republic and the need for the common development and prosperity of all nationalities in the future and includes many comprehensive provisions in various areas. The relevant articles are cited below:

1. Principles regarding the nationality question.

(*a*) The People's Republic of China is a unitary multinational State built up jointly by the people of all its nationalities (Preamble).

(*b*) All nationalities in the People's Republic of China are equal. The State protects the lawful rights and interests of the minority nationalities and upholds and develops the relationship of equality, unity and mutual assistance among all of China's nationalities. Discrimination against and oppression of any nationality are prohibited; any acts that undermine the unity of the nationalities or instigate their secession are prohibited.

---

[1] Report submitted by State (CERD/C/101/Add.2).
[2] *Ibid.* (CERD/C/101/Add.2).

2. On regional autonomy of nationalities.

(*a*) The organs of self-government of national autonomous areas are the people's congresses and people's governments of autonomous regions, autonomous prefectures and autonomous counties (article 112).

(*b*) The organs of self-government of the national autonomous areas independently administer educational, scientific, cultural, public health and physical culture affairs in their respective areas, protect and cull through the cultural heritage of the nationalities and work for the development and flourishing of their cultures (article 119).

(*c*) In performing their functions, the organs of self-government of the national autonomous areas, in accordance with the autonomy regulations of the respective areas, employ the spoken and written language or languages in common use in the locality (article 121).

(*d*) Citizens of all nationalities have the right to use the spoken and written languages of their own nationalities in court proceedings. The people's court and prosecutors' offices should provide translation for any party to court proceedings who is not familiar with the spoken or written languages in common use in the locality.

3. The National People's Congress should include deputies of the minority nationalities.

(*a*) The National People's Congress is composed of deputies elected by the provinces, autonomous regions and municipalities directly under the Central Government, and by the armed forces. All minority nationalities are entitled to appropriate representation (article 59).

(*b*) Minority nationalities are entitled to appropriate representation on the Standing Committee on the National People's Congress (article 65).

# CUBA

## A. Condemnation of racial segregation and *apartheid*
### (*articles 1 and 2 of the Universal Declaration;*
### *article 3 of the International Convention on the Elimination*
### *of All Forms of Racial Discrimination*)[1]

Cuba has supported and co-sponsored many resolutions condemning racism, *apartheid* and zionism.

In addition, Cuba voted in favour of the General Assembly resolution calling for the commuting of the death penalty imposed by a racist court of South Africa on the ANC (African National Congress) patriots Thelli Simon Mogoerane, Jerry Semano Mosololi and Marcus Thabo Notaung.

Cuba also co-sponsored the resolution adopted by the General Assembly requesting the International Monetary Fund to refrain from granting any credits or other assistance to South Africa in response to the application by the South African régime to IMF for a loan of 1 billion dollars.

The Cuban delegation to the thirty-seventh session of the United Nations General Assembly took part in the activities of the Week of Solidarity with the People of Namibia and Their Liberation Movement (SWAPO), which began with a solemn ceremony at United Nations Headquarters on 27 October 1982. It also participated in the Day of Solidarity with South African Political Prisoners at United Nations Headquarters, calling for the release of Nelson Mandela and other South African patriots.

As Chairman of the Movement of Non-Aligned Countries, Cuba circulated a document, in the plenary session of the General Assembly calling on States members of the Movement to co-sponsor the draft resolution for the discussion of the item on the policy of *apartheid* of the Government of South Africa.

At the special session of the Security Council to deal with the question of Namibia, held in May 1982 at Arusha, Tanzania, the Cuban Deputy Minister for Foreign Affairs, Oscar Oramas, on behalf of the Movement of Non-Aligned Countries, urged the Council to call for a just solution to the Namibian problem.

During this period, in the Commission on Human Rights, Cuba has supported a number of resolutions condemning discriminatory practices.

---

[1] Report submitted by State (CERD/C/106/Add.3).

## B. Political rights

*(article 21 of the Universal Declaration;*
*article 5 of the International Convention on the Elimination*
*of All Forms of Racial Discrimination)*[2]

With regard to political rights, it should be pointed out that the Elections Act No. 37/82 has been in force in Cuba since 18 September 1982, replacing Act No. 1305 of 1976 and repealing all provisions of laws and regulations which conflict with the implementation of the provisions of the 1982 Act. This new legislation brings together in one legal text the principles and procedures for the electoral system set forth in chapter XI of the Constitution, which provides for equality of rights for all citizens without distinction as to sex or race in both voting and election.

The new Act, as provided in article 1, governs the following:

(*a*) The election of delegates to the Municipal Assemblies of People's Power;

(*b*) The election by the Municipal Assemblies of delegates to the Provincial Assemblies and deputies to the National Assembly of People's Power;

(*c*) The constitution of the Municipal and Provincial Assemblies of People's Power and the election by them of their Executive Committees;

(*d*) The constitution of the National Assembly of People's Power and the election by it of its President, Vice-President and Secretary, as well as the Council of State;

(*e*) The revocation of elected representatives' mandates by their electors;

(*f*) Elections to fill vacant posts;

(*g*) Nation-wide voting in referendums held by the National Assembly of People's Power.

Articles 3 and 4 govern the right to vote and the requirements for exercising it, respectively.

## C. Promotion of understanding, tolerance and friendship among all nations, racial and ethnic groups

*(article 26 (2) of the Universal Declaration;*
*article 7 of the International Convention on the Elimination*
*of All Forms of Racial Discrimination)*[3]

The Cuban United Nations Association (ACNU), a member of the World Federation of United Nations Associations (WFUNA), undertook the following activity:

On 21 March 1982 a speech was made by Mr. Mawete Joao Baptista, the Angolan Ambassador to Cuba, in commemoration of the International Day for the Elimination of Racial Discrimination.

---

[2] *Ibid.* (CERD/C/106/Add.3).
[3] *Ibid.* (CERD/C/106/Add.3).

In addition, the Cuban Institute for Friendship with Peoples (ICAP) undertook various activities in different provinces of the country.

A meeting of the Bureau of the Co-ordinating Committee of the Non-Aligned Countries was held in Havana from 31 May to 5 June 1982; paragraphs 33 to 71 of its final communiqué analyse the situation in Africa, condemn the policy of racial discrimination and *apartheid* and refer to the pressing need for Namibia to achieve independence.

# CYPRUS

## A. Right to social security

*(article 22 of the Universal Declaration;*
*article 9 of the International Covenant on Economic,*
*Social and Cultural Rights)*[1]

A Social Insurance Law (Law 48) and the Social Insurance (Contribution) (Amendment) Regulations were adopted in 1982.

## B. Right to work

*(article 23 (1) of the Universal Declaration;*
*article 6 of the International Covenant on Economic,*
*Social and Cultural Rights)*[2]

The implementation of the Fourth Emergency Economic Action Plan started in 1982 and is of five years' duration.

The objectives of the Fourth Plan with respect to the labour force are summarized below:

(*a*) The maintenance of conditions of full employment;

(*b*) An increase in labour productivity;

(*c*) An increase in earnings within the margins of the rate of growth of productivity;

(*d*) The elimination of those factors which constrain the participation in economic activity and the complete mobilization of groups of population facing special problems;

(*e*) The more rational distribution of the labour force;

(*f*) The qualitative improvement of the labour force through the provision of technical training;

(*g*) The improvement of working conditions.

---

[1] Report submitted by State (E/1984/7/Add.13).
[2] *Ibid.* (E/1984/7/Add.13).

## C.  Right to just and favourable conditions of work
*(article 23 (1) of the Universal Declaration;*
*article 7 of the International Covenant on Economic,*
*Social and Cultural Rights)*[3]

The Agricultural Works (Safety, Health and Welfare) Regulations were adopted in 1982.

## D.  Right to education
*(article 26 of the Universal Declaration;*
*article 13 of the International Covenant on Economic,*
*Social and Cultural Rights)*[4]

As regards the improvement of the material conditions on teaching staff, the payment of pensions to all retired teachers, together with the old age and other benefits from the social insurance funds, is secured by law. From 1 June 1982, maternity leave has been extended to two months with full pay instead of with half pay, as was the case previously.

## E.  Promotion of understanding, tolerance and friendship among all nations, racial and ethnic groups
*(article 26 (2) of the Universal Declaration;*
*article 7 of the International Convention on the Elimination*
*of All Forms of Racial Discrimination)*[5]

The Cultural Service of the Ministry of Education encourages and supports, by subsidies and technical assistance, all institutions and associations working to develop national culture and traditions, to combat racial prejudices and to promote intra-national and intra-cultural understanding, tolerance and friendship among nations and racial or ethnic groups.

For the same purpose the Cultural Service promotes the participation of Cypriot artists in international artistic events abroad and has established bilateral and multilateral cultural relations with other countries by the signing of cultural agreements and programmes of cultural exchanges. In this way intra-cultural understanding is furthered and popularized.

In all local cultural manifestations organized or aided by the Government all ethnic groups can freely participate. For example in the newly established State collection of contemporary Cypriot art, works by artists of Greek, Turkish, Armenian and British origin are included.

The Public Information Office of the Republic of Cyprus circulated a poster on the occasion of the International Day for the Elimination of Racial Discrimination

---

[3] *Ibid.* (E/1984/7/Add.13).
[4] *Ibid.* (E/1982/3/Add.19).
[5] *Ibid.* (CERD/C/118/Add.13).

on 21 March 1982, and also translated and published in Greek the Lusaka Declaration of the Commonwealth on Racism and Racial Prejudice.

The Public Information Office, moreover, encouraged and helped various associations and unions to organize demonstrations and other events to publicize Cyprus's opposition to all forms of racial discrimination. These events are normally covered by the press.

# DENMARK

## A. Right to social security

*(article 22 of the Universal Declaration;*
*article 9 of the International Covenant on Economic,*
*Social and Cultural Rights)*[1]

Under Act No. 574 of 27 October 1982 on the amendment of certain regulations on adjustment within the social legislation, the provisions on adjustment of death grants under the national health security scheme have been amended.

The rate of partial payment for dental care was reduced from 60 to 50 per cent of the charge fixed under approved agreements to persons secured under group 1 (see Order No. 598 of 19 November 1982 of the Ministry of Social Affairs). By the same order, the rate of partial payment to persons included in a regular dental care scheme was reduced from 70 to 60 per cent of the above charges, and the group previously including persons born in 1945 or later was reduced in such a way that the scheme does not apply in respect of dental care provided after the end of the year in which the person in question attains the age of 30.

The Order of 19 December 1982 on the temporary regulation of partial payments under the National Health Security Scheme reduced the partial payment for physiotherapeutical treatment from four fifths to three fifths of the amount fixed under the agreement in respect of persons protected under group 1; the rate of partial payment for physiotherapy has not been changed since 1 July 1982.

Order No. 430 of 19 August 1982 of the Ministry of Social Affairs extended the provisions under the National Health Security Act on partial payment for chiropody. The scheme only applies to diabetics. The rate of partial payment is four fifths of the charges fixed in respect of persons protected under group 1, in accordance with the agreement entered into between the Negotiating Committee of the Health Security Scheme and Landsforeningen af Statsautoriserede Fodterapeuter (Union of State-Authorized Chiropodists).

Order No. 77 of 10 March 1982 on the waiting period in respect of the right to benefits under the National Health Security Act introduced an extension of the right 'o national health security benefits without a waiting period to government scholarship holders.

Order No. 24 of 25 January 1982 of the Ministry of Social Affairs fixed the annual contribution on the part of the shipowner in respect of seamen engaged in foreign trade to DKr 180, with effect from 1 April 1982. On this basis, the shipowner's contribution is calculated at DKr 0.50 per day of employment.

---

[1] Report submitted by State (E/1984/7/Add.11).

Order No. 732 of 21 December 1982 on national health security in respect of seafarers contains amendments made as a consequence of legislative amendments and the amendment of the Nordic Convention on Social Security, as well as a codification of practice in this area.

The provisions on social pensions are laid down in the Order of the Ministry of Social Affairs of 13 July 1982, with subsequent amendments: No. 417 (Old-Age Pension Act), No. 418 (Invalidity Pension Act) and No. 419 (Widow's Pension Act).

With the adoption of the concept of the social income, Act No. 573 of 27 October 1982 amending the Old-Age, Invalidity and Widow's Pension Acts is, in principle, of greatest importance. This new Act departed from the principle of section 3 of the Old-Age Pension Act, in pursuance of which the basic amount of the old-age pension is payable to persons having attained the age of 67, irrespective of their financial situation. Act No. 573, with effect from 1 January 1984, will make the basic amount in respect of persons aged 67 to 69 years subject to an income adjustment on the basis of income gained by employment. However, an amount equal to DKr 35,600 is not taken into account in the adjustment. This amount is indexed in accordance with section 37. The same Act annulled the right to a deferment increment which had been granted where the claim for an old-age pension was deferred for six months or more from the age of 67.

The Acts of 16 June 1980, 10 March 1982, 9 June 1982 and 21 December 1982 increased the amounts available to the local authorities for providing assistance towards heating costs to pensioners so that the amount as of 1 January 1983 was DKr 2,013 per year in respect of a single pensioner who as of 1 January 1983 was in receipt of the full rate of pension supplement from the local authorities. The increases were made as a result of the high fuel prices and the special fuel taxes. The amount is adjusted in accordance with section 37 of the Old-Age Pension Act.

## B. Trade union rights

*(article 23 (4) of the Universal Declaration;*
*article 8 of the International Covenant on Economic,*
*Social and Cultural Rights)*[2]

The Act of 9 June 1982 on protection against dismissal due to organizational matters provides that an employer shall not be allowed to dismiss an employee for being a member of an organization or a particular organization or for not being a member of an organization or a particular organization. However, this protection does not extend to employees who, on recruitment, knew that the employer regarded membership as a condition for employment, or to employees who, on recruitment, were not members of an organization and after recruitment were informed that membership was a condition for continued employment.

The protection of the Act does not extend to cases in which the undertaking has been set up for the purpose of promoting particular viewpoints of a political, ideological, religious or cultural character or in which the organizational affiliation is of importance to the undertaking.

---

[2] *Ibid.* (E/1984/7/Add.11).

## C.  Right to education
*(article 26 of the Universal Declaration;*
*article 13 of the International Covenant on Economic,*
*Social and Cultural Rights)*[3]

A circular of 26 January 1982 co-ordinated enrolment in certain types of youth education. This scheme was formulated to ensure that applicants for some types of youth education are admitted to the education, that they are given the highest priority and that no applicant is admitted to more than one educational institution. This scheme comprises the Gymnasium, the higher preparatory examination and the first part of the basic vocational education.

This circular is based on a resolution of the Folketing of 4 June 1980, in which it invited the Government to ensure that all young people are guaranteed a form of education. As part of this guarantee, it laid down that a coherent system of guidelines and registration of educational wishes should be established.

---

[3] *Ibid.* (E/1982/3/Add.20).

# DOMINICAN REPUBLIC

### Protection of human rights and fundamental freedoms
*(article 2 of the Universal Declaration;*
*article 2 of the International Covenant on Civil and Political Rights)*[1]

Bearing in mind that on 10 December 1948, the United Nations General Assembly proclaimed the Universal Declaration of Human Rights, the content and substance of which constitutes a catalogue of the rights of mankind, and that the Government of National Unity accords full force to the rights enshrined in that historic Declaration and is anxious that all Dominicans should remember that date as one of mankind's major achievements, the Dominican Government in Decree No. 500 of 22 November 1982 proclaimed 10 December of each year as "Human Rights Day".

Simultaneously, it urged employees in the public and private sectors, professionals, industrialists, tradesmen, students, workers and the general public to commemorate that date with appropriate events in the interests of keeping those rights constantly present in the awareness of Dominican citizens.

In order to supplement Decree No. 500 a Commission to prepare the events to celebrate Human Rights Day has been set up comprising the Attorney-General of the Republic, the Legal Counsel of the Executive, the Human Rights Adviser to the President of the Republic, the Chairman of the Dominican Lawyers' Association and the Chairman of the Dominican Union for the Defence of Human Rights.

---

[1] Report submitted by State (CCPR/C/6/Add.10).

# EGYPT

## Limitation on rights; emergency situations

*(article 29 of the Universal Declaration;*
*article 4 of the International Covenant on Civil and Political Rights)*[1]

Act No. 164 of 1981 amended various provisions of Act No. 162 of 1958 concerning the state of emergency. Those amendments applied to the status of persons detained under the Emergency Act who were given the right to submit a complaint to the President of the Republic or his authorized representative if they had not been released within a period of six months from the date of their arrest or detention.

In the event of the rejection of such complaint or failure to take a decision thereon, the person concerned had the right to submit a new complaint six months after the date of submission of his previous complaint.

With a view to the provision of further safeguards for the freedoms of citizens, Act No. 50 of 1982 amended the above text as follows:

"Everyone arrested or detained under the Emergency Act shall immediately be informed, in writing, of the reasons for his arrest or detention and shall have the right to communicate with anyone whom he wishes to advise of what has happened. He shall also be entitled to avail himself of the services of an attorney and shall be treated in the same manner as any other person held in precautionary custody. The detainee, and any other persons concerned, may lodge a complaint against his arrest or detention if he is not released within 30 days after the date of the said arrest or detention. Such complaint shall be submitted, without payment of any charges, to the Supreme Court of State Security constituted in accordance with the provisions of this Act.

"The Court shall take a substantiated decision on the complaint within 15 days after the date of its submission and after hearing the statements of the person arrested or detained; otherwise it shall order his immediate release.

"If an order is issued for the release of the said person, or if no decision is taken on the complaint within the time-limit specified in the preceding paragraph, the Minister of the Interior may appeal against the release order within 15 days after the date of its issue or of the expiry of the above-mentioned time-limit.

"If the Minister of the Interior appeals against the order, his appeal shall be referred to another court within 15 days after the date of its submission and a decision shall be taken thereon within 15 days after the date of its referral; otherwise the detainee must be released immediately and the court order becomes final in such an event.

---

[1] Report submitted by State (CCPR/C/26/Add.1).

"Anyone whose complaint has been rejected shall be entitled to submit a new complaint 30 days after the date of rejection of the said complaint."

The text of article 6 of the Emergency Act is also amended as follows:

### "Article 6

"Persons acting in violation of orders issued in accordance with the provisions of this Act or committing offences specified in such orders shall be liable to immediate arrest.

"Anyone arrested may lodge a complaint against the order for his arrest with the competent State Security Court and a decision must be taken on his complaint within 30 days after the date of its submission; otherwise the person concerned shall be released immediately.

"The competent court may issue an order for the provisional release of the accused during its consideration of the complaint or during the hearing of the case. The decision of the court shall be final unless challenged by the Minister of the Interior within 15 days after the date of its promulgation in cases where the accused is charged with offences against the internal or external security of the State.

"If the Minister of the Interior appeals against the release order in such cases, his appeal shall be referred to another court within 15 days after the date on which it is lodged and a decision shall be taken on the said appeal within 15 days after the date of its referral; otherwise the accused shall be released immediately and the court order shall be final in such cases."

# EL SALVADOR

## A. Protection of human rights and fundamental freedoms
*(article 2 of the Universal Declaration;*
*article 2 of the International Covenant on Civil and Political Rights)*[1]

One of the most recent measures adopted by the Government of National Unity to guarantee the provisions of the Covenant is the establishment, by Executive Decree No. 30, dated 10 December 1982 and published in the *Diario Oficial,* No. 221, of the same date, of the Human Rights Commission as part of the basic government platform signed by the President of the Republic and by the political parties which are represented in the Constituent Assembly and whose human rights aims are: "To achieve the full implementation of the inalienable rights of the individual and to ensure that the State is an effective guarantor not only of the physical security of the individual, but also of the full development of his personality."

The basic government platform provides for the establishment of three commissions, one of which is the Human Rights Commission. "In order to ensure the protection, implementation and promotion of these rights to the fullest possible extent", a Commission will be established, with the agreement of the Executive, to recommend appropriate measures for the effective observance of human rights, especially those recognized by the Political Constitution and international agreements.

The foregoing principles are enunciated in the preambular paragraphs of the Decree establishing the statutes of the Human Rights Commission.

## B. Right to take part in government
*(article 21 of the Universal Declaration;*
*article 1 of the International Covenant on Civil and Political Rights)*[2]

Decree No. 999, dated 24 February 1982, introduced an amendment extending the suspension of constitutional guarantees, except in the case of political parties, which were authorized to seek electoral support and publish election propaganda without being subject to the restrictions imposed by the suspension of constitutional guarantees.

Decree No. 999 ceased to have effect on 24 March 1982, when constitutional guarantees were restored, thus making it possible for the elections of 28 March to be held in an atmosphere of freedom.

---

[1] Report submitted by State (CCPR/C/14/Add.5).

[2] *Ibid.* (CCPR/C/14/Add.5).

The Government of El Salvador, which is aware of the need to establish more democratic conditions in the country in order to guarantee constitutional stability and the well-being of its inhabitants, set in motion the electoral process that led to the elections of 28 March 1982, in which Salvadorians freely elected their representatives to the Constituent Assembly and entrusted them with the task of drawing up a new Constitution. This new fundamental law of the Republic will be promulgated shortly. Being convinced that the Salvadorian people is fully entitled freely to determine its political status, the Government of El Salvador intends to hold presidential elections at the end of this year. With a view to the election, the Government has, through the Political Commission, the Peace Commission and the Human Rights Commission, appealed to the rebels to lay down their arms and to take part in the electoral campaign.

### C. Limitations on rights; emergency situations
*(article 29 of the Universal Declaration;
article 4 of the International Covenant on Civil and Political Rights)*[3]

On 20 April 1982, by Decree No. 1089, published in the *Diario Oficial,* No. 71, vol. 275, the Revolutionary Government Junta, in consideration of the fact that the electoral process had been completed and that the circumstances which had given rise to Decree No. 155 again obtained, suspended constitutional guarantees once more.

By Decree No. 7, dated 20 May 1982 and published in the *Diario Oficial,* No. 29, vol. 275, the Legislative Assembly, which was elected on 28 March, extended the effects of Revolutionary Government Junta Decree No. 1089 and has subsequently continued to extend the suspension of guarantees in view of the continuing violence in the country and the attacks by subversive groups.

---

[3] *Ibid.* (CCPR/C/14/Add.5).

# ETHIOPIA

### Right to form trade unions

*(article 23 of the Universal Declaration;*
*article 5 of the International Convention on the Elimination*
*of All Forms of Racial Discrimination)*[1]

The establishment of trade unions in Ethiopia is governed by the Trade Unions Organization Proclamation No. 22/1982. This Proclamation is totally different from the Proclamation on ''Peasant Associations Consolidation Proclamation No. 223/1982'' or other laws on the formation of co-operatives. The Trade Unions Organization Proclamation treats thoroughly the conditions of the establishment of trade unions in seven parts which deal, among others, with the objectives and functions of trade unions, their formation, membership, legal personality and administration. Article 14 of this Proclamation dealing with membership specifically states that ''any worker has the right to be a member of a trade union in accordance with this Proclamation; membership shall be voluntary''.

---

[1] Report submitted by State (CERD/C/104/Add.3).

# FINLAND

## A. Elimination of racial discrimination; development and protection of certain racial groups or individuals belonging to them

*(articles 2, 7 and 22 of the Universal Declaration;*
*article 2 (2) of the International Convention on the Elimination*
*of All Forms of Racial Discrimination)*[1]

A provision was included in 1982 in the Law on Children's Day Care, according to which the municipalities are obliged to arrange day care in the mother tongue of a child (Finnish, Swedish or Sami language). The purpose of that provision is primarily to secure the said right to children belonging to a linguistic minority in a given municipality.

## B. Right to work

*(article 23 (1) of the Universal Declaration;*
*article 6 of the International Covenant on Economic,*
*Social and Cultural Rights)*[2]

At the beginning of 1982, the Ministry of Labour undertook the drafting of a new programme on employment and manpower policy (the previous programme dates from 1974), the aim of which is to achieve and maintain full employment. The programme runs until the mid-1990s.

## C. Right to just and favourable conditions of work

*(article 23 (1) of the Universal Declaration;*
*article 7 of the International Covenant on Economic,*
*Social and Cultural Rights)*[3]

The following regulations aimed at improving labour protection, were introduced in 1982:

Decision No. 355/82 of the Council of State concerning work involving exposure to benzene;

Decision No. 356/82 of the Council of State concerning the elimination and supervision of harmful effects due to the use of lead;

---

[1] Report submitted by State (CERD/C/107/Add.3).

[2] *Ibid.* (E/1984/7/Add.14).

[3] *Ibid.* (E/1984/7/Add.14).

51

Decision No. 191/82 of the Council of State concerning protection against hearing impairment caused by work;

Decision No. 769/82 of the Council of State concerning the application of the Labour Protection Act to suspension scaffolding and the inspection thereof;

Decision No. 354/83 of the Council of State concerning loading cranes and the inspection thereof.

The Act concerning the working hours of seafarers on vessels in domestic transport was completely amended in 1982 (No. 248/82). By this Act, the statutory weekly working hours were reduced to 40. The 40-hour week had already been included in collective agreements. The new Act also contains more detailed provisions on the organization of working hours and periods of rest, as well as the maximum lengths of overtime.

## D. Right to take part in cultural life

*(article 27 (1) of the Universal Declaration;*
*article 15 of the International Covenant on Economic,*
*Social and Cultural Rights)*[4]

From the beginning of 1982 the legislation on artists, fellowships and grants was complemented by the possibility of awarding 15-year working fellowships for talented active artists with no permanent working relationship. The long-term fellowships also include a pension guarantee.

---

[4] *Ibid.* (E/1982/3/Add.28).

# FRANCE

## A. Elimination of discrimination based on sex
*(article 2 of the Universal Declaration;*
*article 3 of the International Covenant on Civil and Political Rights)*[1]

Under Act No. 82-596 of 10 July 1982, relating to the spouses of artisans and tradesmen working in the family business, the status of wives of artisans and tradesmen has improved.

Position of women in public service: Act No. 82-380 of 7 May 1982, amending article 7 of the Ordinance of 4 February 1959 concerning the general status of public officials and containing a number of provisions relating to the principle of equality of access to public employment, provides that no distinction shall be made between men and women, subject to the provisions of the Act regarding separate recruitment of men or women to bodies in which the person's sex is a prerequisite for performance of the duties involved.

A list of the bodies in question has been laid down in a Decree of 15 October 1982.

The Act of 7 May 1982 also establishes a procedure whereby the few remaining derogations are reviewed in consultation with the competent joint bodies, on the basis of a report on application of the principle of equality of the sexes in public service that is submitted to Parliament every two years.

## B. Equal protection of the law
*(articles 2 and 7 of the Universal Declaration;*
*articles 2 (1) and (2) and 26 of the International Covenant on Civil and Political Rights)*[2]

Act No. 82-683 of 4 August 1982 repealed article 331, paragraph 2, of the Criminal Code, whereby any person committing an indecent or unnatural act with a minor of the same sex was liable to imprisonment for six months to three years and a fine of 60 francs to 20,000 francs. Such acts, therefore, are now subject to the same penalties, irrespective of the sex of the minor, pursuant, *inter alia,* to articles 331, 331-1 and 333 of the Criminal Code.

---

[1] Report submitted by State (CCPR/C/22/Add.4).

[2] *Ibid.* (CCPR/C/22/Add.4).

## C. Treatment compatible with human dignity

*(article 5 of the Universal Declaration;*
*article 10 (3) of the International Covenant on Civil and Political Rights)*[3]

Special security wings designed to isolate convicted persons considered to be dangerous, and with prison conditions harsher than elsewhere, were abolished by Decree No. 82-191 of 26 February 1982.

## D. Right to all the guarantees necessary for defence

*(article 11 of the Universal Declaration;*
*article 14 (3) of the International Covenant on Civil and Political Rights)*[4]

Legal aid, introduced under the Act of 3 January 1972 as amended by the Act of 31 December 1982, is designed to enable persons with insufficient resources to have access to the law.

It applies to:

All disputes referred to the ordinary courts of law (although in criminal proceedings it is confined to actions brought by a claimant for criminal indemnification and to actions involving persons liable in civil law that are brought before the trial courts);

Disputes brought before the conflicts court, the Council of State and the administrative courts.

Any person accused of an offence, whether before or after committal for trial, may, irrespective of his financial position, ask for a lawyer to be officially assigned to him. Under the Act of 31 December 1982, lawyers who are officially assigned can receive a fee from the State if the resources of such person do not exceed the prescribed ceiling for full legal aid.

## E. Right to freedom of movement and residence

*(article 13 of the Universal Declaration;*
*article 13 of the International Covenant on Civil and Political Rights)*[5]

Decrees have been issued to implement Act No. 81-973 of 29 October 1981, which amends the Ordinance of 2 November 1945 relating to the entry of aliens and the conditions governing their residence in France; they include Decree No. 82-440 of 26 May 1982, governing the various stages in the deportation procedure.

---

[3] *Ibid.* (CCPR/C/22/Add.2).
[4] *Ibid.* (CCPR/C/22/Add.4).
[5] *Ibid.* (CCPR/C/22/Add.4).

## F. Freedom of opinion and expression

*(article 19 of the Universal Declaration;*
*article 19 of the International Covenant on Civil and Political Rights)*[6]

Act No. 82-652 of 29 July 1982, on audio-visual communication, concerns the state radio and television service and all systems for broadcasting programmes and images to the public.

Article 1 of the Act provides that audio-visual communication shall be free. One of the main purposes of the Act is to set out the arrangements for this freedom and this has been done in Title IV, "Audio-visual communication services requiring a declaration or authorization". Hence, anyone can now express his views on radio or television, within the appropriate legal framework.

The Act of 29 July 1982 has not only vested public and private persons with the right to communicate freely but has also strengthened the independence of audio-visual public service agencies. An Audio-visual Communications Board is responsible for ensuring the independence of programme companies and public corporations.

This Act has been made applicable throughout the Overseas Departments.

## G. Right to work; right to just and favourable conditions of work; right to equal pay for equal work

*(article 23 (1) and (2) of the Universal Declaration;*
*article 5 (e) of the International Convention on the Elimination*
*of All Forms of Racial Discrimination)*[7]

The Act of 4 August 1982 establishing regulations concerning labour contracts amended article L.122-35 of the Labour Code by specifying that the internal regulations of enterprises "may not include provisions which jeopardize wage-earners in their employment or their work because of their sex, their family situation, their origins, their opinions or faith, or their handicaps, their professional abilities being equal".

Similarly, such internal regulations "may not impose on people's rights or on individual and collective freedoms restrictions which are not justified by the nature of the task to be performed or proportionate to the purpose sought". Lastly, article L.122-45 states: "No wage-earner may be punished or dismissed because of his origin, his sex, his family situation, his membership of a particular ethnic group, his colour or race, his political opinions, his trade union activities or his religious beliefs."

In addition, the Collective Bargaining Act of 13 November 1982 established the principle of equal treatment for French and alien wage-earners, in particular with regard to employment (Labour Code, art. L.133-5, tenth paragraph).

---

[6] *Ibid.* (CCPR/C/22/Add.4).
[7] *Ibid.* (CERD/C/117/Add.2).

## H.  Right to form trade unions

*(article 23 (4) of the Universal Declaration;*
*article 22 of the International Covenant on Civil and Political Rights)*[8]

The conditions governing the exercise of the right to form trade unions conferred upon public officials were set forth in a directive by the Prime Minister dated 14 September 1970 and subsequently in a decree of 28 May 1982. In particular the decree confers upon any government servant wishing to do so the right to attend, for one hour a month during working hours, a trade union information meeting held in administrative buildings. It also extends the facilities for time off which are granted by the administration to trade union representatives to enable them to perform their functions.

## I.  Right to a social and international order in which human rights can be realized

*(article 28 of the Universal Declaration)*[9]

On 16 April 1982 the declaration of acceptance of the individual right of appeal provided for in article 14 of the International Convention on the Elimination of All Forms of Racial Discrimination was deposited with the Secretary-General of the United Nations.

## J.  Limitations on the exercise of rights and freedoms; emergency situations

*(article 29 of the Universal Declaration;*
*article 4 of the International Covenant on Civil and Political Rights)*[10]

Under Act No. 82-621 of 21 July 1982, concerning the investigation and trial of military offences and offences against the security of the State, which amends the Codes of Criminal Procedure and of Military Justice, the Permanent Courts of the Armed Forces have been abolished.

In the event of a declaration of a state of siege or a state of emergency, territorial courts of the armed forces may be established; they will have the same jurisdiction as in wartime.

---

[8] *Ibid.* (CCPR/C/22/Add.4).
[9] *Ibid.* (CERD/C/117/Add.2).
[10] *Ibid.* (CCPR/C/22/Add.4).

# GERMAN DEMOCRATIC REPUBLIC

## A. Protection of minorities

*(articles 2, 7 and 22 of the Universal Declaration;*
*article 27 of the International Covenant on Civil and Political Rights)*[1]

The Domovina which represents the interests of the Sorbs and observed the 70th anniversary of its foundation in 1982 has a considerable share in the all-round development of the Sorbs. In the period between the 9th and the 10th Federal Congress held in March 1982, it organized 48,424 public functions of all kinds in which 1,373,500 citizens participated.

## B. Right to life, liberty and security of person

*(article 3 of the Universal Declaration;*
*article 6 of the International Covenant on Civil and Political Rights)*[2]

The German Democratic Republic initiated, e.g., the resolution on "Measures to be taken against Nazi, Fascist and neo-Fascist activities and all other forms of totalitarian ideologies and practices based on racial intolerance, hatred and terror", which was adopted at the thirty-seventh United Nations General Assembly.

Based on the internationally accepted principles embodied in article 7 of the Constitution, the Law on the State Frontier of the German Democratic Republic, which was enacted on 25 March 1982 (*Gesetzblatt I*, No. 11, p. 147), gives due consideration to the function of the State frontier with regard to the establishment of a stable peace order throughout Europe and to the actual state of intergovernmental agreements and arrangements concerning all matters in respect of the State frontier.

The Law reaffirms the character of the German Democratic Republic's frontier in terms of international law and provides the legal prerequisites for the inviolability of the State frontier, for security and order in the frontier areas. Security of frontiers and their unqualified recognition proves whether the policy of a State serves peace and, hence, the interests of mankind. It is, therefore, necessary to adopt appropriate measures designed to suppress violations of the frontier and safeguard their inviolability (article 17).

Article 23 of the Constitution of the German Democratic Republic of 7 October 1974 defines the protection of peace and the socialist homeland as a basic right and the honourable obligation of the citizens. For that purpose such fundamental laws as the Defence Act of 13 October 1978 (*Gesetzblatt I*, No. 35, p. 377) and the Military Service Act of 25 March 1982 (*Gesetzblatt I*, No. 12, p. 221) were enacted.

---

[1] Report submitted by State (CCPR/C/28/Add.2).

[2] *Ibid.* (CCPR/C/28/Add.2).

During military service or a corresponding service without weapon training, German Democratic Republic citizens have the same basic rights and duties as are provided under the Constitution for all citizens in general (article 21 of the Act). This also applies to members of construction units of the Ministry of National Defence who, for religious or similar reasons, object to armed service and, therefore, do alternative service in special units.

## C.  Administration of justice: right to protection of the law; right to a fair and public hearing
### (articles 7 to 10 of the Universal Declaration; articles 14 and 15 of the International Covenant on Civil and Political Rights)[3]

The new Law on social courts of 25 March 1982 (*Gesetzblatt I*, No. 13, p. 269) enhances legal security and promotes the civil rights of the citizens. The activity of social courts, i.e. disputes and arbitration commissions, is characterized by a close involvement of the citizens as hearings held before such courts are public and their members are elected and work in an honorary capacity.

As a rule, social courts can finally settle disputes without having administrative authority or powers. The functioning of these courts as part of the system of administration of justice adds to the rule of law and legal security and the protection of the citizens' rights.

The judiciary provides safeguards for the subjective rights of the citizens in other branches of law, such as labour and family law, making sure that the principle of equality as set forth in articles 2 and 3 of the Covenant is observed. On 27 January 1982 the Supreme Court Presidium dealt, for instance, with demands to be made on the elucidation of facts in civil, family and labour law proceedings.

## D.  Right to work
### (article 23 (1) of the Universal Declaration; article 6 of the International Covenant on Economic, Social and Cultural Rights)[4]

On 2 July 1982, the Co-operative Farms Act (*Gesetzblatt I,* No. 25, p. 443) was adopted by the People's Chamber after six months of public discussion and approval at the Twelfth Farmers' Congress.

The Co-operative Farms Act consistently establishes that co-operative farms are fully responsible for the efficient use of their property on the grounds of their juridical and economic independence. The Act contains stipulations which are important for every farm member, above all the right to participate in co-operative work according to their abilities and knowledge (article 31). Similar to the provisions of the Labour Code, article 29 of the Act guarantees to all co-operative farmers the right to work, to participate in farm management and planning, to remuneration according to the quality and quantity of work depending on the economic result of the

---

[3] *Ibid.* (CCPR/C/28/Add.2).
[4] *Ibid.* (E/1984/7/Add.3).

co-operative concerned, to education, leisure time and recreation, to protection of health and working capacity, to old-age and disability care, and to social security in case of illness or accident.

The Ordinance of 4 January 1982 on preparatory courses for young skilled workers to qualify for higher education in the German Democratic Republic (*Gesetzblatt I*, No. 4, p. 103) has opened up another channel to college or university. Accordingly, accomplished young workers may attend a one-year full-time study course at certain institutes of higher learning to achieve university entrance qualifications entitling them to enrolment in a specific branch of study. This presupposes the successful completion of a ten-year general polytechnical secondary education and of vocational training that corresponds to the chosen branch of study, and a good record of vocational and social performance.

The Ordinance of 5 January 1982 on applications for an apprenticeship (*Gesetzblatt I*, No. 4, p. 95) prolongs the period in which an application may be submitted from 6 to 15 days. At the same time, the processing time of applications for an apprenticeship encompassing higher education entrance qualifications was shortened from 21 days to 14, thus giving applicants who are turned down the chance to apply again for training as skilled workers together with the other school-leavers. Such an application is decided on by the employer concerned together with the enterprise Trade Union Committee and the Free German Youth branch.

### E. Trade union rights

*(article 23 (4) of the Universal Declaration;*
*article 8 of the International Covenant on Economic,*
*Social and Cultural Rights)*[5]

A highlight in trade union activity was the tenth Congress of the Confederation of Free German Trade Unions, held at Berlin from 21 to 24 April 1982. It demonstrated the role of trade unions in increasing the say of the working class in economic and other public affairs. FDGB has proved to be an important force in fulfilling economic, cultural and social tasks. By virtue of the comprehensive rights that the Constitution of the German Democratic Republic and the Labour Code vest in the trade unions, they give great attention to the steady improvement of living and working conditions.

The Social Courts Act of 25 March 1982 (*Gesetzblatt I*, No. 13, p. 269) is of great importance for the implementation and protection of the right to work. FDGB played an active part in the elaboration and discussion of the Act, because its operation involves a number of important trade union rights and tasks.

In connection with the Social Courts Act, the Disputes Commission Regulation of 12 March 1982 (*Gesetzblatt I*, No. 13, p. 274) should be mentioned, since it invokes trade union rights and responsibilities.

---

[5] *Ibid.* (E/1984/7/Add.3).

# GERMANY, FEDERAL REPUBLIC OF

## A. Elimination of racial discrimination; development and protection of certain racial groups or individuals belonging to them

*(article 2 of the Universal Declaration;*
*article 2 (2) of the International Convention on the Elimination*
*of All Forms of Racial Discrimination)*[1]

In May 1982, the Federal Minister of Education and Science invited the Sinti associations in the Federal Republic of Germany, a number of experienced practitioners from the school and social work sector, representatives of institutions and school administrations together with a number of experts to conduct special talks on these problems and possible ways of resolving them.

The Minister will carefully evaluate the talks and develop proposed solutions which all the participants—including the Sinti/Rom Gypsies themselves—can help to implement.

## B. Protection against racial discrimination; prohibition of organizations promoting racial discrimination

*(article 7 of the Universal Declaration;*
*article 4 of the International Convention on the Elimination*
*of All Forms of Racial Discrimination)*[2]

The Volkssozialistische Bewegung Deutschlands/Partei der Arbeit (German People's Socialist Movement/Party of Labour), including the Junge Front (Youth Front), was banned on 14 January 1982, under section 3 of the Law on Associations.

## C. Right to an effective remedy

*(article 8 of the Universal Declaration;*
*article 6 of the International Convention on the Elimination*
*of All Forms of Racial Discrimination)*[3]

*Judgement handed down by Rosenheim Local Court on 6 May 1982—reference 3 Ls 11 Js 22155/81*

---

[1] Report submitted by State (CERD/C/91/Add.30).
[2] *Ibid.* (CERD/C/118/Add.19).
[3] *Ibid.* (CERD/C/118/Add.19).

*Facts of the case*

The accused were two brothers, aged 21 and 17, and their 17-year-old friend, a painter, an apprentice mason and an apprentice painter respectively. During the period from 1978 to 1981 the accused had spray-painted political slogans on streets, fences and a number of public buildings. The slogans in question were of a National Socialist nature, such as "Germany awake!", "Jews out!" and "Foreigners out!". They also sprayed National Socialist emblems such as swastikas and other symbols such as "SS", "NSDAP" and "SA".

*Findings*

All three accused were found guilty of repeated illegal use of the symbols of unconstitutional organizations, in conjunction with repeated instigation to racial hatred and incitement of the people as well as damage to property.

The slogans from the Nazi period sprayed by the accused were likely, in the court's view, to cause a breach of the peace and to incite people to hatred against sections of the population.

*Sentence*

The elder of the brothers was sentenced to eight months' detention at a young offenders' institution. He was put on probation on the grounds that he had in the mean time left the National Democratic Party of Germany (NPD) and had evidently begun to appreciate the seriousness of the offences he had committed.

The other accused were sentenced to seven days' detention and to juvenile leisure-time detention respectively. The court made allowances for the fact that the two younger accused had given little thought to their action, which was evidently motivated more by friendship with the older accused than any other grounds.

*Judgement handed down by Koblenz Regional Court on 7 September 1982— reference 101 Js 2545/81-1 Ns*

*Facts of the case*

In 1976, the accused, an 81-year-old pensioner, had produced some 2,000 leaflets, some of which he distributed himself but most of which he made available at cost price to right-wing extremist groups propagating Nazi ideology. For distributing the leaflets, through which he sought to stir up hatred and antipathy towards Jews, including those living in Germany, the accused had been found guilty of incitement of the people. Two years later he decided once again to enlighten the public about the "conservation of the purity of the German race" and the "pernicious influence of Jews on the German nation, its race and culture". He distributed leaflets with titles such as "Zionist humility" and duplicated extracts from certain pamphlets, for instance one entitled "Young people of Europe! What do you know about the founder of the Pan-European Union?" He distributed a number of leaflets to 16- to 19-year-old pupils at the gates of senior secondary schools in order to involve them in discussions on the content of the leaflets and with the intention of winning the pupils over to the opinions expressed in them.

### Findings

The accused was found guilty of incitement of the people (Penal Code, sect. 130). In sentence after sentence of the distributed publications, enmity towards Jews in general, and towards those Jews living in the Federal Republic of Germany, was aroused. The accusations made against the Jews in the pamphlets were formulated in the same way as the atrocity propaganda of the Nazis with its notorious and unfounded claims. The value and human dignity of the Jewish people, as well as their unrestricted right to live as citizens within the community of the State, were disputed. The tenor and purpose of the publications were unmistakable and were recognized by most of the pupils. He was also found guilty of instigation to racial hatred (Penal Code, sect. 131 (1) 1 and 4).

### Sentence (by the court of second instance)

The accused was sentenced to seven months' imprisonment, and the confiscation of the distributed publications was ordered.

The fact that, notwithstanding his previous trial, the accused had wanted to publicize his racist views again and had sought in particular to infect young people with Nazi ideology was found to have aggravated the offence. In the view of the court, the actions of the accused, who had caused an actual breach of public peace and security, must not be played down and ridiculed as the hare-brained scheme of someone unable to face up to present reality. Only the advanced age of the accused justified the passing of a sentence at the lower end of the scale, despite his previous conviction. If the accused had been younger, the sentence would not have constituted due punishment for his renewed serious offence.

### Judgement handed down by Ludwigshafen am Rhein Local Court on 12 November 1982—reference 140 Js ,6763/82 Ls

### Facts of the case

The accused, a 36-year-old mechanic, distributed copies of a leaflet in Ludwigshafen from the DVR Association for the Restoration in Peace of the Unity of Germany and the German People and of Equality with all Nations, for which he was also responsible under press legislation. Over the entire leaflet was stamped diagonally in red the word "fraud". In the accompanying article, the extermination of Jews during the Hitler régime was denied and the indemnification payments made by the Federal Republic of Germany presented as having been fraudulently procured. In a further leaflet entitled "Bloody hands" the accused admonished parents and youths to read the leaflet over and over again while watching films like "that third-rate horror movie *Holocaust*" and to hang it up next to their television sets.

### Findings

The accused was found guilty of incitement of the people, compounded by incitement to racial hatred.

*Sentence*

The accused was fined 120 per diem rates of 50 deutsche mark. In determining the sentence, the court made allowance for the fact that the accused had no previous criminal convictions. It held the crime to have been aggravated by the offence given to many people, particularly to the Jewish people, by the method of presentation which the accused adopted in the leaflets and by the fact that during the proceedings he had neither properly distanced himself from the accusations nor offered any apology.

# HAITI

## A. Principle of equal treatment

*(articles 2 and 7 of the Universal Declaration;*
*articles 2 and 5 of the International Convention on the Elimination*
*of All Forms of Racial Discrimination)*[1]

For the purpose of preventing any kind of discrimination, the Legislature has in the regulations for the civil service, instituted the merit system, which is based on the aptitude, assiduousness and competence of civil servants.

The laws of 30 September and 12 October 1982 on the standardization of the structures of the Haitian public administration and on the civil service were enacted so as to afford guarantees of a proper career for all civil servants and public employees. They are based on the intrinsic value of each individual, the sole criterion for the selection, advancement and retirement pension of the holder of an administrative post.

With reference to legislative measures taken by the Government as regards non-discrimination between individuals, attention should be drawn to the electoral law of 22 October 1982.

To ensure full participation by the rural and urban masses in the communal and the general elections and to enable citizens to vote freely, without any constraint, the electoral law of 22 October 1982 provides for the establishment of *ad hoc* registration bureaux and for voting booths in all of the rural areas. It provides for registration of voters, acceptance of voters' identification cards, a ban on trafficking in votes, a specified period for the electoral campaign, a court procedure for settling electoral disputes, and so on.

## B. Treatment compatible with human dignity

*(article 5 of the Universal Declaration;*
*articles 2 and 5 of the International Convention on the Elimination*
*of All Forms of Racial Discrimination)*[2]

*Decree of 7 April 1982 bringing the criminal laws in force into line with the International Conventions signed and ratified by the Government of Haiti.*

*Article 2.* In cases of sentences to hard labour or rigorous imprisonment, the work required of the prisoner shall depend on actual need and shall be carried out in

---

[1] Report submitted by State (CERD/C/116/Add.2).

[2] *Ibid.* (CERD/C/89/Add.2).

the general interest, in decent and humane conditions, taking account of the prisoner's health and physical and mental ability.

*Article 3.* In cases of sentences to ordinary imprisonment, the prisoner shall, depending on the state of his health, be assigned to organized labour in a centre operating under the supervision of the Prison Administration, with the co-operation of the Department of Social Affairs.

The prisoner shall be free to choose activities with a bearing on his usual occupation and commensurate with his abilities.

His wishes shall be recorded in a document signed by him and the prison director.

If the prisoner does not know how to write, he shall sign by means of a fingerprint.

*Article 7.* Depending on the availability of funds, suitable quarters shall be provided in every prison for persons who are being held in pre-trial detention or who have been convicted of crimes of opinion, breaches of discipline at work or political offences.

Such detainees and prisoners may receive visits from their families, friends, and lawyers at times to be specified by the prison director.

They shall be subject to the rules and regulations relating to the maintenance of order and security within the prison and may, like any other detainees and prisoners, be punished for disciplinary offences.

*Article 9.* Article 17 of the Penal Code is hereby amended to read:

"*Article 17:* Sentences of life imprisonment shall entail the loss of civil and political rights as of the date of enforcement, subject to the legal effects of pardon, commutation of sentence, rehabilitation and amnesty."

*Article 10.* Article 18 of the Penal Code is hereby amended to read:

"*Article 18:* A temporary prison sentence entailing the loss of civil and political rights shall, *de jure*, be subject to the legal prohibitions provided for in article 28 of the Penal Code for the duration of the sentence, subject to the conditions provided for in the preceding article."

## C. Right to education

*(article 26 of the Universal Declaration;*
*(article 5 of the International Convention on the Elimination*
*of All Forms of Racial Discrimination)*[3]

The Government of Haiti has taken a number of measures in the area of education which are designed to promote action to combat racial discrimination.

In this connection, mention should be made of the Decree of 5 April 1982, which made the teaching of Creole compulsory in primary schools throughout the Republic of Haiti.

---

[3] *Ibid.* (CERD/C/89/Add.2).

# HOLY SEE

### Promotion of understanding, tolerance and friendship
### among all nations, racial and ethnic groups
*(article 26 (2) of the Universal Declaration;*
*article 7 of the International Convention on the Elimination*
*of All Forms of Racial Discrimination)*[1]

The Holy See's own action to oppose racial discrimination, is, above all, a work of education of conscience guided by the light of the Gospel. Thus the action of the Holy See in this area is illustrated from the principal papal documents. It is not of course an exhaustive list.

Address of His Holiness Pope John Paul II to the Diplomatic Corps accredited to the Holy See, 16 January 1982 (*L'Osservatore Romano*, English edition, No. 4, 25 January 1982, p. 2):

"The conviction is gaining ground daily in public opinion that the peoples must be able to choose freely the social organization to which they aspire for their own country, and that this organization should be in conformity with justice, in respect of freedom, religious faith, and human rights in general. It is a commonly shared conviction that no people should be treated by other peoples as subordinate or as an instrument, in defiance of equality which is inscribed in human conscience and recognized by the norms of international law."

Address of His Holiness Pope John Paul II to the President of the Federal Republic of Nigeria, 12 February 1982 (*L'Osservatore Romano*, English edition, No. 7, 15 February 1982, p. 3):

"It is my conviction that all Africa, when allowed to take charge of its own affairs, without being subjected to interference and pressure from any outside powers or groups, will not only astound the rest of the world by its achievements, but will be able to share its wisdom, its sense of life, its reverence for God with other continents and nations, thus establishing that exchange and that partnership in mutual respect that is needed for the true progress of all humanity.

"I therefore desire to pay homage to the significant contribution which the Nigerian nation has made and is making in the first place to the African continent. You forcefully stand up for political freedom and for the right of all peoples to self-determination. You spare no efforts to help remove all discrimination against people because of their colour, race, language or social status."

---

[1] Report submitted by State (CERD/C/91/Add.17).

Address of His Holiness Pope John Paul II to South African Bishops on their *Ad limina* visit, 27 April 1982 (*L'Osservatore Romano*, English edition, No. 19, 10 May 1982, p. 19):

"But there is more. I wish to thank you in the name of Christ and his Church for all your dedicated efforts on behalf of peace. You have striven vigorously to help implant the peace of Christ in human hearts, in families, in communities that have racial differences and are faced with serious racial discrimination, and throughout your nations. By its very nature, your work for peace, situated as it is in the historical framework of your local situations, has had to be concerned for freedom and for everything that freedom entails. You have worked conscientiously and perseveringly for justice and for human dignity rightly insisting on non-violence and the need for reconciliation among brothers and sisters—so that all people may enjoy the freedom of the children of God, that freedom for which Christ set us free (cf. Gal. 5:1). In fulfilling your ministry, you have endeavoured to apply fundamental Christian principles, some of which I alluded to in the context of the 1981 World Day of Peace: 'Without a deep and universal respect for freedom, peace will elude man . . . Freedom is wounded when the relationships between peoples are based not on respect for the equal dignity of each but upon the right of the most powerful . . .' (Message of 8 December 1980, No. 2). And again: 'The freedom of the individual finds its basis in man's transcendent dignity: a dignity given to him by God, his Creator, and which directs him towards God . . . To be free is to be able to choose and to want to choose; it is to live according to one's conscience.'

"In particular, I know that you are looking forward with positive hope to the difficult but necessary process that must result in a just and peaceful solution to the problem of Namibia for the good of its people. I am close to you in this pastoral concern of yours and I continue to keep this intention in my heart and to remember it in my prayers."

# HUNGARY

## A. Condemnation of racial segregation and *apartheid*

*(articles 1 and 2 of the Universal Declaration;*
*article IV of the International Convention on the Suppression*
*and Punishment of the Crime of* Apartheid)[1]

Solidarity mass rallies were held to observe the Africa Day in 1982 and the Liberty Day of South Africa in the presence of representatives of the African National Congress. Meetings were also held on the occasion of the 70th anniversary of the foundation of the ANC. On the Days of Namibia in the past two years peace rallies were organized with thousands of participants. Solidarity events included the observance of Solidarity Day in the presence of ANC and South West African Peoples' Organization representatives. The policy of scholarship grants to students of ANC and SWAPO for secondary and higher education in Hungary has been continued in the period 1982-1983. Voluntary relief supplies are dispatched annually to the refugee camps of ANC and SWAPO.

## B. Right to social security

*(article 22 of the Universal Declaration;*
*article 9 of the International Covenant on Economic, Social and Cultural Rights)[2]*

In 1982, new measures were introduced in respect of the child-care allowance scheme: a mother or a father bringing up her or his child alone is entitled to a child-care allowance until the child reaches three years of age or, in the case of continuing illness or a serious handicap, six years of age, provided that, within two years immediately prior to childbirth, the parent:

(*a*) Has been in employment working at least four hours a day; or

(*b*) Has been covered by insurance as an outside worker; or

(*c*) Has been a member of an industrial co-operative, working at least four hours a day.

After the child reaches one year of age, the father is also entitled to avail himself, instead of the mother, of the benefit of the child-care allowance (Decree No. 10/1982 (IV.16) of the Council of Ministers).

---

[1] Report submitted by State (E/CN.4/1984/36/Add.7).

[2] *Ibid.* (E/1984/7/Add.15).

# ICELAND

## Right to an effective remedy
*(article 8 of the Universal Declaration;*
*article 6 of the International Convention on the Elimination*
*of All Forms of Racial Discrimination)*[1]

The post of ombudsman which was established on an experimental basis in the Ministry of Justice was discontinued in 1982. An analysis of the results of the experiment demonstrated that the post was not an alternative to existing mechanisms. The question of an ombudsman of the Althing is included in the continuing deliberations on the revision of the Constitution.

---

[1] Report submitted by State (CERD/C/118/Add.20).

# INDIA

### A. Condemnation of racial segregation and *apartheid*

*(articles 1 and 2 of the Universal Declaration; articles IV and VI
of the International Convention on the Suppression
and Punishment of the Crime of* Apartheid)[1]

India participated in an International Conference on Women and *Apartheid*, held in Brussels, Belgium, from 17 to 19 May 1982, organized by the Special Committee against *Apartheid* in co-operation with the International Committee of Solidarity with the Struggle of Women in South Africa and Namibia.

The Government of India has also adopted necessary measures to disseminate information among people regarding the evils of racial discrimination and *apartheid*. Apart from giving due publicity to the enactment of the Anti-*Apartheid* (United Nations Convention) Act, the various publicity media have been devoting time for publicizing various aspects of the abhorrent practice of *apartheid*. The All India Radio and the Door Darshan (Television Centre) have been broadcasting/telecasting programmes on the subject.

The Government of India has been contributing every year to: (*a*) the United Nations Institute for Namibia; (*b*) the United Nations Trust Fund for South Africa; (*c*) the United Nations Educational and Training Programme for southern Africa; (*d*) the United Nations Fund for Namibia; and (*e*) the Trust Fund for Publicity against *Apartheid*.

### B. Elimination of racial discrimination; principle of equal treatment

*(articles 2 and 7 of the Universal Declaration;
article 2 of the International Covenant on Civil and Political Rights)[2]*

The Constitution of India guarantees that "the State shall not discriminate against any citizen on grounds of religion, caste, race, place of birth or any of them". Article 14 of the Constitution strikes at arbitrariness in State action and ensures fairness and equality of treatment. (*Nand Lal* v. *Punjab*, 1982, 1, SCR, 718 at p. 724.)

---

[1] Report submitted by State (E/CN.4/1983/24/Add.6).

[2] *Ibid.* (CCPR/C/10/Add.8).

## C. Equal protection of the law

*(article 7 of the Universal Declaration;*
*articles 9 and 14 of the International Covenant on Civil and Political Rights)*[3]

Protection of life, and personal liberty are guaranteed under article 21 of the Indian Constitution which lays down that no person shall be deprived of his life or personal liberty except according to the procedure established by law. The Supreme Court held that the procedure contemplated by article 21 must be "right and just and fair and not arbitrary, fanciful or oppressive; otherwise it would be no procedure at all and the requirement of article 21 would not be satisfied". (*Special Courts Bill case*, 1979, AIR, 1979, SC 478 at p. 516.) Further, the procedure contemplated under article 21 must satisfy article 14 which guarantees to every person equality before law or the equal protection of the laws within the territory of India. The Supreme Court held in *Nand Lal* v. *Punjab* (1982, 1, SCR, 718 at p. 724):

"Article 14 strikes at arbitrariness in State action and ensures fairness and equality of treatment. The principle of reasonableness, which, legally as well as philosophically, is an essential element of equality or non-arbitrariness, pervades article 14 like a brooding omnipresence and the procedure contemplated by article 21 must answer the test of reasonableness in order to be in conformity with article 14."

## D. Freedom of movement

*(article 13 of the Universal Declaration;*
*article 12 of the International Covenant on Civil and Political Rights)*[4]

The rights enshrined in article 19 of the Constitution are subject to the operation of any existing law imposing reasonable restrictions on them in the interests of the general public or for the protection of the interests of any scheduled tribe. "The interests of the general public" may enable the legislature to impose restrictions to deal with acts that are aimed at breach of public order or security of the State or those acts which have a tendency to cause these effects. With regard to the standard of reasonable restrictions the Supreme Court laid down in the case of *Bishambar Dayal Chandra Mohan* v. *State of UP* (AIR, 1982, SC 33 at p. 35):

"The expression 'reasonable restriction' signifies that the limitation imposed on a person in enjoyment of the right should not be arbitrary or of an excessive nature, beyond what is required in the interests of the public. The test of reasonableness, wherever prescribed, should be applied to each individual statute impugned, and no abstract standard, or general pattern of reasonableness can be laid down as applicable in all cases. The restriction which arbitrarily or excessively invades the right cannot be said to contain the quality of reasonableness and unless it strikes a proper balance between the freedom guaranteed in article 19 (1) (*g*) and the social control permitted by cl. (6) of article 19, it must be held to be wanting in that quality."

---

[3] *Ibid.* (CCPR/C/10/Add.8).
[4] *Ibid.* (CCPR/C/10/Add.8).

# IRAQ

## A. Condemnation of racial segregation and *apartheid*
*(articles 1 and 2 of the Universal Declaration;*
*articles III, V and VI of the International Convention on the Suppression*
*and Punishment of the Crime of* Apartheid)[1]

The information media, comprising the press, radio and television, attach considerable importance to the campaign against racism and *apartheid* to which special coverage is given with a view to providing readers, listeners and viewers with a wide range of news and information concerning the struggle of peoples against *apartheid* and colonialism.

The information media cover all conferences concerning the campaign against racism. The media also publish the texts of conventions dealing with human rights and the suppression of racist crimes on occasions such as the anniversary of the Universal Declaration of Human Rights, the International Day for the Elimination of Racial Discrimination, and the Week of Solidarity with the People of Namibia and Their Liberation Movement.

## B. Right to social security
*(article 22 of the Universal Declaration;*
*article 9 of the International Covenant on Economic,*
*Social and Cultural Rights)[2]*

Decision of the President of the Court of Cassation of Iraq, dossier No. 166/Labour/1982, serial No. 145, and decision of the President of the Court of Cassation of Iraq, dossier No. 66/67/Labour/1982, standardized, serial No. 149, have been adopted in relation to the social security system.

## C. Right to work
*(article 23 of the Universal Declaration;*
*article 6 of the International Covenant on Economic,*
*Social and Cultural Rights)[3]*

Decision of the President of the Court of Cassation of Iraq, dossier No. 258/Labour/1982, serial No. 101, and decision of the President of the Court of Cassation of Iraq, dossier No. 208/Labour/1982, serial No. 237, relate to the right to work.

---

[1] Report submitted by State (E/CN.4/1983/24/Add.10).

[2] *Ibid.* (E/1984/6/Add.3).

[3] *Ibid.* (E/1984/6/Add.3).

# ISRAEL

### Right to an effective remedy against discrimination

*(article 8 of the Universal Declaration;
article 6 of the International Convention on the Elimination
of All Forms of Racial Discrimination)*[1]

The following Supreme Court judgements deal with the concept of equality, illegal discrimination and permissible differentiation:

HCJ 720/82. *Elizur-Religious Sports Association, Nahariya Branch* v. *City of Nahariya and others*

The appellant, alleging discrimination, had contested a local authority's distribution amongst interested parties, of the hours of access to and use of a municipal facility (swimming pool). In its unanimous acceptance of the appeal, the Court dwelt on the universal and elementary obligation of the State authorities to act with fairness and avoid arbitrariness, prejudice, bias and unreasonableness in its dealings. The concept of equality, a means for achieving justice, must guide the authorities in their fair and just behaviour. While the rule of thumb is that equals must be treated equally, the question is always begged: who are equals? The determination of who are equals requires consideration of the just aim one wishes to achieve and strictly relevant criteria.

Accordingly, in order to achieve the just result, one may be required to act not on a strictly equal basis.

HCJ 141/82. *M. K. Rubinstein and others* v. *Speaker of the Knesset*

The petitioners, members of the Knesset, alleged that a law which purported to amend, retroactively, the Party Finance Law 1973, thereby effectively altering the rules of finance that were in force prior to the elections of the tenth Knesset, resulted in a breach of the principle of equality in the Israeli elections as entrenched in section 4 of the Basic Law: the Knesset. In accepting the petition, the Supreme Court elaborated on the principle of equality as a substantive and not a formal concept, adjusting to time and society and often represented by terms such as rights, reasonableness, justice and fairness. In the context of the Israel election system (of proportional representation), the aim is equal opportunity and not merely "one man, one vote". A provision of law that retroactively establishes an unequal distribution of public finances amongst the Knesset factions leads to inequality of political rights thereby injuring legitimate expectations. In such instance the rights and expectations of the petitioner are deemed worthy of a protective remedy from the High Court of Justice.

---

[1] Report submitted by State (CERD/C/113/Add.2).

# ITALY

## A. Elimination of racial discrimination; development and protection of certain racial groups or individuals belonging to them

*(articles 2 and 7 of the Universal Declaration;*
*article 2 (2) of the International Convention on the Elimination*
*of All Forms of Racial Discrimination)*[1]

In 1982 the Italian Parliament began to consider various bills aimed at achieving an overall protection of the Slovene minority through the codification of its rights, as already happens for the German-speaking minority in the Alto Adige region, for the Ladin-speaking minority and for the French-speaking minority in the Valle d'Aosta region.

So far as the minority groups of ancient installation are concerned, mention should be made of the fact that in 1982 the Parliament began to study various proposals relating to these groups generally considered or specifically dealt with, as the Friulian, the Sardinian and the Provençal groups. The proposals are consolidated in a single text, entitled "Special measures to safeguard linguistic groups".

## B. Right to work

*(article 23 of the Universal Declaration;*
*article 5 of the International Convention on the Elimination*
*of All Forms of Racial Discrimination)*[2]

The Government bill on the employment in Italy of foreign workers from outside EEC countries has been approved in 1982 by the Senate and, by the end of the same year, was in course of discussion in the House of Commons.

Considering the urgent need of at least regularizing the cases of underground work which most deserve to be taken into account, the Ministry of Labour and Social Insurance gave instructions to the Provincial Labour Offices so as to prevent further defaults on the part of the employers and to rectify the omissions already come in being. The Ministry authorized the employment of foreign workers from outside EEC countries arrived in Italy before 31 December 1981. The employer has to obtain at the Provincial Labour Office, an authorization which is granted independent of any checks, the availability of EEC or national manpower included, on the following conditions:

(*a*) The date of entry of the worker has to result from the temporary residence permit issued by the police in expectation of a regular employment contract;

---

[1] Report submitted by State (CERD/C/104/Add.2).

[2] *Ibid.* (CERD/C/104/Add.2).

(*b*) As envisaged by previous instructions of the Ministry of Labour, the employer has to prove he has deposited the air ticket necessary to ensure the worker's return journey to his country of birth or provenance. The following categories are exempted from such bonds: foreign workers married to Italian women; refugees issued, by a commission operating at the Ministry of Foreign Affairs, with a statement attesting their status; citizens of countries sharing their borders with Italy; employees of foreign air or shipping lines, even in the case their nationality be different from that of the companies employing them.

## C. Right to an adequate standard of living

*(article 25 (1) of the Universal Declaration;*
*articles 11 and 12 of the International Covenant on Economic,*
*Social and Cultural Rights)*[3]

### Right to adequate food

Inspired by the sensitivity shown by public opinion and the Italian political forces, the Government first announced, on suitable occasions (at the Ottawa summit of the industrialized countries, at the United Nations Conference on the Least Developed Countries held at Paris, and at the FAO conference, held in Rome, from 26 to 29 April 1982), a meeting for the fight against world hunger, to be followed by a successive meeting at the ministerial level.

In the final summary of the meeting of the World Food Council, which met from 20 to 24 June 1982, there was praise for the initiative of the Italian Government in mobilizing greater and more co-ordinated efforts among the donor countries in the fight against hunger in the world.

### Right to adequate housing

Law No. 94 concerning the financing of the second four-year period of the 10-year plan was adopted on 25 March 1982.

This law provides for the allocation, for purposes of investment in home-building, of about 14,000 billion lire (equal to about $US 10 million).

### Right to health

In 1982, the Ministry of Labour instituted a National Commission for voluntarism problems to prepare a *legge quadro* on voluntarism.

In a recent international seminar on health economy, organized in Italy in September 1982 by the Centro Europeo di Studi Economici e Sociali (CESES) (European Centre of Economic and Social Studies), a comprehensive report was presented on Italy, also containing an analysis of the critical reflections so far formulated on the present state of the Italian health economy, with a contribution of new orientations regarding the various implementation strategies of the health reform, the objectives which it pursues remaining unchanged.

---

[3] *Ibid.* (E/1980/6/Add.31).

## D.  Right to education

*(article 26 of the Universal Declaration;*
*article 5 of the International Convention on the Elimination*
*of All Forms of Racial Discrimination)*[4]

Foreign children are generally provided for through bilateral agreements. As for children subjects of EEC countries, the Italian legislation accepted (Presidential Decree No. 727 of 1982) a community instruction according to which it is their right to be received in the Italian elementary school, where they also enjoy special supports so as to learn the Italian language and to treasure their mother tongue.

_____

[4] *Ibid.* (CERD/C/104/Add.2).

# JAPAN

## Right to social security
*(article 22 of the Universal Declaration;*
*article 9 of the International Covenant on Economic,*
*Social and Cultural Rights)*[1]

The amendment of the National Pension Scheme in 1981, in accordance with the entry into force for Japan of the Final Act and Convention relating to the Status of Refugees, contained a clause abolishing the nationality requirement which had been a part of this scheme (the amendment became effective in January 1982).

Based on the Children's Allowance Law, the Children's Allowance Scheme was established in January 1972.

This scheme exists to contribute to a stable family life and to promote the healthy growth of the children who will one day be the mainstay of society by paying an allowance to persons bringing up children. There are approximately 2.5 million children qualifying for this allowance. The nationality requirement was abolished in January 1982, in accordance with the amendment of the Children's Allowance Act in 1981 in accordance with the entry into force for Japan of the Final Act and Convention relating to the Status of Refugees).

------------

[1] Report submitted by State (E/1984/6/Add.6).

# KUWAIT

## Right to just and favourable conditions of work

*(article 23 of the Universal Declaration;*
*article 5 (e) of the International Convention on the Elimination*
*of All Forms of Racial Discrimination)*[1]

The labour legislation in force in the State of Kuwait attaches considerable importance to the welfare of both national and non-national manpower which enjoy the full protection of the law.

Any loopholes that might have been observed in the labour legislation currently in force will soon be closed by the new draft legislation concerning employment in the private sector for the study of which a tripartite commission (consisting of representatives of the Government and of employees' and employers' organizations) has been established under the terms of Ministerial Decision No. 58 of 1982.

---

[1] Report submitted by State (CERD/C/118/Add.3).

# LAO PEOPLE'S DEMOCRATIC REPUBLIC

## Elimination of racial discrimination
(*article 2 of the Universal Declaration;
article 2 of the International Convention on the Elimination
of All Forms of Racial Discrimination*)[1]

Equality and solidarity among the national ethnic groups have always been re-affirmed in the various resolutions and decisions of the Lao People's Revolutionary Party (PPRL). For example, a resolution of the third Congress of the PPRL, of 27 March 1982, concerning policies and tasks involved in improving the administrative power of popular democracy and strengthening the collective sovereignty of the multi-ethnic people, refers to, among other things:

"pursuing the expansion of the Front of National Unity, strengthening the solidarity of the various ethnic groups and religions, and creating conditions favourable to the participation, on an equal footing, of all such groups in the work of national defence and construction, with the same rights and the same duties".

---

[1] Report submitted by State (CERD/C/105/Add.4).

# LESOTHO

## A. Right to life, liberty and security of person
### (*article 3 of the Universal Declaration*)[1]

The Amnesty Act extends a royal pardon to nationals outside Lesotho who would otherwise have had to stand trial for criminal offences.

## B. Prohibition of inhuman or degrading treatment or punishment
### (*article 5 of the Universal Declaration*)[2]

The rights of persons held under section 12 (3) (*a*) of the Internal Security Act, 1974, were spelt out in a number of decisions by the Lesotho High Court. Thus, an individual held under the section which permits incarceration for up to 60 days for "having committed or being about to commit a crime," must be held at a place precisely identified in the detention order and he has a right to be visited by a Judicial Officer (a Magistrate) over stated periods.

## C. Protection of the family, motherhood and childhood
### (*articles 16 (3) and 25 (2) of the Universal Declaration*)[3]

Important statutes which bear upon human rights, and which have been passed by the Lesotho National Assembly, the Children's Protection Act under which special children's courts are to be established for dealing with matters such as neglect of children and the commission of offences by juveniles, namely persons aged eighteen and under; a Married Civil Servants' Pension Bill which is intended to admit married women to the pensionable establishment and eliminate a provision which discriminated against them on the grounds of sex; and a law to legalize a man's customary law wives in cases where a man has more than one wife married, variously, under the Lesotho law and custom and under the Roman-Dutch law. The position, as it was before this statute, was that customary law marriages could not subsist side by side with those of Roman-Dutch law.

---

[1] Contribution submitted by State.
[2] *Ibid.*
[3] *Ibid.*

# LUXEMBOURG

### Promotion of understanding, tolerance and friendship among all nations, racial and ethnic groups
*(article 26 (2) of the Universal Declaration;*
*article 7 of the International Convention on the Elimination*
*of All Forms of Racial Discrimination)*[1]

The Luxembourg Government is aware of the importance of educational and cultural measures to promote understanding between the indigenous population and, in particular, recent immigrants.

Accordingly, advisory offices have been set up at the commune level. In addition, the State subsidizes advisory committees to which immigrants may apply. Mention might also be made of other facilities provided by the State, such as meeting rooms for the use of immigrant associations, special radio and television broadcasts, appropriate language courses, encouragement to participate in cultural events, and so on.

---

[1] Report submitted by State (CERD/C/103/Add.2).

# MADAGASCAR

### A. Condemnation of racial discrimination, segregation and *apartheid*

*(articles 1 and 2 of the Universal Declaration;*
*articles 2 and 4 of the International Convention on the Elimination*
*of All Forms of Racial Discrimination;*
*articles IV and V of the International Convention on the Suppression*
*and Punishment of the Crime of* Apartheid)[1]

*Act No. 82/013 of 11 June 1982 supplementing the Penal Code (new article 115)*

*Article 1.*   A new article 115, to read as follows, shall be inserted in the Penal Code:

"*Article 115.*   Anyone who, because of a person's origin, colour, sex, family situation, actual or presumed membership or non-membership of a particular ethnical group, nation, race or religion, has knowingly denied to that person the enjoyment of a right to which that person is entitled, shall be liable to imprisonment for a period of one month to one year or to a fine of 50,000 to 250,000 francs, or both.

"The above penalties shall be doubled if the offences have been committed by a public official or by a citizen in charge of a public ministry in the exercise of or in connection with his functions.

"In the cases referred to in the two preceding paragraphs, if the perpetrator of the offence proves that he has acted on the order of his superiors in matters coming within their competence and in which he had to comply with their orders as his superiors, only the superior officers having issued the order shall be liable to the corresponding penalties.

"This article shall not apply to the distinctions, exclusions, restrictions or preferences laid down by the laws or regulations distinguishing between Malagasy nationals and non-nationals."

*Article 2.*   This Act shall be published in the *Journal Officiel* of the Republic. It shall take effect as a law of the State.

### B. Right to an effective remedy

*(article 8 of the Universal Declaration;*
*article 6 of the International Convention on the Elimination*
*of All Forms of Racial Discrimination)[2]*

Order No. 82-019 relating to the powers of the Supreme Court in its general supervision of the administration of justice lays down the conditions and methods

---

[1] Reports submitted by State (CERD/C/91/Add.29;  E/CN.4/1985/26/Add.4).

[2] Report submitted by State (CERD/C/118/Add.10).

for the exercise by the Supreme Court of general supervision over the administration of justice. Its principal provisions are as follows:

The First President of the Supreme Court directs and co-ordinates the supervision which the elected body exercises over the activities of judges and those of courts of appeal and courts of first instance.

The supervision exercised by the body over courts of appeal and courts of first instance aims at checking the extent to which these courts observe the rules governing their operation and the extent to which each judge respects the applicable rules of procedure and of law and fulfils his professional and ethical obligations.

In the interests of the correct application of the law, the First President of the Supreme Court may make such observations or recommendations as he sees fit to judges subject to this supervision.

On no account may the supervision, observations or recommendations be such as to impair the independence of the judge's decisions.

The body's supervisory functions are exercised through missions of inspection, inquiry, verification or information, carried out from documents or *in situ*, either within a general programme drawn up by the First President of the Supreme Court, or at the request of the People's National Assembly, the Supreme Council of the Revolution or the Minister of Justice, or on the initiative of the First President in consequence of facts or irregularities brought to his attention.

A report is made on the result of such supervision, drawing attention to any deficiencies, delays and shortcomings in order to identify the causes and establish responsibility.

The report must conclude by recommending measures to improve or correct the situation and to penalize any irregularities.

As the First President of the Supreme Court exercises supervision over the judges, so also the Government Attorney of the Supreme Court is responsible for the general supervision of the activities of the public prosecutor's department and of the judicial police throughout the Republic.

Thus, when the Government Attorney has knowlege of a breach of the law by an officer of justice or an officer of the judicial police, he must admonish the officer and draw his attention to his error or act of negligence.

If the admonition is without effect, he institutes proceedings against the person responsible.

When the First President or the Government Attorney of the Supreme Court has knowledge of a decision taken in flagrant violation of the law, he lodges an objection with the authority which took the decision.

The objection suspends all proceedings pending before the court that are concerned with the application of the decision.

If the authority concerned does not rescind or modify its decision within a month, the case may be brought before or returned to the competent court by any interested party.

With regard to the right of personal safety, the law guarantees citizens against arbitrary arrest and detention. There are, however, certain exceptions to meet the requirements of law and order. In the case of arrest for the purposes of a preliminary police inquiry, a police officer may detain a suspect for up to 48 hours for the purposes of the inquiry. Detention may be prolonged for an additional period of 48 hours at the most on the authorization of the responsible official of the public prosecutor's department.

Similarly, officials of the public prosecutor's department may remand persons charged with offences in custody for a maximum period of 15 days (warrant of committal).

The responsible officials of the public prosecutor's department (public prosecutors, their deputies and heads of section) may order persons being proceeded against for an offence to be remanded in custody for the purposes of the preliminary investigation. The duration of the remand in custody may not exceed the maximum of the penalty incurred.

Despite these exceptions, necessitated by the proper administration of justice, the judicial procedure provides certain safeguards against arbitrary detention. Release on bail during preliminary investigation may be requested by accused persons.

# MALTA

## A. Right to a nationality

*(article 15 of the Universal Declaration;
article 5 of the International Convention on the Elimination
of All Forms of Racial Discrimination)*[1]

Since the question of citizenship comes up quite often it may be pertinent that, leaving apart those individuals who become citizens of Malta as of right by birth, no racial discrimination is practised and the only conditions which need to be met are those found in the Constitution and the relevant Act. Thus since 1981, the 279 persons who were registered or naturalized as citizens come from various nations such as Australia; Canada; German Democratic Republic; Germany, Federal Republic of; Guyana; India; Ireland; Italy; Philippines; Poland; United Kingdom and Colonies (majority) and United States of America. Some of those registered or naturalized were also stateless.

## B. Promotion of understanding, tolerance and friendship among all nations, racial and ethnic groups

*(article 26 (2) of the Universal Declaration;
article 7 of the International Convention on the Elimination
of All Forms of Racial Discrimination)*[2]

Maltese schools celebrate a number of international days proclaimed by specialized agencies of the United Nations, World Children's Day, World Telecommunications Day, etc. These involve teaching about human rights both directly and indirectly. Maltese schools also take part in competitions sponsored by United Nations agencies (Universal Postal Union, International Telecommunication Union, etc.). UNESCO and WHO International Years have also been celebrated on a national scale. Schools are invariably supplied with posters, films and other United Nations literature as available and allowed to organize their own festivities. As Human Rights Day, however, falls close to Malta's Republic Day (13 December) the latter's festivities and ceremonies tend to overshadow the former's in schools, though in some they may be combined.

Teaching about human rights not only features on the syllabuses of both primary and secondary schools but may be said to permeate through the system, for example, in religious instruction and in school projects in geography, history, social studies, etc. Direct teaching at the primary level generally takes place in projects

---

[1] Report submitted by State (CERD/C/90/Add.9).
[2] *Ibid.* (CERD/C/90/Add.11).

(principally, the UNESCO Associated Schools Project on International Understanding) and the celebration of United Nations Days.

The Malta Constitution which is the basis of Maltese education and is taught in civics/social studies lessons throughout the system is based on the Universal Declaration of Human Rights.

The Department of Education has compiled a series of civics textbooks for secondary schools to be used in accordance with the syllabuses of instruction. Page 26 of one of the textbooks (Malta—Ir-Repubblika Taghna) used in Form III, contains a reproduction of the Universal Declaration of Human Rights with the caption "The Constitution of the Republic of Malta, like that of other democratic countries, enfolds the Universal Declaration of Human Rights, adopted by the United Nations on the 10th December 1948".

*Activities carried out in government and private schools*

Most schools in Malta celebrate United Nations Days and the celebrations include aspects of the Universal Declaration of Human Rights.

A number of government and private primary schools take part in the UNESCO Associated Schools Project on International Understanding.

There are over 600 expatriate students in Maltese schools. These are found mainly in private schools but also in the university and technical/trade schools. They include (*a*) Palestinian and (*b*) Zimbabwean students at the university and in government technical schools studying in Malta under government agreements; students from China, France, Italy, the Republic of Korea and the Libyan Arab Jamahiriya, etc. studying in government institutions under cultural agreements; and students from many European and African countries studying in private schools. There are also summer schools in the teaching of English for foreign students run by the Education Department. Students come from many European and North African countries.

There are expatriate teachers in government schools. These include Libyans, Egyptians, Tunisians, Iraqis and Kuwaitis (all engaged in the teaching of Arabic which is compulsory in secondary schools), Czechs, Poles, Belgians, Italians, French and British (who teach various academic subjects at secondary and upper secondary levels).

English and Arabic (besides Maltese) are compulsory subjects in Maltese secondary schools. Students can also choose one or two languages from Italian, French and German as optional subjects.

# MAURITIUS

## Realization of economic rights

*(article 22 of the Universal Declaration;*
*article 5 of the International Convention on the Elimination*
*of All Forms of Racial Discrimination)*[1]

The Government has set up a State Trading Corporation to ensure fair, regular and equitable distribution of essential commodities, such as rice, flour and petrol and their availability at reasonable prices and to compete with monopolistic trade in the interest of consumers (the State Trading Corporation Act 1982).

---

[1] Report submitted by State (CERD/C/106/Add.8).

# MEXICO

## A. Right to all the guarantees necessary for defence

*(article 11 of the Universal Declaration;*
*article 14 (3) (b) of the International Covenant on Civil and Political Rights)*[1]

The contents of article 14, subparagraph 3 (*b*), of the Covenant are covered in article 20, paragraph IX, of the Constitution, which states that an offender shall be heard "in his own defence, either personally or by counsel, or by both, as he may desire. Should he have no one to defend him, a list of official counsel shall be submitted to him, in order that he may choose one or more to act in his defence. If, after being called upon to do so at the time of his preliminary examination, the accused does not wish to name any counsel for his defence, the court shall take such action for him". Furthermore, according to article 134 *bis*, paragraph 4, of the addendum to the Code of Criminal Procedure for the Federal District, published in the *Diario Oficial* of 29 December 1982, "An arrested person may, immediately upon his arrest, appoint counsel or a person whom he trusts to undertake his defence. Failing such appointment, the Public Prosecutor shall assign him counsel *ex officio.*"

## B. Right to work

*(article 23 (1) of the Universal Declaration;*
*article 6 of the International Covenant on Economic,*
*Social and Cultural Rights)*[2]

Article 123 of the Constitution provides that every person is entitled to suitable work that is socially useful. Likewise, article 3 of the Federal Labour Act embodies the general principle that work is a social right and obligation, and lays down the peremptory obligation that any person offering employment should do so in conditions of freedom and dignity, in the broadest sense of those terms, with a view to safeguarding the lives and health not only of workers, but also of their families, and enabling them to enjoy decent economic standards. It is therefore prohibited to discriminate between workers on grounds of race, sex, age, religious or political belief or social status.

On 29 December 1982, article 40 of the Organic Law of the Federal Public Administration was revised. The article now defines the responsibilities of the Ministry of Labour and Social Welfare, which include monitoring the observance and implementation of the provisions contained in article 123 of the Constitution, in the Federal Labour Act and in its own by-laws, setting up and managing the national

---

[1] Report submitted by State (CCPR/C/22/Add.1).

[2] *Ibid.* (E/1984/6/Add.2).

employment service, overseeing its activities and collecting general statistics on labour matters, in accordance with the procedures established by the Programme and Budget Division.

With respect to the formulation of employment plans, article 9 of the current by-laws of the Ministry of Labour and Social Welfare gives the Co-ordination Unit for Labour Policy, Research and Statistics responsibility for gathering and analysing employment statistics.

## C. Trade union rights

*(article 23 (4) of the Universal Declaration;*
*article 8 of the International Covenant on Economic,*
*Social and Cultural Rights)*[3]

Under the Presidential Decree of 1 September 1982, if a private bank is nationalized, its employees are entitled to form unions.

---

[3] *Ibid.* (E/1984/6/Add.2).

# MONGOLIA

**Right to social security**

*(article 22 of the Universal Declaration;*
*article 9 of the International Covenant on Economic,*
*Social and Cultural Rights)*[1]

In 1982, a standard pension age equal to that for manual and non-manual workers in State institutions and enterprises was instituted for members of agricultural combines.

---

[1] Report submitted by State (E/1984/7/Add.6).

# NETHERLANDS

## A. Prohibition of discrimination or incitement to it

*(articles 2 and 7 of the Universal Declaration;*
*article 4 of the International Convention on the Elimination;*
*of All Forms of Racial Discrimination)*[1]

In December 1982 the Rotterdam Magistrates' Court found a football supporter guilty of making anti-semitic remarks during a match. He was fined f.1,000 (suspended) with the proviso that he donate f.500 within six months to the *Stichting '40-'45*, which assists victims of World War II.

## B. Elimination of racial discrimination; development and protection of certain racial groups or individuals belonging to them

*(articles 2 and 22 of the Universal Declaration;*
*articles 2 and 5 of the International Convention on the Elimination*
*of All Forms of Racial Discrimination)*[2]

Parliament is considering a bill presented on 11 June 1982 which seeks to amend articles 15 and 16 of Book 2 of the Civil Code and article 140 of the Criminal Code to make it easier to take action against legal persons whose aims or activities are contrary to public order or morality. A legal person whose aim is to discriminate or to support discrimination on the grounds of race or whose actual activities are directed towards this end must be deemed to offend against public order. The Bill requires the court, at the requisition of the public prosecutions department, to ban and dissolve any legal person which it finds to be acting contrary to public order and morality. The court will also determine the date on which the ban is to enter into force. The ban on the legal person is an established fact once the civil court has handed down its decision, which point is of importance for the criminal court and administrative bodies.

Under article 140 of the Criminal Code it is a punishable offence to take part in the activities of a legal person whose aim is to commit offences and of other prohibited legal persons. The amendment extends this provision to participation in organizations which do not have the status of a legal person.

A study of housing for Moluccans in the Netherlands was commissioned in 1982. Extra resources were allocated in 1982 to a number of municipalities which have large populations of Moluccans, to cover the relatively high costs of improving their housing.

---

[1] Report submitted by State (CERD/C/106/Add.11).

[2] *Ibid.* (CERD/C/106/Add.11).

On 21 December 1982 the Supreme Court upheld the verdict of the Den Bosch Court of Appeal of 10 November 1981 that foreigners seeking accommodation had been discriminated against by a housing association. Statistics revealed that only a very small number of homes had been allocated to foreigners. The President of the Den Bosch District Court had ruled on 20 February 1981 that discrimination had not been sufficiently proved. The Supreme Court took a different view, ruling that numerical or statistical differences, such as those proved to exist in this case could be considered by the court as sufficient proof of discrimination. Differences of this sort constitute *prime facie* evidence of discrimination, and the burden of proof then rests on the accused to show that the disparities are based on legally acceptable considerations.

### C.  Right to an effective remedy
*(article 8 of the Universal Declaration;*
*article 6 of the International Convention on the Elimination*
*of All Forms of Racial Discrimination)*[3]

Since 1 January 1982 persons who feel they have been badly treated by civil servants or police officers may lodge a complaint with the national ombudsman. A number of the complaints submitted since that date have concerned some form of discrimination.

The ombudsman functions independently of the Government. If he believes that a complaint warrants legal measures, he refers the complainant to the appropriate agencies. Where this is not the case he investigates the complaint himself to ascertain whether the behaviour in question was correct or not in that particular instance. He then presents his findings and opinion in a public report which is sent to the Government department and the official concerned and to the complainant. The ombudsman reports annually to the Upper and Lower Houses of Parliament. It is hoped that publication of the reports will encourage the authorities concerned to show the utmost care and consideration in their dealings with the public. A publicity campaign using brochures and television spots has been mounted to inform the public of this facility.

The Netherlands made the declaration required by article 14 of the Convention in 1971. This article, which came into force on 3 December 1982, established the right of complaint for individuals and groups under Netherlands jurisdiction. Following the introduction of this procedure the Government issued a press communiqué calling the public's attention to the possibility of seeking international redress by lodging a complaint with the Committee once all available local remedies have been exhausted. A number of governmental bodies and non-governmental organizations have also been informed of the new procedures.

---

[3] *Ibid.* (CERD/C/106/Add.11).

## D. Political rights

*(article 21 of the Universal Declaration;*
*article 5 of the International Convention on the Elimination*
*of All Forms of Racial Discrimination)*[4]

In mid-1982 the Judicial Department of the Council of State (the highest administrative court) made a number of pronouncements on the registration of the Nederlandse Volksunie, the Glimmerveen List and the Centrum Partij as names of parties for the municipal council elections. The Judicial Department ruled that pursuant to articles G1 to G3 of the Franchise Act decisions on applications for the registration of the names of parties for elections may take no account of the substance and dissemination of their political programmes. What was to be taken into consideration, however, was the way in which such programmes were propagated and the behaviour of such political groups if the rights of others were thereby infringed. Everything pointed to the conclusion that the Nederlandse Volksunie had acted in a way which could only be judged contrary to public order and morality. The same could not, in the Department's view, be said of the behaviour of the Centrum Partij.

The Franchise Act deals only with the name and description of political parties which can be given at the top of a list of candidates. Participation in elections is an entirely separate issue and, subject to a number of formal requirements, is open to all persons entitled to vote.

For a list of candidates to be valid the law requires only that it contain the signatures of a specified number of voters from an electoral district. In accordance with the Constitution, the Franchise Act provides no grounds for challenging a list of candidates other than the relevant formal requirements. The Judicial Department further held that the Central Electoral Office is not authorized to exclude individuals or lists on the basis of political or other convictions, whether illegal or not. Only the criminal courts may in certain cases deprive a member of the electorate of the right to vote or to stand for office.

---

[4] *Ibid.* (CERD/C/106/Add.11).

# NEW ZEALAND

## A. Condemnation of racial segregation and *apartheid*

(*articles 1 and 2 of the Universal Declaration;*
*article 3 of the International Convention on the Elimination*
*of All Forms of Racial Discrimination*)[1]

In July 1982 a New Zealand insurance company with interests in South Africa disposed of its holdings; there is now, to the best of the Government's knowledge, no New Zealand company with investments in South Africa. The Government has continued actively to discourage sporting contacts in accordance with the Gleneagles Agreement and the basic principles of United Nations resolutions on the subject. As is shown by the register issued by the United Nations Special Committee against Apartheid, there has been no significant New Zealand sporting contact with South Africa in 1982.

## B. Protection against arbitrary interference with privacy

(*article 12 of the Universal Declaration;*
*article 17 of the International Covenant on Civil and Political Rights*)[2]

Among statutory provisions which attempt to protect privacy, mention can be made of section 227 of the International Companies Act 1981-1982.

## C. Freedom of opinion and expression

(*article 19 of the Universal Declaration;*
*article 19 of the International Covenant on Civil and Political Rights*)[3]

*Tokelau*

The Official Information Act 1982 is designed to make official information more freely available and to provide for proper access by each person to official information relating to that person but it also protects official information to the extent consistent with the public interest and the preservation of personal privacy. It reverses the presumption found in the Official Secrets Act 1951 which it replaced and enacts a statutory presumption that official information is to be made available to the public unless there is good reason for withholding it. Reasons for withholding in-

---

[1] Report submitted by State (CERD/C/106/Add.10).

[2] *Ibid.* (CCPR/C/10/Add.13).

[3] *Ibid.* (CCPR/C/10/Add.11).

formation include the likelihood of prejudice to the security, defence or international relations of New Zealand, the maintenance of law and order and the protection of the privacy of the individual.

## D. Right to take part in the conduct of public affairs

*(article 21 of the Universal Declaration;*
*article 25 of the International Covenant on Civil and Political Rights)*[4]

*Tokelau*

Employment in the Tokelau Public Service provides the only regular source of income in Tokelau. In order to ensure that this income is distributed equitably the Faipule (island head) agreed to begin rotating all wage-worker positions from March 1983. This will increase the number of families who are supported by a Public Service wage earner.

## E. Promotion of understanding, tolerance and friendship among all nations, racial and ethnic groups

*(article 26 (2) of the Universal Declaration;*
*article 7 of the International Convention on the Elimination*
*of All Forms of Racial Discrimination)*[5]

In 1982 the biennial evaluation of the scheme for itinerant teachers of Maori took place. The evaluation showed that the scheme had been effective in encouraging the learning of Maori in primary schools. Approximately 30,250 children were involved in 1982, a slight decrease on previous years. The itinerant teachers of Maori have been concentrated in a smaller number of schools to enable them to provide a more intensive service to fewer teachers. Other schools run their own Maori language programmes independently of the scheme.

Recruiting larger numbers of Maori students into teacher training courses for primary and secondary schools is a priority. In 1982, 8 per cent of new entrants (52) into primary teachers' college courses were Maori students; the aim is to achieve 10 per cent. Eleven Maori students (3 per cent) enrolled for secondary teacher training in 1982. Fostering cross-cultural awareness and skills in the Maori language is regarded as an important element of teacher training.

---

[4] *Ibid.* (CCPR/C/10/Add.11).
[5] *Ibid.* (CERD/C/106/Add.10).

# NICARAGUA

## A. Condemnation of racial segregation and *apartheid*

*(articles 1 and 2 of the Universal Declaration;*
*article 3 of the International Convention on the Elimination*
*of All Forms of Racial Discrimination)*[1]

The Revolutionary Government, conscious of its international commitments and bearing in mind that *apartheid* is a crime against humanity, has tabled a bill in the Council of State condemning *apartheid* and any form of racial discrimination.

## B. Elimination of racial discrimination; development and protection of certain racial groups or individuals belonging to them

*(articles 2 and 26 of the Universal Declaration;*
*article 2 (2) of the International Convention on the Elimination*
*of All Forms of Racial Discrimination;*
*article 27 of the International Covenant on Civil and Political Rights)*[2]

The Revolutionary Government, bearing in mind the multiplicity of ethnic groups and languages that is a feature of Nicaraguan society, organized a campaign in the Miskito, Sumo and Creole English languages which reached 12,664 illiterate persons and reduced the illiteracy rate by about 12.07 per cent.

A further purpose of this campaign was to protect the specific linguistic characteristics of Nicaraguans living the Atlantic coast region.

The International Indian Treaty Council visited, in February and March 1982, several Miskito villages and the communities set up for relocation purposes. The mission was granted access to all the areas that it wished to visit and to the prisons in order to speak with Miskito inmates.

All those interviewed agreed that the absence of due process, in most cases, was the result of the National Emergency Law, itself a result of the military activities of forces outside the area.

While problems did exist for the Miskitos, the International Indian Treaty Council found many positive aspects in the relations between the Government of Nicaragua and the Indians.

Health services have been greatly improved, some now being provided where none existed before.

---

[1] Report submitted by State (CERD/C/103/Add.1).
[2] *Ibid.* (CERD/C/103/Add.1; CCPR/C/14/Add.3).

New ground was broken in education with the introduction of bilingual programmes in Spanish, Miskito and English. The Council found that there are 36 Miskito Indians training to be teachers under this programme.

It also found impressive agricultural programmes for eliminating tree-felling and slash-and-burn methods and for promoting ecological techniques.

Another area in which great progress has been made in the disbandment of the governmental bureaucracy dealing with the Indians, the Nicaraguan Institute for the Atlantic Coast, and the assignment of its personnel to the Miskito communities.

The International Indian Treaty Council also found that more and more Miskitos were participating in the governmental process and that many high-ranking military officers and civil servants are Miskitos.

The major development since the last mission of inquiry in December 1981 was the great resurgence in the sense of indigenous identity on the Pacific coast due to the efforts of the Government to eliminate racism *vis-à-vis* the Indians and, on the contrary, to make them feel proud of being Indians.

## C. Administration of justice

*(articles 7, 8, 10 and 11 of the Universal Declaration; articles 2, 3, 9 and 14 of the International Covenant on Civil and Political Rights)*[3]

There have been some changes in the administration of justice introduced by Decrees Nos. 1045 of 22 April 1982, 1153 of 9 December 1982 and 1159 of 15 December 1982. The purpose of these decrees is to expedite judicial proceedings, thus providing an additional guarantee of the rights of citizens.

With respect to the penal legislation in force in Nicaragua there have been a number of reforms. These were introduced by Decree No. 942 of 1 February 1982, superseding the existing law relating to customs evasion and smuggling, which had been in force since 1884, and Decree No. 1074 of 6 July 1982 amending and reformulating, with the intervention of the Council of State, the Maintenance of Order and the Public Security Act.

Where penal procedure is concerned, Decree No. 1130 of 5 October 1982 introduced a first partial reform of the principles of criminal proceedings, designed to make the dispensing of prompt and speedy justice a reality under a procedure providing maximum guarantees of impartiality for the accused. The first steps are aimed at incorporating the principles of sound assessment of evidence, public monopoly of penal proceedings except in the case of private-law offences, and trial by jury for persons accused of parricide, infanticide, murder in the first degree, endangerment of persons and violation of persons over 14 years of age where the penalty applicable is more than a correctional one.

---

[3] *Ibid.* (CCPR/C/14/Add.3).

## D. Right not to be subjected to arbitrary arrest or detention

*(article 9 of the Universal Declaration)*[4]

The legislation governing criminal procedure has been amended during the period of revolutionary government basically in order to reduce the time spent in detention during preliminary inquiries or to provide maximum guarantees for the person or persons in detention so as to prevent any abuse. Furthermore, under Decree No. 1130, any person held in detention before the start of criminal proceedings must be placed at the disposal of the Attorney-General, who may, if necessary, take steps to prevent their rights from being infringed.

## E. Right to a fair trial

*(articles 10 and 11 of the Universal Declaration)*[5]

On 10 November 1982 by Decree No. 1130 a substantial reform of criminal procedure was approved; this empowers the Office of the Government Attorney to take criminal proceedings for offences publicly or privately.

With this amendment the whole process of investigation is made subordinate to the control of the Office of the Government Attorney. This law increases the guarantees of a fair trial for detainees.

## F. Right to a nationality

*(article 15 of the Universal Declaration;*
*article 24 of the International Covenant on Civil and Political Rights)*[6]

Advances have been made with respect to legislation relating to nationality. They include the promulgation of the Regulations under the Nationality Act of 1 February 1982 and the adoption of the Aliens Act (Decree No. 1032) and the Migration Act (Decree No. 1031), both of 29 April 1982.

## G. Protection of the family, motherhood and childhood

*(articles 16 (3) and 25 (2) of the Universal Declaration;*
*article 5 of the International Convention on the Elimination*
*of All Forms of Racial Discrimination;*
*articles 23 and 24 of the International Covenant on Civil and Political Rights)*[7]

The rights of the family, the rights of the child and women's rights have been a subject of concern to the Government of Nicaragua. Evidence of this can be seen in the establishment of the Bureau for Women's Affairs under Decree No. 1091 of 28

---

[4] *Ibid.* (CERD/C/103/Add.1).

[5] *Ibid.* (CERD/C/103/Add.1).

[6] *Ibid.* (CCPR/C/14/Add.3).

[7] *Ibid.* (CERD/C/103/Add.1; CCPR/C/14/Add.3).

July 1982, and in the Act regulating Mother-Father and Child Relations (Decree No. 1065 of 24 June 1982).

On 3 July 1982, *La Gaceta* No. 155 published Decree No. 1065—Act Governing Relations between Mother, Father and Children. This Act does away with the unilateral criterion for the exercise of paternal authority (paternal principle) and guarantees the absolute equality of the spouses in all respects.

As Nicaraguan citizens, the inhabitants of the indigenous communities enjoy each and every one of the rights enunciated, especially in an area of such fundamental importance for social development as the protection of the family.

## H. Right to own property

*(article 17 of the Universal Declaration;*
*article 5 of the International Convention on the Elimination*
*of All Forms of Racial Discrimination)*[8]

The right to own property, and the ways in which that right may be exercised under current Nicaraguan law, were also approached from a social standpoint. A number of provisions relating to the holding of shares in distributed property were aimed at giving effect to property rights within the framework of legality. Examples are Decree No. 923 of 14 January 1982 and Decree No. 1017 of 2 March 1982 amending it; the Regulations thereunder, issued on 14 August 1982; and the addition to article 1 of the Act (Decree No. 1117 of 29 September 1982). Mention should also be made of Decree No. 1170 of 30 December 1982, which clarified Decrees Nos. 3, 38 and 282 by stating that the confiscations and disposals of property referred to in paragraph 519 of the report were not retroactive.

By Decree No. 1079 of 22 July 1982, the Government of Nicaragua ordered the issue of titles for plots and dwellings in the Tasba Pri settlements.

## I. Freedom of thought, conscience and religion

*(article 18 of the Universal Declaration;*
*article 18 of the International Covenant on Civil and Political Rights)*[9]

Mention should be made of the statement issued by a group of Moravian bishops to mark Christmas 1982, in which they expressed the gratitude of the authorities of their Church for the efforts of the Revolutionary Government to assist the inhabitants of the Atlantic coast. Mention should also be made, at a practical level, of the community-oriented programmes which are carried out jointly by the mass organizations, Catholic priests and Moravian bishops and the Government of National Reconstruction.

---

[8] *Ibid.* (CERD/C/103/Add.1; CCPR/C/14/Add.3).

[9] *Ibid.* (CCPR/C/14/Add.3).

## J.  Realization of economic, social and cultural rights
*(articles 1 and 22 of the Universal Declaration;*
*article 1 of the International Covenant on Civil and Political Rights)*[10]

The right to education and culture, sports and recreation have received atten-tion from the Government of the Republic. This was reflected in the adoption of the Act for the Promotion of Sports and Culture among Youth (Decree No. 937) and of the Act to Regulate Sports, Physical Education and Physical Recreation Activities (Decree No. 957). Mention may also be made of the Act for the Encouragement and Promotion of Production Practices in Higher Education (Decree No. 1151 of 6 December 1982), the Act for the Protection of the Cultural Patrimony of the Nation (Decree No. 1142 of 22 November 1982) and the Regulations of the Film Classification Board (of 30 December 1982).

## K.  Right to social security
*(article 22 of the Universal Declaration;*
*article 1 of the International Covenant on Civil and Political Rights;*
*article 9 of the International Covenant on Economic,*
*Social and Cultural Rights)*[11]

Social security is a constant goal of the Government of Nicaragua. Benefits were extended during the past year to various sectors. Other measures included the adop-tion of the Social Security Act (Decree No. 974 of 11 February 1982) and the General Regulations thereunder (Decree No. 975 of the same date) and, in the context of in-ternational relations, the approval and ratification of the Treaty of the Ibero-American Social Security Community (Decree No. 1090 of 28 July 1982).

The new Social Security Act, which was considered and discussed by the State Council in 1981 and adopted in March 1982, lays down the objectives and functions deriving from the concept of social security, which has been recognized and pro-claimed by the Sandinist People's Revolution as a right inherent in the human per-son.

## L.  Labour law
*(article 23 of the Universal Declaration)*[12]

There have been a number of advances in labour law. ILO Conventions Nos. 137 of 1973, concerning dock labour, 122, concerning employment policy, 135, con-cerning workers' representatives, 119, concerning the guarding of machinery, 117, concerning basic aims and standards of social policy, 139, concerning prevention and control of occupational hazards caused by carcinogenic substances and agents, and 138 of 1973, concerning minimum age, were all incorporated in Nicaraguan

---

[10] *Ibid.* (CCPR/C/14/Add.3).
[11] *Ibid.* (CCPR/C/14/Add.2 and 3; E/1984/6/Add.9).
[12] *Ibid.* (CCPR/C/14/Add.3).

legislation; a clear sign of the firm intention of the present Government to improve labour law. Notable advances have also been made, as a result of the impetus imparted by the intervention of the Ministry of Labour, with regard to labour disputes and collective contracts.

### M. Limitations on the exercise of rights and freedoms; emergency situations
(*article 29 of the Universal Declaration;*
*article 4 of the International Covenant on Civil and Political Rights*)[13]

On 14 April 1982, the Governing Junta found itself obliged to extend the state national emergency for a further month, from 15 April to 15 May 1982.

Article 2 of the operative part of the Decree stated that, in addition to the exceptions specified in Decree No. 996, the suspension of rights and guarantees did not apply to political rights under article 25 (*b*), (*c*) and (*d*) of the Statute on the Rights and Guarantees of Nicaraguans, to the rights of the family under article 34 of the Statute or to the rights of the child under article 35. The escalation in the number of attacks from Honduran territory confirms that the state of national emergency imposed by the Act of 15 March 1982 was not adequate to the purpose of restoring the minimum normality compatible with peaceful national development.

Since the reasons which had led to the previous extension of the state of emergency continued to obtain, the Governing Junta decided on 30 April 1982, by Decree No. 1043, to extend it for a further 30 days from 15 May 1982. In April 1982 there was an upward trend in the number and nature of the attacks on the Republic.

On 11 June 1982, the Government was obliged to extend the state of emergency for a further 30 days, from 15 June, with the same express limitations as regards alienable rights. This action was taken through Decree No. 1056.

By Decree No. 1061 of 21 June 1982, the Governing Junta of National Reconstruction, on the initiative of the Council of State itself, temporarily suspended the application of article 14 of the Fundamental Statute for the duration of the national emergency. Under that provision, laws drafted by the Governing Junta were to be submitted to the Council of State, which is empowered to veto them within the period stipulated therein. Article 2 of the Decree extends the period within which the Council of State can propose changes in the laws, and hence the time-limit after which laws are considered to have been tacitly approved. The Decree also left in suspense the application of article 20 of the General Statute of the Council of State.

On 12 July 1982, the Government of the Republic of Nicaragua found itself obliged once again to extend the state of national emergency, having regard to both the continuation of the previously reported plans for destabilization and the need to carry out the tasks necessitated by the disaster resulting from the rains. The relevant Decree (No. 1071) also made mention of the increase in tension in the Central American area.

The Government of the Republic issued, on 26 July, Decree No. 1082 extending the state of emergency for a further six months.

---

[13] *Ibid.* (CCPR/C/14/Add.3).

During the months of September, October and November 1982, 42 criminal attacks, forming part of the campaign to destabilize the Nicaraguan Government, from Honduran territory necessitated the declaration under the state of emergency of a military emergency zone consisting of the territory of 24 municipalities in the Departments of Chinandega, Madriz, Nueva Segovia, Jinotega and Zelaya, adjacent to the frontier zone. It was so ordered by Decree No. 1132 of 4 November 1982.

## N.  Prevention of terrorism; protection of rights and freedoms
### (*article 30 of the Universal Declaration*)[14]

Against the background of the flagrant increase in acts of aggression, the Governing Junta put into effect, by Decree No. 1074 of 6 July 1982, the Maintenance of Order and Public Security Act, as amended and reformulated by the Council of State.

---

[14] *Ibid.* (CCPR/C/14/Add.3).

# NIGER

## A. Right to work

*(article 23 of the Universal Declaration;*
*article 5 of the International Convention on the Elimination*
*of All Forms of Racial Discrimination)*[1]

Further to Act No. 67-029 of 20 September 1967 setting the penalties for the unlawful exercise of non-wage-earning occupational activities by foreigners, the Government of the Niger adopted, on 29 April 1982, Decree No. 82-65/PCMS/MC/MI establishing the régime governing the exercise of non-wage-earning occupational activities by foreigners. Decree No. 82-66/PCMS/MC/MI of the same date contains the list of occupations which foreigners are prohibited from exercising or whose exercise by them is restricted.

## B. Right to education

*(article 26 of the Universal Declaration;*
*article 5 of the International Convention on the Elimination*
*of All Forms of Racial Discrimination)*[2]

At the congress it held from 5 to 10 August 1982, the Women's Association of the Niger decided to take part in efforts to teach all women in the Niger to read and write.

---

[1] Report submitted by State (CERD/C/91/Add.34).
[2] *Ibid.* (CERD/C/91/Add.34).

# NIGERIA

## A. Elimination of racial discrimination

*(article 2 of the Universal Declaration;*
*article 2 of the International Convention on the Elimination*
*of All Forms of Racial Discrimination)*[1]

The Electoral Act of 1982 Section 16 provides a restriction on formation of political parties by ensuring that no Association by whatever name called shall function as a political party unless its membership is open to every Nigerian citizen irrespective of his place of origin, ethnic group, sex or religion, and an association which is desirous of being registered as a political party by the Commission shall only be considered as being open to every Nigerian citizen if its name, emblem or motto has no ethnic or religious connotation and does not give the appearance that the association's activities are confined to a part only of the geographical area of Nigeria.

## B. Political rights

*(article 21 of the Universal Declaration;*
*article 5 of the International Convention on the Elimination*
*of All Forms of Racial Discrimination)*[2]

Political right to participate in elections is granted by Section I of the Electoral Act of 1982 to every citizen of Nigeria of 18 years of age regardless of his race, origin or colour.

---

[1] Report submitted by State (CERD/C/91/Add.35).
[2] *Ibid.* (CERD/C/91/Add.35).

# NORWAY

## A. Elimination of racial discrimination; development and protection of certain racial groups or individuals belonging to them

*(articles 2 and 22 of the Universal Declaration;*
*article 2 (2) of the International Convention on the Elimination*
*of All Forms of Racial Discrimination)*[1]

### Development Fund for the Central Sami Settlement Areas

The purpose of the Fund is to promote measures of economic, social and cultural value in the Sami settlement areas. Support is given in the form of grants, loans or guarantees for loans.

The Board of the Fund has five members and is appointed by the Government. Four of the members are Sami. A proposal has been made that the Fund should be permanent and placed under the Norwegian Lapp Council as of 1 January 1982.

It is proposed that from 1982, through the budget of the Ministry of Local Government and Labour, a three-year trial scheme be implemented for interpreter service under the direction of individual municipalities or county municipalities. This will ensure Sami and Norwegian speakers an equal level of service, and will offer the same possibilities for taking part in the decision-making processes in the various communities.

## B. Right of asylum

*(article 14 of the Universal Declaration;*
*article 5 of the International Convention on the Elimination of All Forms*
*of Racial Discrimination)*[2]

Work with refugees has been reorganized with the establishment on 1 July 1982 of a Government Refugee Agency, which is now responsible for the reception and establishment of refugees.

The Refugee Agency enters into agreements with each municipality concerning the reception of refugees, and the refugees are now as a rule received directly by the municipalities, which are responsible for their future integration.

Through the County Governors, the Refugee Agency and the Ministry of Health and Social Affairs therefore are responsible for providing advisory services to the municipalities in the form of courses and material.

---

[1] Report submitted by State (CERD/C/76/Add.2).

[2] *Ibid.* (CERD/C/107/Add.4).

# PERU

## A. Right to life, liberty and security of person; prohibition of forced labour

*(articles 3 and 4 of the Universal Declaration;*
*article 8 of the International Covenant on Civil and Political Rights)*[1]

Supreme Decree No. 023-82-JUS contains the following articles relating to work:

Article 212, paragraph (*c*) states: The following are exempt from the obligation to work:

(*a*) Convicted offenders over 60 years of age.

(*b*) Convicted offenders suffering from any infirmity duly verified by the prison medical services rendering them unfit to work.

(*c*) Pregnant women convicts from the sixth month of pregnancy to the second month after confinement duly certified by the prison medical services.

Notwithstanding the foregoing, convicted offenders in any of the above categories wishing to work voluntarily may engage in work of their choice provided it is not harmful to their health and they are authorized to do so in writing by the prison medical services.

## B. Treatment of offenders

*(article 5 of the Universal Declaration;*
*article 7 of the International Covenant on Civil and Political Rights)*[2]

Supreme Decree No. 023-82-JUS (Prison regulations), article 198, states:

1. The working day, the time-table, overtime, the weekly rest day, leave and holidays shall be organized in accordance with the provisions of the legislation in force.

2. The working day, time-table and overtime shall, if the régime of the establishment so permits, be calculated for employment and wage purposes and for the purposes of the remission of sentences on the basis of the hours actually worked.

---

[1] Report submitted by State (CCPR/C/6/Add.9).
[2] *Ibid.* (CCPR/C/6/Add.9).

## C. Right to an effective remedy

*(article 8 of the Universal Declaration;*
*article 6 of the International Convention on the Elimination*
*of All Forms of Racial Discrimination;*
*article 2 of the International Covenant on Civil and Political Rights)*[3]

To give effect to one of the basic provisions of the Constitution, the authorities adopted Act No. 23385, 1982, namely, the Act establishing the Court of Constitutional Guarantees, the body which is solely responsible for monitoring the Constitution, ruling on the partial or total unconstitutionality of acts, legislative decrees, general regional regulations and municipal ordinances that are in conflict with the Constitution and hearing appeals against decisions to deny *habeas corpus* and *amparo*, once legal remedies have been exhausted.

Act No. 23506, which was promulgated on 7 December 1982, is known as the *Habeas Corpus* and *Amparo* Act; it provides for remedies which guarantee the exercise of constitutional rights and which may be claimed in respect of acts or omissions which are attributable to the State and the public authorities and which constitute breaches of their obligations.

## D. Protection of privacy

*(article 12 of the Universal Declaration;*
*article 17 of the International Covenant on Civil and Political Rights)*[4]

A plea of self-defence exonerates the defendant provided that it complies with the conditions set out in article 85 (2) viz.: there must have been an unlawful attack, the means employed to prevent or repel it must be reasonable and no provocation must have been offered by the person defending himself.

Included in this provision is the case of a person taking steps to prevent someone from attempting to enter or entering his house or dwelling place by breaking in or using surreptitious or violent means, as provided in the amendment introduced by Law No. 23404 promulgated on 27 May 1982.

## E. Right to social security; realization of economic, social and cultural rights

*(article 22 of the Universal Declaration;*
*article 1 of the International Covenant on Civil and Political Rights)*[5]

Article 71 of the recently promulgated General Industries Act (Law No. 23407) states: "Industrial enterprises established or subsequently established in frontier or forest areas shall be liable only for contributions to the Peruvian Social Security In-

---

[3] *Ibid.* (CERD/C/90/Add.7; CCPR/C/6/Add.9).

[4] *Ibid.* (CCPR/C/6/Add.9).

[5] *Ibid.* (CCPR/C/6/Add.9).

stitute, import duties, save as provided in the preliminary title, article VI, of this Law, and municipal taxes. Industrial enterprises established in frontier or forest areas shall be liable only for taxes and contributions expressly mentioned therein and hence shall be exempt from any other taxes which have been or may be levied, including those that require an express provision for exemption.''

## F.  Right to work

*(article 23 (1) of the Universal Declaration;*
*article 5 of the International Convention on the Elimination*
*of All Forms of Racial Discrimination)*[6]

Under Act No. 23285 of 16 October 1981, which is enforced by the Supreme Decree of 21 May 1982, a 50 per cent accounting rebate is granted to public or private enterprises or agencies which hire physically, sensorially or intellectually handicapped persons as part of their total work force.

## G.  Trade union rights

*(article 23 (4) of the Universal Declaration;*
*article 8 of the International Covenant on Economic,*
*Social and Cultural Rights)*[7]

The right of workers in the public sector to form trade unions is protected under article 61 of the Constitution and under its Seventeenth General and Transitional Provision, which are governed by Supreme Decree No. 003-82-PCM of 22 January 1982, Supreme Decree No. 026-82-JUS of 13 April 1982, and Executive Resolution No. 134-82-INAP/DIGESNAP of 18 May 1982, establishing, *inter alia*, that such trade unions shall be registered with the National Public Administration Institute.

## H.  Right to education

*(article 26 of the Universal Declaration;*
*articles 2 and 5 of the International Convention on the Elimination*
*of All Forms of Racial Discrimination)*[8]

Act No. 23384 of 18 May 1982, namely the General Education Act, guarantees the inherent right of every person in Peru to an education which will promote his full development and that of society, without distinction as to the sex, race, religious belief, political affiliation, language, family responsibilities or marital, social or economic status of the pupil or his parents, and pays particular attention to underprivileged sectors of the population, groups where indigenous languages predominate and other similar situations.

---

[6] *Ibid.* (CERD/C/90/Add.7).

[7] *Ibid.* (E/1984/6/Add.5).

[8] *Ibid.* (CERD/C/90/Add.7).

# PHILIPPINES

## A. Condemnation of racial segregation and *apartheid*
### (*articles 1 and 2 of the Universal Declaration*)[1]

In keeping with its commitments to support the promotion of effective international action to secure national liberation, freedom, human dignity and peace, the Philippines hosted recently the Regional Conference on Action against *Apartheid* on 24-26 May 1982 in Manila. The Conference was the first ever to be held in the Asia-Pacific region in 30 years.

The Manila Declaration on Action against *Apartheid* which was adopted at the close of the Conference contained decisions on regional action to suppress racist régimes, such as the intensification of all forms of assistance to the oppressed peoples of South Africa and Namibia and their national liberation movements, in close co-operation with the Organization of African Unity; full implementation of the United Nations mandatory arms embargo against South Africa; effective enforcement of the embargoes imposed by oil exporting States to prevent supplies of oil to South Africa; cessation of loans to and investments in South Africa and the implementation of the other economic measures recommended by the United Nations; and the implementation of sports, cultural and other boycotts against South Africa.

## B. Right to work
### (*article 23 (1) of the Universal Declaration;*
### *article 6 of the International Covenant on Economic,*
### *Social and Cultural Rights*)[2]

Presidential Decree No. 442, otherwise known as the Labour Code of the Philippines, provides for the so-called clearance and report requirement, so that before an employer can terminate the employment of a worker, the former has to file a clearance with the Ministry of Labour and Employment. In most cases clearance is required, otherwise only a report is filed. The provision under an earlier Presidential Decree (No. 21) was that this clearance must first be filed with the MOLE within 10 days from the expected date of dismissal. The provision has been incorporated in P.D. No. 442.

Presidential Decree No. 442, with its implementing rules, was amended by Batas Pambansa Bilang 130, dated 31 May 1982. The amendment did away with the clearance and report and provided that before an employer can terminate the services of a worker, the former must notify said worker of the grounds of termination

---

[1] Contribution submitted by State.

[2] Report submitted by State (E/1984/7/Add.4).

within 30 days from the expected date of termination. Within that period, the employee should be given the opportunity to meet the grounds of his termination and present evidence in his behalf. If the employer is not satisfied with the explanation of the worker, then he can terminate the services of the latter. However, the worker is not precluded from filing an action for illegal dismissal with the National Labour Relations Commission. Rule XIV of the implementing rules of Batas Pambansa Bilang 130 describes the procedural process for filing such action.

For protection against arbitrary termination of employment, the employer may terminate the employee only on grounds provided by law. These grounds are found in section 15 of Batas Pambansa Bilang 130, which amended articles 283 and 284 of the Labour Code:

"Article 283 (Termination by employer). An employer may terminate an employment for any of the following just causes:

"(a) Serious misconduct or wilful disobedience by the employee of the lawful orders of his employer or representative in connection with his work;

"(b) Gross and habitual neglect by the employee of his duties;

"(c) Fraud or wilful breach by the employee of the trust reposed in him by his employer or duly authorized representative;

"(d) Commission of a crime or offence by the employee against the person of his employer or any immediate member of his family or his duly authorized representative; and

"(e) Other causes analogous to the foregoing."

This provision shows that the law is definite about the grounds on which an employer may terminate an employment. These grounds are considered just causes.

A series of presidential decrees and wage orders have been issued concerning the increase of remuneration of workers. This measure is in line with the policy of the State to protect wages, incomes and employment against domestic inflation.

## C. Trade union rights
*(article 23 (4) of the Universal Declaration;*
*article 8 of the International Covenant on Economic,*
*Social and Cultural Rights)*[3]

Batas Pambansa Bilang 130 introduces a new Labour Relations Law. Significant features brought about by the passage of this law include:

(i) Elimination of the certification requirement for collective agreements;

(ii) Reduction of membership requirement for union registration;

(iii) Elimination of clearance requirement for dismissals at the initiative of the employer;

(iv) Introduction of the concept of labour-management committees;

(v) Streamlining dispute settlement by expanding the jurisdiction of the grievance machinery;

---

[3] *Ibid.* (E/1984/7/Add.4).

(vi) Restoration of the right to strike and lockout, providing rules for observance thereof.

Batas Pambansa Bilang 227, or the Anti-Scab and Picketing Law, defines the scope of lawful picketing and regulates the hiring of scabs or replacements for workers in cases of strikes. Also, Batas Pambansa Bilang 227 provides the sanctions with which the demonstrated violence and illegal acts at picket lines can be prevented or stopped;

Recent judicial pronouncements touching on trade union rights are enunciated in the cases described below.

### *Eastland C. v. Noriel (February 1982)*

The lack of the required 30 per cent vote of employees in a petition for certification election is not of itself a bar to an order for such election by the Bureau of Labour Relations Director, provided there is no abuse of discretion.

### *People's Industrial and Commercial Employees and Workers' Organization et. al. v. People's Industrial and Commercial Corporation et al. (March 1982)*

The question to be resolved is whether or not the petitioner's act of disaffiliating themselves from the mother federation constitutes an act of disloyalty to the union which would warrant their expulsion and consequently their dismissal from the company in pursuance of the union security clause embodied in the collective bargaining agreement. There is no merit to the contention that the act of disaffiliation is disloyalty to the union. The federation and the union are two different entities, notwithstanding the fact that it was the federation which negotiated the collective agreement for and on behalf of the employees, for which reason it actively initiated the dismissal of the individual petitioners. A local union does not owe its existence to the federation to which it is affiliated. It is a separate and distinct voluntary association owing its creation and continued existence to the will of its members. The very essence of self-organization is for the workers to form a group for the effective enhancement and protection of their common interests. By so disaffiliating themselves, therefore, the employees cannot be covered by the union security clause embodied in the CBA, and thus cannot be dismissed from employment.

### *Free Telephone Workers' Union v. Philippine Long Distance Telephone Company (April 1982)*

Peaceful picketing cannot be restrained because the same is part of the freedom of speech. Orders prohibiting picketing must be understood to refer only to picketing through the use of illegal means.

To the same effect is the decision in *Philippine Commercial and Industrial Bank v. Philnabank Employees Association* (105 SCRA 314).

### *National Federation of Sugar Workers (NFSW) v. Ovejera et al. (May 1982)*

Upon failure of the company to comply with the union's demand for bonus payments pursuant to an earlier compromise agreement, NFSW filed a notice of strike. Six days after, they went on strike, and the next day a report of the strike vote was filed. Labour Arbiter Ovejera declared the strike illegal because of failure on the part of the union to observe the 15-day period and the filing of strike notice required by Batas Pambansa Bilang 130 which are mandatory. Non-compliance with these requirements render a strike illegal. In requiring a strike notice and cooling-off period, the intent of the law is to provide an opportunity for mediation and conciliation. So, too, the 7-day strike vote. Its submission gives assurance that the strike vote has been taken and if the report concerning it is false, the majority of the members can take appropriate remedy before it is too late.

### *Pepsi-Cola Labour Union* v. *National Labour Relations Commission and Pepsi-Cola, Naga City (June 1982)*

A certification election was held in the Pepsi plant in Naga, where the petitioner garnered 128 votes out of 131, with the losing labour union contesting the election. In the meantime, the petitioner-union filed a notice of strike, claiming Pepsi refused to bargain. Pepsi countered that it was willing to, but that there was as yet no final decision on the appeal of the other labour union. When the petitioner-union actually struck, Pepsi filed a complaint of unfair labour practice and illegal strike which the National Labour Relations Commission upheld. On review, the Supreme Court held that, although the strike was indeed illegal, it could not discount the presence of good faith on the part of the rank and file union members, since the union had obtained 128 out of 131 votes, so as to be justifiably considered their sole bargaining representative. There is no proof that all the union members participated in the strike. The ones who deserve punishment are the officers of the union who staged the strike in defiance of the orders of the med-arbiter. Hence, the petition must be granted, and the company should reinstate all the persons mentioned in the Labour Arbiter's decision under the same terms and conditions of employment except for the officers of the union.

The right to strike and lockout, including the corresponding restrictions on the exercise thereof, are embodied in Batas Pambansa Bilang 130 and 227, which amended certain articles in the Labour Code. The following provisions are pertinent: article 264 (Strikes, picketing, and lockouts); article 265 (Prohibited activities).

# PORTUGAL

## A. Right to security of person

*(article 3 of the Universal Declaration;*
*article 5 (b) of the International Convention on the Elimination*
*of All Forms of Racial Discrimination)*[1]

### Decree-law No. 458/82, on the criminal investigation police

The purpose of Decree-law No. 458/82, which establishes the organization of the criminal investigation police, is to impose certain duties upon its officials and agents, in keeping with the need to respect the rights, freedoms and guarantees of citizens.

### (a) Special duties

The personnel who conduct or carry out a criminal investigation:

Must act with integrity, impartiality and dignity and strongly oppose any act of corruption;

Must not engage in acts of torture, inhuman, cruel or degrading treatment and must ignore or refuse to comply with orders or instructions entailing such acts;

Must act decisively but without using force.

Any official who refuses to carry out an order or instruction involving acts of torture or inhuman, cruel or degrading treatment is not liable to disciplinary proceedings.

### (b) Use of firearms

This is permitted only as an extreme measure of restraint and specifically:

Where assault on a policeman or third party is imminent or in progress;

To arrest or prevent the escape of a person suspected of having committed a serious crime, particularly if that person is making use of firearms, bombs, grenades or explosives;

To imprison a person who has escaped or who is the subject of an order or warrant of arrest for a crime punishable by a custodial sentence of more than three years or to prevent the escape of a person who has been duly detained or imprisoned;

To free hostages;

To prevent a serious and imminent attack on public facilities whose destruction would cause extensive damage.

The use of firearms is prohibited if it endangers third parties, except in the case of self-defence or necessity.

---

[1] Report submitted by State (CERD/C/101/Add.8).

The use of a firearm must, however, be preceded by a clear and audible warning, provided the occasion and circumstances so permit. Such a warning may be given by firing a shot in the air if there is no danger of wounding anyone and only where a warning might not be clear and audible.

A criminal investigation official who uses a firearm must provide any wounded persons with first-aid as soon as possible.

Lastly, the use of a firearm must be reported in writing to the superior officer as soon as possible, even if no harm has been done.

## B. Right to an effective remedy

*(article 8 of the Universal Declaration;*
*article 6 of the International Convention on the Elimination*
*of All Forms of Racial Discrimination)*[2]

Since its entry into force, the International Convention on the Elimination of All Forms of Racial Discrimination may be invoked in and applied by the Portuguese courts.

## C. Right to education

*(article 26 (1) of the Universal Declaration;*
*article 13 of the International Covenant on Economic,*
*Social and Cultural Rights)*[3]

Decree-law No. 35/82 concerning the termination of the installation procedures for the new universities established under Decree-law No. 402/73, was adopted on 4 February 1982.

As regards the award of grants at the higher education level, mention can be made of Decree-law No. 3/82 of 8 February 1982 concerning the creation, within the framework of the Ministry of Education, of the "Francisco Sá Carneiro" and "Adelino Amaro da Costa" grants.

A number of measures have been taken with a view to improving the material conditions of teaching staff, such as the establishment by Decree-law No. 125/82 of 22 April 1982, of the National Education Board under the auspices of the Ministry of Education and Universities; as a consultative organ, the Board gives advice, upon the Minister's request, respecting matters on which its guidance is desirable, in accordance with the provisions of the draft legislation on the bases of the educational system; the creation in the State universities (by Decree-law No. 188/82 of 17 May 1982) of statutory administrative machinery competent to perform administrative and financial management functions.

---

[2] *Ibid.* (CERD/C/101/Add.8).
[3] *Ibid.* (E/1982/3/Add.27).

## D. Right to take part in cultural life
*(article 27 (1) of the Universal Declaration;*
*article 15 of the International Covenant on Economic,*
*Social and Cultural Rights)*[4]

Decree-law No. 105/82 of 8 April 1982 concerns the establishment of the Institute of Tropical Scientific Research (IICT), within the framework of the Ministry of Education and Universities.

The number of cultural agreements and agreements on scientific and technological co-operation concluded with other countries has increased from five in 1973 (Belgium, France, Germany, Federal Republic of, Spain and United Kingdom) to 45 in 1982. Thirty-seven programmes of co-operation have already been put into effect.

## E. Right to a social and international order in which human rights can be realized
*(article 28 of the Universal Declaration)*[5]

The International Convention on the Elimination of All Forms of Racial Discrimination was approved, for the purposes of accession thereto, by Act 7/82 of the Assembly of the Portuguese Republic, dated 29 April 1982, and came into force for Portugal on 23 September 1982.

---

[4] *Ibid.* (E/1982/3/Add.27).
[5] *Ibid.* (CERD/C/101/Add.8).

# REPUBLIC OF KOREA

**Condemnation of racial segregation and** *apartheid*
*(articles 1 and 2 of the Universal Declaration;*
*article 3 of the International Convention on the Elimination*
*of All Forms of Racial Discrimination)*[1]

President Chun Doo Hwan unreservedly condemned the policy of *apartheid* and the régime of South Africa in joint communiqués with the leaders of Gabon, Kenya, Nigeria and Senegal in 1982 when he made state visits to those countries.

The Government had suspended exchanges with the South African régime, including diplomatic relations. Important measures taken by the Government include the rejection of issuing visas to groups or individual participants from South Africa in the following events held in Seoul, namely:

(*a*) International Amateur Basketball Championship in 1982;

(*b*) International Trade Fair in 1982;

(*c*) World Media Conference in 1982.

---

[1] Report submitted by State (CERD/C/113/Add.1).

# RWANDA

## A. Elimination of racial discrimination; principle of equal treatment

*(articles 2 and 7 of the Universal Declaration;*
*articles 2 and 5 of the International Convention on the Elimination*
*of All Forms of Racial Discrimination)*[1]

Article 28 of Decree-law No. 06/82, of 7 January 1982, provides that judges shall have, among other duties, that of "serving the cause of justice with fidelity, devotion, integrity, objectivity and impartiality, without any discrimination whatsoever, particularly with regard to race, colour, origin, ethnic group, clan or social position".

The five-year (1982-1986) plan defines endogenous development in terms of a development strategy and provides that the efforts undertaken shall be directed, in the first instance, towards meeting the essential needs of the various categories of the population, by placing special emphasis on the development of the least privileged social stratas with the stated intention of securing a better social and economic balance permitting more homogeneous internal development.

## B. Promotion of understanding, tolerance and friendship among all nations, racial and ethnic groups

*(article 26 (2) of the Universal Declaration;*
*article 7 of the International Convention on the Elimination*
*of All Forms of Racial Discrimination)*[2]

From primary school to secondary school, respect for human rights is taught systematically to Rwandese children in civic education classes.

At the higher education level, instruction in human rights is given in the Faculty of Law of the National University of Rwanda, in a section of constitutional law entitled "Public Freedoms". Instruction is based on the Constitution of the Rwandese Republic.

Refresher courses for judicial personnel are regularly organized by the Ministry of Justice. The list of subjects taught at such courses includes constitutional law and law relating to the individual. The teaching of human rights has also been included in the curricula of military schools.

In the sphere of information, national radio also plays a leading role in educating the public in respect for human rights. For example, the positions adopted

---

[1] Reports submitted by State (CERD/C/88/Add.4; CERD/C/115/Add.2).
[2] *Ibid.* (CERD/C/88/Add.4).

by Rwanda at international or regional meetings, particularly the condemnation of
the racial segregation practised by the Pretoria régime in South Africa and Namibia,
are broadcast to the public in the two official languages, Kinyarwanda and French.

# SEYCHELLES

**Right to education**

*(article 26 of the Universal Declaration;*
*article 5 of the International Convention on the Elimination*
*of All Forms of Racial Discrimination)*[1]

The education system is essentially administered under the Education Act, 1982.

---

[1] Report submitted by State (CERD/C/103/Add.3).

# SOLOMON ISLANDS

**Right to an effective remedy**

*(article 8 of the Universal Declaration;
article 6 of the International Convention on the Elimination
of All Forms of Racial Discrimination)*[1]

In 1982 the Rules Committee amended the High Court (Civil Procedure) Rules 1964 in pursuance of section 18 (6) of the Constitution to provide for the procedure of commencing proceedings in the High Court for alleged contravention of constitutional rights and freedoms.

Sections 17 and 18 of the Constitution were invoked in 1982 in the case of *Fr. Fugui and others* v. *Solmac Ltd* in which the applicants who are customary landowners alleged unlawful occupation of their land by the respondent.

The High Court refused the application on the Court's interpretation of section 8 of the Constitution (compulsory acquisition of property).

---

[1] Report submitted by State (CERD/C/101/Add.1).

# SPAIN

## A. Protection of human rights and fundamental freedoms

(*article 2 of the Universal Declaration;*
*article 2 of the International Covenant on Civil and Political Rights*)[1]

Among instruments in force in the field of the promotion and protection of human rights, mention can be made of the rules of the Congress of Deputies of 10 February 1982, articles 40-53 and the Senate Rules of 26 May 1982, articles 49-68.

## B. Prohibition of slavery, servitude and forced labour

(*article 4 of the Universal Declaration;*
*article 8 of the International Covenant on Civil and Political Rights*)[2]

Article 30 of the Constitution provides as follows:

"1. Citizens have the right and the duty to defend Spain.

"2. The law shall determine the military obligations of Spaniards and shall regulate, with the proper safeguards, conscientious objection as well as other grounds for exemption from compulsory military service; it may also, when appropriate, impose a form of social service in lieu thereof.

"3. A civilian service may be established with a view to accomplishing objectives of general concern.

"4. The duties of citizens in the event of grave risk, catastrophe or public calamity may be regulated by law."

In view of some doubts which were initially raised regarding the effectiveness of the right to conscientious objection in the absence of legislation to give effect to it, the Constitutional Court has established:

"It is true that, where this legally stipulated reservation is concerned, until such time as the regulations are produced the constitutional provisions may have only a minimum content which, in the present case, would have to consist in the provisional suspension of enlistment, but that minimum content must be protected since otherwise the protection provided for in article 53 (2) of the Constitution would be lacking in effect and that would lead to the complete

---

[1] Report submitted by State (CCPR/C/32/Add.3).
[2] *Ibid.* (CCPR/C/32/Add.3).

denial of a right which enjoys the maximum constitutional protection under our legal order. Delay in the fulfilment of the duty which the Constitution imposes on the legislature cannot impair a right recognized in it. Hence, in order to fulfil the constitutional provisions, it is necessary to state that the conscientious objector is entitled to have his enlistment deferred until the procedure is devised which may permit the full enjoyment of his right of objection." (Constitutional Court judgement No. 15/1982 of 23 April 1982.)

## C. Equality before the law

*(article 7 of the Universal Declaration;*
*article 26 of the International Covenant on Civil and Political Rights)*[3]

The Constitutional Court has made very numerous pronouncements on the content of the right to equality:

"Article 14 of the Constitution, in establishing the general principle that Spaniards are equal before the law, establishes a subjective right to obtain equal treatment, imposes an obligation on the public authorities to implement that equal treatment and, at the same time, restricts the legislative power and the power of organs responsible for the application of legal norms." (Constitutional Court judgement No. 49/1982 of 14 July 1982. Constitutional Court judgement No. 2/83 of 24 January 1983 is to the same effect.)

It is a right which "is binding upon and applicable to not only the Administration and the Judiciary, but also the Legislature, as can be deduced from articles 9 and 53 of the Constitution." (Constitutional Court judgement of 2 July 1981. The Constitutional Court judgements of 10 November 1981 and No. 59/1982 of 28 July 1982 are to the same effect.)

According to the Constitutional Court:

"The general rule of equality before the law contained in article 14 of the Constitution involves, in the first place, equality in the treatment given by the law or equality in the law, and from this point of view it constitutes a limit imposed upon the exercise of legislative power, but likewise equality in the application of the law, which requires that an individual organ cannot arbitrarily change the tenor of its decisions in cases which are substantially equal and that when the organ in question considers that it must depart from its precedents it has to show adequate and reasonable cause for so doing." (Constitutional Court judgement No. 49/1982 of 14 July 1982.)

Not all inequality constitutes discrimination (inequality which is constitutionally forbidden), but only such inequality as is not reasonably justified, and provided that there is no attempt to establish or require equality in illegality (Constitutional Court judgements Nos. 37/1982 of 16 June 1982 and 43/1982 of 6 June 1982).

---

[3] *Ibid.* (CCPR/C/32/Add.3).

## D. Administration of justice

*(articles 10 and 11 of the Universal Declaration;*
*articles 14 and 15 of the International Covenant on Civil and Political Rights)*[4]

*Right of all persons to equality before the judges and courts*

The jurisprudence of the Constitutional Court already contains a very well considered doctrine on this point.

"The right to the effective protection of the judges and courts includes the right to obtain a decision founded in law. The decision must be on the merits, whether or not it is favourable to the claims made, if all the procedural requirements for this are satisfied." (Constitutional Court judgement No. 11/1982 of 29 March 1982.)

"The right to effective protection is not exhausted by the requirement that the person concerned should have access to the courts of justice, can express and defend his legal claim before them on a footing of equality with the other parties, and can be free to bring any evidence that might be procedurally appropriate and admissible; nor is it limited to guaranteeing that a decision on the merits, founded in law, whether or not favourable to the claim formulated, will be obtained if all the procedural requirements for this are satisfied. It also requires that the judicial decision should be implemented and that the applicant should be restored in his right and compensated, where appropriate, for the damage sustained; otherwise judicial decisions and the acknowledgement of the rights which they entail in favour of specific parties would be converted into mere declarations of intent." (Constitutional Court judgement No. 32/1982 of 7 June 1982.)

"Whether or not a person is undefended must be assessed in each instance, since nobody should be injured in his legitimate rights or interests by a sentence without having been able to defend himself . . ."

"A plea of no defence may be warranted if evidence that is relevant and material to the decision in the case is submitted in time and in due form and the judge in the case rejects it without providing a remedy for the lack of a defence by other evidential means." (Constitutional Court judgement No. 50/1982 of 15 July 1982.)

*Right to a hearing by a competent, independent and impartial tribunal*

In its judgement No. 47/1982 of 12 July 1982 the Constitutional Court ruled that:

"Article 24 of the Constitution affirms the right of the accused to enjoy, among other guarantees, the guarantee that he will be tried by the ordinary judge predetermined by law. Consequently, there is a connection between the rules by which the judge is determined and article 24 of the Constitution. These rules are not restricted to those establishing the limits of the jurisdiction and competence of judicial bodies. There are also the rules relating to the specific suitability of a given judge in a particular case, the most important of which is

---

[4] *Ibid.* (CCPR/C/32/Add.3).

the rule of impartiality, which is measured not only by the subjective criteria of level-headedness and rectitude, but also by the criteria of disinterestedness and neutrality. Thus it must be borne in mind that the right to make use of the means of defence and the right to be tried by the judge predetermined by law include the right to challenge those officials in connection with whom it is felt that there are grounds deemed in law to be circumstances that detract from individual suitability or from the conditions that make for impartiality and neutrality. The right to formulate a challenge entails, in principle, that the claim has to be substantiated in accordance with the relevant procedure provided for by law and that the decision on the issue thus raised should not be taken by the same judges who are the subject of the challenge, but by other judges to whom consideration of the matter is delegated by law.

*Right to a public hearing*

The legislature may regulate the restriction of the right to a public hearing for reasons of morality, as in the case of article 680 of the Criminal Prosecution Act (Constitutional Court judgement No. 62/1982 of 15 October 1982).

Moreover, article 120 (1) of the Spanish Constitution provides that "Judicial proceedings shall be public, with the exception of those provided for in the laws of procedure". There is also some constitutional jurisprudence on this article in conjunction with article 20 (1) of the Spanish Constitution, which guarantees the right to information. Judgement No. 30/1982 of 1 June 1982 states that:

"The principle that judicial proceedings shall be public, which is guaranteed by article 120 (1) of the Constitution, implies that persons additional to those actually present in the courtroom should be aware of them and that they may be generally distributed. Such distribution can be made effective only by the presence of the mass media, in so far as their presence enables them to acquire the information at its source and to transmit it to persons . . . who cannot otherwise obtain it. This role of natural intermediary played by the mass media . . . is augmented in the case of events which, by their importance, can affect everyone and which therefore have particularly widespread social repercussions, as is undoubtedly the case with the action with which were are concerned."

*Presumption of innocence*

"The right to the presumption of innocence cannot be understood when strictly confined to the prosecution of allegedly criminal conduct; it also has to be appreciated that it is dominant in the adoption of any administrative or judicial decision based on the circumstances or conduct of persons and the resulting assessment of which gives rise to a sanction or restriction on their rights" (Constitutional Court judgement No. 13/1982 of 1 April 1982).

*Right to be informed of the nature and cause of the charges*

A judgement of the Constitutional Court, No. 9/1982 of 1 March 1982, contains the following passage:

"The campaign to secure a public trial based on specific charges, including an adversary stage and attended by full guarantees began in continental Europe towards the second half of the eighteenth century, in contradistinction to the old type of inquiry, and it has continued with partial but cumulative successes up to the present time, as is exemplified by various principles contained in article 24 of our Constitution . . . In particular, reference must be made to the fact that accused persons may not go undefended (article 24 (1) and to the right of all persons 'to be informed of the charges brought against them' (article 24 (2))—principles which cannot be interpreted in isolation but by viewing the second with reference to the first and by placing both within the overall meaning of article 24 as a whole and within the above-mentioned historical process . . . According to the most widely disseminated doctrine, the purpose of the indictment (*escrito de calificación*) referred to in article 650 of the Criminal Prosecution Act and of the indictment (*escrito de conclusiones*) referred to in article 729 of the Code of Military Justice is to serve as a framework for the proceedings by establishing which fact or facts constitute the subject-matter of the charge and by indicating to the accused the content of the incrimination and the evidence on which it is to be based, so that the accused can adequately prepare his defence. Consequently, any inconclusiveness in the provisional indictment with regard to the punishable acts in question may give rise to an imprecise, vague and even inadequate charge and may therefore lead to a situation in which the accused is unable to defend himself, since he will be able to do so effectively and to submit the evidence that he considers appropriate only in so far as he is aware of the concrete statement of the facts . . . The right which all persons have to be informed of the charges brought against them is a guarantee that there will be a balance between the prosecution and the accused in criminal proceedings. Any tilting of this balance against the accused, such as happens when the latter does not know specifically which punishable acts are attributed to him, can lead to a situation in which he is unable to defend himself . . ."

On various occasions the Supreme Court, too, has applied the constitutional principle of the right to information with which we are now concerned (for example, in the judgement of its fourth section dated 31 May 1982).

## Right to adequate preparation of one's defence

The right "to the use of the evidence pertinent to the defence" is guaranteed by article 24 (2) of the Spanish Constitution.

The Supreme Court has also expressed itself on this matter, for example in its judgements of 22 May and 9 June 1982. In this latter judgement it declared that in order for a violation of article 24 of the Constitution to be recognized, it is necessary, among other requirements, that the evidence rejected should have been submitted in a procedurally correct manner and that it "should be both materially and functionally relevant—that is to say, that it should have a connection with the subject-matter of the proceedings and with the purpose thereof", so that its rejection produces a "defencelessness contrary to the essence of the proceedings, as specified in the above-mentioned article 24 of the Constitution".

## Right to legal assistance

With reference to the right to the assistance of a lawyer, the Constitutional Court has declared that:

"Among the rights guaranteed by article 24 (2) of the Constitution . . . is the right to the assistance of a lawyer. This is certainly not a right that has been incorporated in the law by our Constitution, since it was known to our law, as it was to that of other peoples, long ago. In its traditional operation, it is easy to perceive the connection between this right and the institution of the trial itself . . .; because of this connection the passivity of the person entitled to the right has to be made good by the court . . . for whose own proceedings, and not only for the purpose of better protecting the rights and interests of the defendant, the presence of a lawyer is necessary. This traditional operation matches the traditional concept of the State subject to the rule of law, in which the latter is understood to be fulfilled merely if fundamental rights are secured in a formal manner. In so far as this traditional concept of the State subject to the rule of law does not cover all aspects of the notion of the social State subject to the rule of law incorporated in our Constitution, it is obvious that the existing rules regarding the assistance of a lawyer have to be interpreted in conformity with this latter notion and further supplemented.

"The idea of the social State subject to the rule of law (article 1 (1) of the Spanish Constitution, which states that 'Spain is hereby established as a social and democratic State subject to the rule of law . . .') and the overall scope of article 9 (2) (It is incumbent upon the public authorities to promote conditions which ensure that the freedom and equality of individuals and of the groups to which they belong may be real and effective . . .') undoubtedly require that the arrangements made to give effect to the right to be assisted by a lawyer should not be such that the material guarantee of its exercise by needy persons rests upon a *munus honorificum* of professional lawyers, since such arrangements are defective . . . The fact that the arrangements made to give effect to the right—in other words, the material guarantee thereof—may be defective does not, however, annul or impair the right itself, which, like the other rights set forth in article 24, is guaranteed by the remedy of *amparo* with the scope stipulated by law, and thus, when it is established in law, there is an understanding that it will be provided free of charge." (Constitutional Court judgement No. 42/1982 of 5 July 1982.)

## Right to a review by a higher tribunal

Constitutional Court judgement No. 42/1982 of 5 July 1982 states that:

"The International Covenant on Civil and Political Rights—in conformity with which the principles relating to the fundamental rights recognized by the Constitution have to be interpreted pursuant to the provisions of article 10 (2) of the Constitution—provides, in article 14 (5), that everyone convicted of a crime shall have the right to his conviction and sentence being reviewed by a higher tribunal according to law. This provision incorporated in our domestic law . . . is not sufficient, in itself, to create non-existent remedies, but it imposes an obligation to consider that the guarantees in criminal proceedings to which general reference is made in article 24 (2) of the Constitution include the guarantee of an appeal to a higher tribunal and that, consequently, all the provisions of our law of criminal procedure have to be interpreted in the sense most favourable to a remedy of that kind."

*Right to the application of the principle of* non bis in idem

Organic Law No. 7/82 of 13 July 1982 regulated crimes and administrative offences involving smuggling and put an end to the possibility, which had until then existed, that two sentences might be imposed for the same act, contrary to the general principle of *non bis in idem*, which now really forms part of subjective law.

*Right to the application of the principle of the statutory nature of offences and their punishment and to the retroactivity of the most lenient law*

"The general matter of retroactivity . . . does not flow from article 25 of the Constitution outside the field of crimes and offences: it is dealt with in article 9 and as such is not subject to the remedy of *amparo*, although it may be grounds for a claim of unconstitutionality." (Constitutional Court judgement No. 68/1982 of 22 November 1982.)

"The principle of the statutory nature of offences and their punishment is not violated in cases in which classification of the crime involves concepts, the exact definition of which allows an element of discretion, particularly, in cases which relate to the protection of legal values recognized in the international context into which our Constitution, in keeping with article 10 (2) thereof, falls, and in cases in which the definition of such values is of a dynamic and evolutionary nature which may vary according to the period and country involved." (Constitutional Court judgement No. 62/1982 of 15 October 1982.)

"The rule (article 25 (1) of the Spanish Constitution) expressly mentions felonies, misdemeanours or administrative offences and for that reason it is not directly applicable to simple offences of a civil nature in which classification and criminalization do not apply so strictly." (Constitutional Court judgement No. 73/1982 of 2 December 1982.)

## E. Protection against arbitrary interference with privacy
### (*article 12 of the Universal Declaration;*
*article 17 of the International Covenant on Civil and Political Rights*)[5]

The right to honour, to personal and family privacy and to personal reputation is in addition developed by Organic Law No. 1/1982 of 5 May 1982.

According to Constitutional Court judgement No. 73/1982 of 2 December 1982:

"The right to privacy is not violated if limitations are placed on an individual's liberty as a consequence of legal duties and relationships imposed by the law, since privacy is a sphere of refuge guarded against access by others and it is not in itself directly related to the freedom to form relationships with other individuals or the right to friendship."

---

[5] *Ibid.* (CCPR/C/32/Add.3).

## F. Right of asylum; right of aliens faced with possible expulsion from a State;

*(article 14 of the Universal Declaration;*
*article 13 of the International Covenant on Civil and Political Rights)*[6]

The instrument of ratification, dated 21 April 1982, of the European Convention on Extradition (Paris, 13 December 1957) was published in the *Boletín Oficial del Estado* of 8 June 1982, and the instrument ratifying (on 2 June 1982) European Agreement No. 31 on the Abolition of Visas for Refugees (Strasbourg, 20 April 1959) was published in the *Boletín* of 22 July 1982.

## G. Freedom of thought, conscience and religion

*(article 18 of the Universal Declaration;*
*article 18 of the International Covenant on Civil and Political Rights)*[7]

### Religious and ideological freedom

The Constitutional Court has stated, *inter alia*, the following:

"There are two basic principles in our political system which determine the attitude of the State towards outward religious observances and the whole relationship between the State and churches and confessions; the first is religious freedom, interpreted as a subjective right of a fundamental nature which manifests itself in the recognition of an area in which the individual is permitted to act as he chooses; the second is the principle of equality, enshrined in articles 9 and 14, from which it follows that it is not possible to practise any form of discrimination or difference in the legal treatment of citizens on the grounds of their ideologies or their beliefs and that all citizens shall enjoy religious freedom on equal terms. In other words, the principle of religious freedom recognizes the right of citizens to act in this area with total immunity from coercion by the State or any social group so that the State denies itself any participation with citizens as a principal in acts or gestures of religious significance and the principle of equality which is the consequence of the principle of freedom in this area means that the religious opinions of those who enjoy this right cannot justify any difference in their legal treatment." (Constitutional Court judgement No. 24/1982 of 13 May 1982, legal conclusion No. 1.)

"The fact that the State provides facilities for individuals in the armed forces to practise the catholic religion not only does not constitute a breach of the Constitution: on the contrary it affords individuals and communities the possibility of effectively exercising their right to worship. It does not violate the right to freedom of religion or of worship, since all citizens who are members of the armed forces are free to accept or reject the religious facilities provided; it should be understood that it likewise does not violate the right of equality, since the mere fact of providing religious facilities for Catholics does not exclude the provision, in due measure, of such facilities, which they can claim as a basic

---

[6] *Ibid.* (CCPR/C/32/Add.3).
[7] *Ibid.* (CCPR/C/32/Add.3).

right, to members of other confessions. Hence, only if the State should refuse to comply with requests to that effect would it infringe the right under consideration." (Constitutional Court judgement No. 24/1982, legal conclusion No. 4.)

"Article 16 (3) of the Constitution states that 'there shall be no State religion' and therefore prohibits . . . that religious values or interests shall constitute criteria for measuring the legitimacy or justice of the rules and acts of the public authorities. At the same time the constitutional rule quoted prohibits any type of confusion between religious and public functions." (Constitutional Court judgement No. 24/1982 of 13 May 1982.)

## Freedom of conscience

"Both legal writers and comparative law affirm the link between conscientious objection and freedom of conscience. In respect of theory, conscientious objection constitutes a specific form of freedom of conscience which assumes not only the right to develop one's own conscience freely but also to act in a manner consistent with its behests . . ." (Constitutional Court judgement No. 15/1982 of 23 April 1982.)

## H. Freedom of opinion and expression
### (article 19 of the Universal Declaration; article 19 of the International Covenant on Civil and Political Rights)[8]

## Content of the right

The right freely to express and disseminate thoughts, ideas and opinions is "above all, a freedom, in that it basically signifies the absence of interference or meddling by State authorities in the process of communication. Nevertheless, on another plane it signifies the recognition and the guarantee of that fundamental political education which consists in free public opinion, indissolubly linked with political pluralism, which is a fundamental value and a requirement of the democratic State. Article 20 of the Constitution defends freedom in the formation and development of public opinion, since freedom in the expression of thoughts and ideas and in the dissemination of information is a necessary premise of free public opinion, . . . The freedom of expression . . . is primarily a freedom which all citizens enjoy equally and which protects them from any interference whatsoever by the public authorities that does not rest upon the law, including protection against the law itself if it attempts to fix limits other than those allowed by the Constitution . . ." (Constitutional Court judgements Nos. 12/82 of 16 March 1981 and 74/82 of 7 December 1982.)

## Limits to the right

The problem of determining whether public morality may be a limit established by the legislature, or whether such a limit will affect the essential content of the freedom of expression,

---

[8] *Ibid.* (CCPR/C/32/Add.3).

"can be easily resolved on the basis of article 10 (2) of the Constitution, given that in the Universal Declaration of Human Rights, as in the International Covenant on Civil and Political Rights adopted in New York in 1966 . . . and in the Rome Convention of 4 November 1950, it is provided that the legislature may set limits for the purpose of meeting the just requirements of morality (article 20 of the Declaration), for the protection of public morality (article 19, (3) (b) of the Covenant) for the protection of morals (article 10 of the Rome Convention) . . ." (Constitutional Court judgement No. 62/1982 of 15 October 1982.)

The Supreme Court has also made repeated pronouncements on the subject —for example, its judgements of 13 February, 22 June, 3, 14 and 24 July 1982, etc. On 19 January 1982 it was established that the rights of freedom of expression and information presuppose

"the duty to make objective reports, at the same time supplying proof, of acts that are breaches of social obligations of the life of the community in the domains of subsistence, culture, recreation or administration, in an effort to promote a climate of opinion and even to foster a pressure group in public opinion tending to the rectification or alleviation of those acts".

### I.  Freedom of peaceful assembly
*(article 20 of the Universal Declaration;*
*article 21 of the International Covenant on Civil and Political Rights)*[9]

In cases of meetings in public places and of demonstrations, it is sufficient to give prior notification to the authorities, who can ban them only when there are well-founded grounds to expect a breach of public order, involving danger to persons or property. Thus, this regulation undoubtedly contrasts with the approach taken by pre-constitutional law, by which the right was regulated starting from a prior general prohibition of its exercise except when authorized by the Civil Governor of the Province, since the Constitution enshrines this fundamental right without making it subject to discretionary assessment and to an enabling instrument under the implicit power of the Administration, laying down as a cause of prohibition a threat to public order through the existence of a specific danger" (Constitutional Court judgement No. 36/1982 of 16 June 1982).

### J.  Political rights
*(article 21 of the Universal Declaration;*
*article 25 of the International Covenant on Civil and Political Rights)*[10]

The latest general election was held on 28 October 1982, and victory went to the Spanish Workers' Socialist Party (Partido Socialista Obrero Español), which today forms the Government. Local elections have also been held, as have elections to the Legislative Assemblies of the 17 Autonomous Communities from which have come

---

[9] *Ibid.* (CCPR/C/32/Add.3).
[10] *Ibid.* (CCPR/C/32/Add.3).

the various Executive Councils or Autonomous Governments, in accordance with the respective Statutes of Autonomy.

## K. Right to social security

*(article 22 of the Universal Declaration;*
*article 9 of the International Covenant on Economic,*
*Social and Cultural Rights)*[11]

Regulations adopted since the promulgation of the Spanish Constitution include the following: Act No. 13/1982 of 7 April, on the social integration of the handicapped; Royal Decree No. 2609/1982 of 24 September, on the assessment and certification of disability status under the social security system.

Coverage under the special scheme for self-employed persons (governed by Decree No. 2530/1970 of 20 August, as amplified by Royal Decree No. 2504/1980 of 24 October) has been gradually broadened through the adoption of various regulations to include new occupational groups, such as self-employed graduates of advanced commercial institutions who are members of their professional association (Order of 18 January 1982); self-employed mining engineers and experts who are members of their professional association (Order of 1 April 1982), and self-employed chartered accountants who are members of their professional association (Order of 13 April 1982).

Prior to being amended by Act No. 13/1982 of 7 April, the General Social Security Act defined major disability as being the condition of the complete invalid who, in addition, requires the help of another person to perform the most essential human actions, such as moving, dressing, eating and so on. Under provision 5 of Act No. 13/1982, major disability does not necessarily imply permanent total incapacity for all work.

An important innovation in the certification and review of disability has been introduced by Royal Decree No. 2609/1982 of 24 September, on assessment and certification of disability status in the social security system, and by the Order of 23 November 1982, on the procedure to be followed by the National Social Security and Social Services Institutes in assessing and certifying cases of disability.

Act No. 13/1982 of 7 April, on the social integration of the handicapped, has retained in its entirety the rehabilitation benefit of the General Act. Nevertheless, it should be noted that article 35, paragraph 2, of Act No. 13/1982 provides that "persons receiving the rehabilitation benefit under the social security system may also qualify for the supplementary measures referred to in the preceding paragraph". The measures referred to mean that the occupational rehabilitation benefits may be supplemented by other measures to assist the recipient to achieve the maximum level of personal development and promote his integration into society.

---

[11] *Ibid.* (E/1984/7/Add.2).

## L. Right to work

*(article 23(1) of the Universal Declaration;*
*article 6 of the International Covenant on Economic,*
*Social and Cultural Rights)*[12]

ILO Convention No. 147 concerning minimum standards in merchant ships was ratified on 10 April 1978 and published on 18 January 1982.

An assistance programme for women with family responsibilities was formerly governed by Royal Decree No. 723/1980 of 11 April (*Official Gazette*, 23 April 1980), on promoting the employment of women with family responsibilities, which has been replaced by Royal Decree No. 1445/1982 of 25 June (*Official Gazette*, 1 July 1982), dealing with various employment promotion measures, among them the said assistance programme.

Under the latter Royal Decree, a woman with family responsibilities is one who has a dependent spouse, or dependent children, parents or other relatives by blood or marriage up to and including the third degree and, if applicable, by adoption. It also establishes the following programmes:

(*a*) Vocational training programme;

(*b*) Programme for the promotion of labour co-operatives which provide services needed by women as a result of their incorporation into the work force;

(*c*) Programme for the promotion of self-employment of women with family responsibilities.

For specific reasons arising out of the current situation of the labour market, the following early retirement systems have been established:

Early retirement governed by the Royal Decrees approving redeployment plans established in pursuance of the provisions of Act No. 21/1982 of 9 June (*Official Gazette*, 19 June 1982), on measures for industrial deployment;

Early retirement governed by the Order of 15 March 1982 (*Official Gazette*, 25 March 1982) for workers whose employers are not subject to industrial redeployment plans and who cease to work for them prior to reaching the age set for voluntary retirement.

Royal Decree No. 1445/1982 of 25 June, was adopted and amended by Royal Decree No. 3887/1982 of 29 December; the latter deals with various employment promotion measures and consolidates the provisions governing all types of contracts, as well as the rules on employment promotion incentives.

That Royal Decree establishes a flexible procedure for temporary contracts (in force up to 31 December 1982 and later extended to 31 December 1983), subject to limitations by reference to the number of permanent staff at the work centres, employing a scale which goes from 5 per cent for a staff exceeding 1,000 to 50 per cent—which can be raised to 100 per cent subject to advising the Provisional Directorate of INEM—for a permanent staff of from 1 to 25.

Measures are provided for in Royal Decree No. 1445/1982 with a view to encouraging the creation of jobs in the occupational sectors and regions worst hit by

---

[12] *Ibid.* (E/1984/7/Add.2).

unemployment; they take the form of granting specified benefits to employers engaging for an indefinite period unemployed workers who are registered with the employment offices.

Royal Decree No. 1445/1982 regulates the employment by public authorities of workers who are drawing unemployment benefits, without their forfeiting the amounts that they receive on that account, for temporary work of social utility that meets the following requirements:

(a) That it is socially useful and of benefit to the community;

(b) That it lasts no longer than five months;

(c) That it is performed within the area served by the employment office with which the worker is registered;

(d) That it is suited to the unemployed worker's physical capacities and skills.

Once the labour legislation—primarily the Workers' Charter and the Basic Employment Act—was in place, Royal Decree No. 1314/1982 of 18 June, on the organization and functions of the National Employment Institute, was enacted (*Official Gazette,* 29 June 1982). The Decree, having described the structure of the Institute's territorial services, identifies the employment offices as the executing agencies of its provincial departments, with the following functions:

(a) To register workers seeking employment;

(b) To receive and respond to offers of and requests for employment;

(c) To register and, where appropriate, approve contracts of employment;

(d) To receive the documentation on unemployment benefits;

(e) Such other functions as are specifically assigned to them.

The various training, further training and retraining programmes and schemes are carried out in the National Employment Institute's own centres and in duly authorized centres co-operating with it.

Among its functions, as enunciated in article 43 of the Act, the National Employment Institute is required to promote workers' training in close co-ordination with employment policy by providing suitable refresher, further training and, where appropriate, retraining schemes.

The above functions are also reflected in article 1.2. (c) of Royal Decree No. 1313/1982 of 18 June on the organization and functions of the Institute, which in addition to vocational training schemes, develops regulated training programmes.

It is necessary to review Royal Legislative Decree No. 1/1982, of 15 January 1982 (*Official Gazette,* 3 February 1982), a contingency measure, by which the Special Unemployment Protection Fund provided for in section 3.2 of the National Employment Agreement of 9 June 1981 was established.

The Fund is intended to cater for extraordinary and urgent situations not provided for under the Basic Employment Act and the Unemployment Benefit Regulations, by providing financial assistance, in particular a special allowance at a rate equal to 75 per cent of the minimum inter-occupational wage, to be drawn over a minimum period of one month and a maximum period of three months, which can be extended to six months.

The Fund was initially endowed with 15,000 million pesetas and was scheduled to cease operations on 31 December 1982; however, under the terms of Royal

Legislative Decree No. 23/1982 of 29 December 1982 (*Official Gazette*, 31 December 1982) its existence was extended until such time as its assets are exhausted.

By Royal Decree No. 3064/1982 of 15 October 1982 (*Official Gazette*, 20 November 1982) entitlement to receive unemployment benefit was extended to certain workers included in group II of the General Regulations of the Seamen's Social Security Act who prior to that time had been ineligible.

## M. Right to just and favourable conditions of work

*(article 23 (1) of the Universal Declaration;*
*article 7 of the International Covenant on Economic,*
*Social and Cultural Rights)*[13]

ILO Convention No. 150 concerning labour administration: role, functions and organization was ratified on 13 February 1982 and published on 10 December 1982.

Royal Decree No. 577 of 17 March 1982 concerns the structure and competence of the National Occupational Safety and Health Institute.

ILO Convention No. 152 concerning occupational safety and health in dock work was ratified on 13 February 1982.

Royal Decree of 12 August 1982 approved the regulations on health protection against ionizing radiation.

Order of 30 August 1982 approved the instruction relating to oil refineries and petrochemical plans, as a supplement to the Safety and Health Regulations for oil refineries and petroleum product storage depots.

Order of 19 July 1982 and the Resolution of 30 September 1982 concerns working conditions applicable to the handling of asbestos.

Royal Decree of 5 March 1982 approved national regulations and the supplementary rules on the carriage of dangerous goods by rail.

Royal Decree No. 281/1981 of 27 November, specifying which holidays are national holidays for the purpose of release from work has been amended in part by Royal Decree No. 3866/1982 of 29 December.

## N. Right to form and join trade unions

*(article 23 (4) of the Universal Declaration;*
*article 21 of the International Covenant on Civil and Political Rights)*[14]

The Constitutional Court has stated that:

"The right to trade union freedom comprises not only the right of individuals to found trade unions and join those of their choice but also the negative right of not joining, which is clearly defined by the graphic expression that nobody may be compelled to join a trade union." (Constitutional Court judgement No. 68/1982 of 22 November 1982.)

---

[13] *Ibid.* (E/1984/7/Add.2).
[14] *Ibid.* (CCPR/C/32/Add.3).

Likewise, it covers:

"The right of established trade unions . . . to carry out the functions that may reasonably be expected of them in accordance with the democratic character of the State and with . . . the essential content of that right. It must therefore be understood that the right recognized by article 28 of the Spanish Constitution is the right of freely established trade unions to carry out the role and the functions of workers' trade unions which are set out in article 7 of the Constitution, so that they shall contribute to the defence and protection of the interests of the workers." (Constitutional Court judgement No. 70/1982 of 29 November 1982.)

Since there are many trade union federations,

"The problem arises of determining which of them should represent the interests of the workers . . . To meet this problem, the law uses the criterion of the greatest degree of representativeness in identifying the unions that are entitled to defend the rights of the workers in collective bargaining or with organs of the Administration." (Constitutional Court judgement No. 65/1982 of 10 November 1982.)

Similar expressions are used in article 4 (3) of the ILO Convention of 9 July 1948 and article 3 (5) of the Constitution of the ILO (Constitutional Court judgement No. 53/1982 of 22 July 1982).

# SRI LANKA

## A. Prohibition of torture or cruel, inhuman or degrading treatment or punishment

*(article 5 of the Universal Declaration;*
*article 7 of the International Covenant on Civil and Political Rights)*[1]

The Government of Sri Lanka has further reiterated its commitment to freedom from torture or cruel, inhuman or degrading treatment or punishment by depositing with the Centre for Human Rights of the United Nations, on 2 September 1982, a Declaration on the Protection of All Persons from Being Subjected to Torture and Other Cruel, Inhuman or Degrading Treatment or Punishment, adopted by the General Assembly on 9 December 1975 (resolution 3452 (XXX)).

## B. Right to take part in government

*(article 21 of the Universal Declaration;*
*article 5 of the International Convention on the Elimination of All Forms of Racial Discrimination)*[2]

The first presidential election under the 1978 Constitution was held in 1982 and candidates from all the recognized political parties representing different political views and ideologies contested the election. A referendum to seek a people's mandate to extend the period of office of the present parliament for a further period of six years was also held in 1982.

## C. Promotion of understanding, tolerance and friendship among all nations, racial and ethnic groups

*(article 26 (2) of the Universal Declaration;*
*article 2 of the International Covenant on Civil and Political Rights)*[3]

The Government of Sri Lanka, in response to a request made by the United Nations Organization, has decided to introduce the teaching of human rights in all schools. The programme of teaching has been prepared by the Ministry of Education in association with the Centre for Human Rights. According to this programme, human rights will be taught in the junior secondary grade as a subject of social studies. The first phase of this programme commenced in January 1983 in grades 6, 7

---

[1] Report submitted by State (CCPR/C/14/Add.6).
[2] *Ibid.* (CERD/C/101/Add.6).
[3] *Ibid.* (CCPR/C/14/Add.4).

and 8. In 1984 it will be extended to grades 9 to 10. Thereafter, it will be introduced into the senior secondary grade.

Apart from the teaching of human rights in schools, the Centre for Human Rights also organized an all-island poster competition on human rights and an all-island quiz competition on human rights with the objective of fostering among schoolchildren humanitarian attitudes of mutual respect and tolerance and of creating a greater awareness of the articles in the Universal Declaration of Human Rights.

# SWEDEN

## A. Elimination of racial discrimination

*(article 2 of the Universal Declaration;*
*article 2 of the International Convention on the Elimination*
*of All Forms of Racial Discrimination)*[1]

In September 1982, a Government Commission was entrusted with the task of investigating the possibilities of strengthening the legal position of the Samis in regard to reindeer breeding. The Commission shall also consider the need for a special Sami organ to represent the Samis on various matters. Furthermore, the Commission shall propose measures in order to preserve and develop the Sami language.

## B. Prohibition of incitement to racial discrimination

*(article 7 of the Universal Declaration;*
*article 4 of the International Convention on the Elimination*
*of All Forms of Racial Discrimination)*[2]

In 1982, the Swedish Supreme Court passed a judgement in a case regarding agitation against an ethnic group. The accused, who was the manager of a camping-ground, had put up a sign at the entrance with the text "Gypsies may not enter the camping". The Supreme Court found that the text expressed contempt for an ethnic group in accordance with section 8 of chapter 16 of the Penal Code and that the accused was guilty of an offence under that provision.

In another case the Chancellor of Justice instituted criminal proceedings against the responsible editor of two programmes of the local radio of Stockholm on the charge of agitation against an ethnic group. Certain pejorative expressions regarding members of a racial group had been used in the programmes, and the Stockholm District Court sentenced the editor to two months' imprisonment. An appeal against the judgement of the District Court has been lodged with the Svea Court of Appeal.

In December 1982 the Chancellor of Justice instituted another prosecution against a person for press libel (agitation against an ethnic group). The accused, who was charged with anti-semitic statements in printed publications, was at that time already detained on remand as being suspected of agitation against an ethnic group. The detained person is now undergoing a forensic psychiatric examination.

A decision was taken by the Chief State Prosecutor on 1 November 1982 to the effect that cases regarding the offences of agitation against an ethnic group (section 8

---

[1] Report submitted by State (CERD/C/106/Add.2).

[2] *Ibid.* (CERD/C/106/Add.2).

of chapter 16 of the Penal Code) and unlawful discrimination (section 9 of chapter 16 of the Penal Code) shall be dealt with by prosecutors at a high level. Those prosecutors have also been called upon to work for a uniform adjudication.

## C. Right to work

*(article 23 (1) of the Universal Declaration;*
*article 6 of the International Covenant on Economic,*
*Social and Cultural Rights)*[3]

The Security of Employment Act has been adopted in 1982.

## D. Right to just and favourable conditions of work

*(article 23 (1) of the Universal Declaration;*
*article 7 of the International Covenant on Economic,*
*Social and Cultural Rights)*[4]

Sweden has ratified, in August 1982:

The ILO Convention (No. 154) on Promotion of Collective Bargaining;

The ILO Convention (No. 155) concerning Occupational Safety and Health and the Working Environment;

The ILO Convention (No. 156) concerning Equal Opportunity and Equal Treatment for Men and Women Workers: Workers with Family Responsibilities;

The ILO Convention (No. 47) on the Reduction of Hours of Work to 40 a Week.

---

[3] *Ibid.* (E/1984/7/Add.5).

[4] *Ibid.* (E/1984/7/Add.5).

# SWITZERLAND

**Right to a social and international order in which human rights can be realized**
*(article 28 of the Universal Declaration)*[1]

In time of armed conflict, persons under house arrest or who have been interned enjoy the protection afforded by the Geneva Convention relative to the Protection of Civilian Persons in Time of War of 12 August 1949, ratified by Switzerland on 31 March 1950, and by the two Protocols additional to the Geneva Convention, adopted on 8 June 1977 and ratified by Switzerland on 17 February 1982.

---

[1] Contribution submitted by State.

140

# UGANDA

## Elimination of racial discrimination

*(articles 2 and 7 of the Universal Declaration;
article 2 (1) of the International Convention on the Elimination
of All Forms of Racial Discrimination)*[1]

By the Immigration (Cancellation of Entry Permits and Certificates of Residence) Decree, 1972, the military régime expelled *en masse* people of Asian origin or descent from Uganda. By the Declaration of Assets (Non-Citizen Asians) Decree, 1972, and the Declaration of Assets (Non-Citizen Asians) (Amendment) Decree, 1972, the military régime also expropriated without compensation properties of the said persons of Asian origin or descent. Those properties were allocated on the authority of various decrees to the Government, private individuals, institutions or organizations.

Following the restoration of parliamentary democracy, the Government promptly initiated a review of the decrees mentioned in the preceding paragraph on the grounds, *inter alia*, that they may have been discriminatory. Consequently, in November 1982, the Parliament adopted the Expropriated Properties Act 1982. Under that Act any property or business expropriated by the military régime became revested in the Government under the management of the Ministry of Finance.

The Act empowers the Ministry of Finance to transfer any such property or business to the former (Asian) owner upon verification of claim to title or ownership and commitment by the owner to return to Uganda, repossess and effectively manage the same. It further provides for compensation to any owner who, though able to verify claim to title or ownership, does not wish to return, repossess and manage the property or business.

---

[1] Report submitted by State (CERD/C/71/Add.2*).

# UKRAINIAN SOVIET SOCIALIST REPUBLIC

## A. Condemnation of racial segregation and *apartheid*

*(articles 1 and 2 of the Universal Declaration;*
*article 3 of the International Convention on the Elimination*
*of All Forms of Racial Discrimination;*
*articles IV, VI and VII of the International Convention on the Suppression*
*and Punishment of the Crime of* Apartheid)[1]

In the Ukrainian SSR there is widespread social activity aimed at condemning *apartheid* and racism, unmasking its crimes and supporting the peoples of southern Africa and their national liberation movements which are waging a heroic and unceasing struggle against the remnants of colonialism, racism and *apartheid* on the African continent. Mass assemblies and meetings of representatives of the public are held every year in towns of the Ukrainian SSR with the participation of manual and non-manual workers, eminent figures from the worlds of science, culture and the arts, and foreign students, *inter alia*, from countries of Africa, Asia and Latin America, attending educational establishments in the Ukrainian SSR. These gatherings mark international days proclaimed by the United Nations. The holding of such events helps to mobilize public opinion in support of the just struggle for independence of the oppressed peoples of South Africa and Namibia and educates the public in a spirit of opposition to colonialism, racism and *apartheid* and of solidarity with the national liberation movements of southern Africa.

## B. Right to social security

*(article 22 of the Universal Declaration;*
*article 9 of the International Covenant on Economic,*
*Social and Cultural Rights)[2]*

On 1 November 1982, one-off cash grants were introduced in the Republic for mothers at work or in full-time education upon the birth of the first, second and third child, and a monthly child-care allowance, paid until the child becomes one year old, was also introduced.

---

[1] Report submitted by State (E/CN.4/1983/24/Add.11).
[2] *Ibid.* (E/1984/7/Add.9).

# C. Right to work

*(article 23 (1) of the Universal Declaration;*
*article 6 of the International Covenant on Economic,*
*Social and Cultural Rights)*[3]

By its decision on 23 March 1982, the Council of Ministers of the Ukrainian SSR approved the regulations concerning job placement arrangements for general secondary school-leavers and other young people who do not continue in full-time education. Under these regulations, job placement activities are organized by special youth employment commissions together with local labour bodies on the basis of established job placement plans, with account being taken of the wishes of the young people, their practical training and the recommendations of the schools.

---

[3] *Ibid.* (E/1984/7/Add.9).

# UNION OF SOVIET SOCIALIST REPUBLICS

## A. Treatment of prisoners

*(article 5 of the Universal Declaration;*
*article 10 of the International Covenant on Civil and Political Rights)*[1]

On 26 May 1982 the Supreme Soviet of the USSR adopted a Decree on the further improvement of criminal and corrective-labour legislation, providing for more widespread use of forms of criminal punishment not involving deprivation of liberty.

Under article 1 of the Decree, a court may, when sentencing a first offender to imprisonment for a period not exceeding three years, taking into account the nature and threat to society involved in the offence, the personality of the accused and other circumstances of the case, and also the possibility of his reform and rehabilitation without isolation from society, suspend execution of the sentence for a period of between one and two years. The court may in this case suspend also the enforcement of additional penalties.

On conclusion of the period of suspension of the sentence the court may, at the instigation of the supervisory organ responsible for the behaviour of the convicted person, and depending on his attitude to work or training and his behaviour during the period of suspension of the sentence by the court, decide to release the convicted person from the punishment imposed or to require him to serve the period of imprisonment imposed by the original sentence.

## B. Protection against arbitrary interference with privacy

*(article 9 of the Universal Declaration;*
*article 17 of the International Covenant on Civil and Political Rights)*[2]

In order to enhance the guarantees of observance of the constitutional rights of citizens (under article 56 of the Constitution of the USSR), the Decree of the Presidium of the Supreme Soviet of the RSFSR of 3 December 1982 on the introduction of amendments and additions to the Criminal Code of the RSFSR made violation of the secrecy of citizens' telephone conversations and telegraphic communications a criminal offence (article 135 of the Criminal Code of the RSFSR and corresponding articles in the Criminal Codes of the other Union Republics).

---

[1] Report submitted by State (CCPR/C/28/Add.3).
[2] *Ibid.* (CCPR/C/28/Add.3).

## C. Freedom of association; trade union rights

*(articles 20 and 23 (4) of the Universal Declaration;*
*article 22 of the International Covenant on Civil and Political Rights)*[3]

Various changes were made to the existing USSR trade union statutes at the seventeenth Congress of USSR trade unions in 1982, aimed at extending the competence of trade unions in deciding matters relating to the utilization of labour and material resources, the protection of mothers and children, the provision of healthy and safe working conditions, the increased production and fair distribution of consumer goods, the control of their utilization, etc.

## D. Right to social security

*(article 22 of the Universal Declaration;*
*article 9 of the International Covenant on Economic,*
*Social and Cultural Rights)*[4]

Pregnancy and childbirth allowances for women cover full earnings. The need has been recognized to increase in the near future the length of post-maternity leave for women to 10 weeks with full pay, and for an extension in the near future of the period during which an allowance is paid for the care of a sick family member.

## E. Right to just and favourable conditions of work

*(article 23 (1) of the Universal Declaration;*
*article 7 of the International Covenant on Economic,*
*Social and Cultural Rights)*[5]

On 19 August 1982, the Central Committee of the Communist Party of the Soviet Union and the Council of Ministers of the USSR adopted the decision entitled "Additional measures to improve public health care". This decision significantly increased the responsibility of the heads of enterprises and organizations for the strict observance of sanitary rules and norms and labour safety standards and for the implementation of health measures designed further to improve workers' conditions of work and of leisure. It has been proposed that plans for the social and economic development of enterprises should provide measures to improve disease prevention and the health of manual and non-manual workers, and to reduce further the incidence of occupational injuries and diseases.

On 7 January 1982, the Central Committee of the Communist Party of the Soviet Union, the Council of Ministers of the USSR and the All-Union Central Council of Trade Unions adopted a joint decision, entitled "Measures for the further improvement of treatment in sanatoria and health resorts and of leisure for

---

[3] *Ibid.* (CCPR/C/28/Add.3).
[4] *Ibid.* (E/1984/7/Add.7).
[5] *Ibid.* (E/1984/7/Add.7).

working people and the development of a network of trade-union health resorts"
which provided for the implementation in 1982-1985 and in the period up to 1990 of
an extensive programme of measures aimed at the further improvement of treatment
in sanitoria and health resorts and of the leisure of working people, expansion of the
network of sanatoria and health resorts and leisure establishments, primarily of the
specialized sanatoria for the treatment of patients with cardio-vascular diseases,
locomotive, digestive, nervous and kidney diseases, and sanatoria and health resort
establishments for parents and children. In 1982, 60 million people visited sanatoria,
holiday hotels, rest homes and tourist centres.

# UNITED KINGDOM OF GREAT BRITAIN AND NORTHERN IRELAND

## A. Protection of human rights and fundamental freedoms

*(article 2 of the Universal Declaration;*
*article 2 of the International Convention on the Elimination*
*of All Forms of Racial Discrimination)*[1]

### Bermuda

In May 1982, Bermuda's first Human Rights Commission was established under the Human Rights Act 1981.

### Jersey

The Administrative Decisions (Review) Regulations referred to in the initial report, have now been converted into permanent legislation as the Administrative Decisions (Review) (Jersey) Law, 1982.

## B. Elimination of racial discrimination

*(article 2 of the Universal Declaration;*
*article 5 of the International Convention on the Elimination*
*of All Forms of Racial Discrimination)*[2]

As from 1 March 1982, and following a successful pilot study, information on the ethnic origins of people held in Prison Department establishments is also being collected centrally. This will make it possible to assess such matters as the distribution of ethnic groups among different types of establishment to a greater degree of accuracy than is possible at present. This may have implications for prison administrations as well as for dietary arrangements, community links and library material.

The Community Programme for the Long-Term Unemployed is run by the Employment Division (ED) of the Manpower Services Commission and was launched on 1 October 1982. Like its predecessor, the Community Enterprise Programme (CEP), the Community Programme provides temporary work opportunities on projects of benefit to the community for adults who have been unemployed for some time. Eligible persons aged 18 to 24 must have been unemployed for at least six

---

[1] Reports submitted by State (CERD/C/118/Add.7; CCPR/C/32/Add.5).
[2] *Ibid.* (CERD/C/91/Add.24; CERD/C/118/Add.7).

months out of the last nine months or more and those aged 25 and over have been unemployed for 12 months out of the last 15 months.

By providing work experience and a recent reference it is hoped that a spell on the programme will enable participants to improve their chances of competing for and obtaining permanent jobs on the open labour market.

### C. Elimination of racial discrimination; development and protection of certain racial groups or individuals belonging to them

*(articles 2 and 22 of the Universal Declaration;*
*article 2 of the International Convention on the Elimination*
*of All Forms of Racial Discrimination)*[3]

In February 1982 the Secretary of State for the Environment asked one of his Parliamentary Under Secretaries of State to take ministerial responsibility for all matters concerned with race relations which fall within the Department of the Environment's sphere of interests. The Government recognize that many aspects of the Department's work are vital for the development of good race relations and for helping to cure racial disadvantage. In addition to the Urban Programme, aspects of housing policy and other local authority programmes are also important.

### D. Treatment of prisoners

*(article 5 of the Universal Declaration;*
*article 10 (3) of the International Covenant on Civil and Political Rights)*[4]

The Criminal Justice Act 1982 abolished imprisonment for those aged under 21. In place of sentences of imprisonment and Borstal training, there is a new custodial sentencing structure. No young offender may be sentenced to custody unless the court is satisfied that no other method of dealing with the offender is appropriate, because it appears to the court that he or she is unable or unwilling to respond to non-custodial penalties, or because the protection of the public or the seriousness of the offence mean that a non-custodial sentence cannot be justified.

### Isle of Man

Following the abolition of Borstal training in England and Wales, consequent upon the Criminal Law Act 1982 of Parliament, where a sentence of Borstal training is imposed on a young person in the Isle of Man it is treated in England and Wales as a youth custody sentence and he or she serves that sentence in England or Wales.

---

[3] *Ibid.* (CERD/C/91/Add.24).
[4] *Ibid.* (CCPR/C/32/Add.5).

## E. Right not to be subjected to arbitrary arrest or detention

*(article 9 of the Universal Declaration;*
*article 9 of the International Covenant on Civil and Political Rights)*[5]

*Guernsey*

In practice, a person charged and detained by the police will appear before a magistrate within 48 hours of his arrest (not counting Sunday). Cases of detention before trial are carefully monitored by the Prosecuting Authorities and the Magistrates. Generally a person will not be remanded in custody for a period of more than seven days at a time. Preventive detention is not used. The Guernsey courts generally adopt the principles laid down in English Law when considering whether or not to admit an accused person to bail pending his trial. If it is necessary to detain a man in custody pending his trial, every effort is made to expedite the trial. A review of cases before the courts in 1982 where persons were committed for trial on indictment before the Royal Court has been carried out and four persons had to be kept in custody pending their trial. One case was disposed of five months after arrest. A second was disposed of six months after arrest. In this case there were problems due to serious illness of one of the police officers and changes of plea on the part of the accused. The other two cases were disposed of more speedily. In all cases custodial sentences were imposed and these took account of periods in custody pending trial.

## F. Right to all the guarantees necessary for defence

*(article 11 of the Universal Declaration;*
*article 14 (3) (d) of the International Covenant on Civil and Political Rights)*[6]

Legal aid in criminal proceedings is governed by the Legal Aid Act 1974, Part II, and the Legal Aid Act 1982, Part II, and normally consists of representation by a solicitor, and counsel where necessary, and includes advice on preparing the case. The power to grant legal aid is exercisable where it appears to the court desirable to do so in the interests of justice and, subject to means, the court must make an order in certain cases, e.g., where a person is committed for trial on a charge of murder. An order must not be made unless it appears to the court that the disposable income and disposable capital of the person concerned are such that he requires assistance in meeting the costs which he may incur. Where a doubt arises whether an order should be made for the giving of aid to any person, the doubt must be resolved in that person's favour. A legally assisted person whose disposable income and disposable capital exceed the limits prescribed in relation to such income and capital will be required to make a payment in respect of the cost of legal aid granted to him.

---

[5] *Ibid.* (CCPR/C/32/Add.5).
[6] *Ibid.* (CCPR/C/32/Add.5).

## G.  Protection of the family
*(article 16 (3) of the Universal Declaration;*
*article 23 (1) of the International Covenant on Civil and Political Rights)*[7]

By section 3 of the Administration of Justice Act 1982, which replaced new sections 1 to 4 of the Fatal Accidents Act 1976, persons treated by the deceased as a parent or child, or persons living with the deceased in the same household may also be the beneficiaries of an action for damages in respect of death.

## H.  Right to social security
*(article 22 of the Universal Declaration;*
*article 9 of the International Covenant on Economic,*
*Social and Cultural Rights)*[8]

### Cash sickness benefits

Related legislation is as follows:

(*a*)  The Social Security and Housing Benefits Act 1982;

(*b*)  The Social Security and Housing Benefits Act 1982 (Commencement No. 1) Order 1982 (SI 1982 No. 893);

(*c*)  The Statutory Sick Pay (General) Regulations (SI 1982 No. 894);

(*d*)  The Statutory Sick Pay (Mariners, Airmen and Persons Abroad) Regulations 1982 (SI 1982 No. 1349);

(*e*)  The Statutory Sick Pay (Adjudication) Regulations 1982 (SI 1982 No. 1400);

(*f*)  Report to Parliament by the Secretary of State.

The Social Security (Medical Evidence, Claims and Payments) Amendment Regulations 1982 (SI 1982 No. 699), which came into operation on 14 June 1982, introduced self-certification for spells of incapacity lasting seven days or less, and for the first seven days of longer spells, into the State system for the payment of sickness, injury, invalidity benefit and non-contributory invalidity pension. Before the regulations were made, they were considered by the Social Security Advisory Committee. The Committee presented its report on the regulations (Cmnd. 8560) to the Secretary of State for Social Services in May 1982.

### Employment injury benefits

The Social Security and Housing Benefits Act 1982 became law on 28 June 1982. Section 39 of this Act gives effect to two of the proposals in the White Paper entitled "Reform of the Industrial Injuries Scheme". From 6 April 1983, injury benefit is abolished and disablement benefit will commence after a waiting period of 90 days (15 weeks) rather than as now after 26 weeks or when incapacity for work ceases. Although injury benefit is abolished from 6 April 1983, provided statutory

---

[7] *Ibid.* (CCPR/C/32/Add.5).

[8] *Ibid.* (E/1984/7/Add.20).

sick pay is not in payment, sickness benefit will be available without contribution conditions where incapacity stems from an industrial accident or prescribed disease.

During 1982, legislation was brought in to include in the list of prescribed diseases occupational asthma in workers exposed to any of seven groups of sensitizing agents (SI 1982 No. 249, Social Security (Industrial Injuries) (Prescribed Diseases) Amendment Regulations 1982). Legislation was also passed to extend the rights of appeal in pneumoconiosis and byssinosis cases (SI 1982 No. 566, Social Security (Industrial Injuries) (Prescribed Diseases) Amendment No. 2 Regulations 1982).

The following reports by the Industrial Injuries Advisory Council were published:

(a) Occupational deafness (Cmnd. 8749), November 1982, recommending extension of the present cover for occupational deafness as a prescribed disease.

(b) Asbestos-related diseases without asbestosis (Cmnd. 8750), November 1982, recommending prescription of certain asbestos-related diseases for asbestos workers who do not have detectable asbestosis.

Two further reports were produced by the Industrial Injuries Advisory Council but were not published. These recommended that streptococcus suis and extrinsic allergic alveolitis should be prescribed as industrial diseases.

## Unemployment benefits

### Part-time and voluntary work

The Social Security (Unemployment, Sickness and Invalidity Benefit and Credits) Regulations 1982 (SI 1982 No. 96). From 8 March 1982 it has been easier for unemployed people to do a certain amount of work—including voluntary work—without losing benefit; the subsidiary occupation earnings limit was raised from 75p to £2 a day and there was some relaxation of the availability condition, though the basic principle that, to be entitled to benefit, a claimant must be available for work was maintained.

### Introduction of voluntary registration for work

From 18 October 1982 unemployed people over age 18 have no longer been required to register for work at a jobcentre (or Employment Office) as a condition of entitlement to benefit. (Young people are still required to register, which they normally do at Careers Offices.) The essence of the test of availability for work has not been changed.

### Rules for claiming unemployment benefit

The Social Security (Claims and Payments) Amendment No. 2 Regulations (SI 1982 No. 1344). Where claims control procedures can be operated effectively, claimants whose employment is not terminated but temporarily stopped can be awarded benefit for up to 13 weeks without having to attend the benefit office after the claim is established. Such claimants formerly had to attend the benefit office each week. This change reduces administration for the benefit office and saves inconvenience for the claimant.

These changes came into effect on 19 October 1982 with other purely technical alterations.

### Requirement for unemployment benefit claimants to attend for an interview with an unemployment review officer

The Social Security (Unemployment, Sickness and Invalidity Benefit) Amendment No. 2 Regulations 1982 (SI 1982 No. 1345). From 18 October 1982 Unemployment Review Officers, who had hitherto worked with unemployed people claiming supplementary benefit, are now also working with people claiming unemployment benefit. The regulations were amended to provide for benefit to be disallowed if an unemployment benefit claimant failed without good cause to attend an interview with an Unemployment Review Officer in connection with obtaining employment. (Regulations already provided for disallowance of benefit where a claimant failed to attend such an interview at a jobcentre.)

### Family benefits

With effect from 31 May 1982, the Child Benefit (General) Amendment Regulations 1982 provide for child benefit not to be paid for any week in which a young person is gainfully employed full-time or receiving an allowance under a Government training scheme or remuneration in excess of provision for fares, tools, etc., from an employer. Payment of child benefit is restored if the young person becomes unemployed or leaves a sponsored training course before the end of the school holidays. During 1982, about 350,000 young people were affected by the change in legislation.

### Invalid care allowance

The Social Security (Invalid Care Allowance) Regulations 1982 (SI No. 1493), effective from November 1982. A person is entitled to invalid care allowance for any pay day in which he is caring for a severely disabled person if, among other things, he is not gainfully employed and earning a prescribed amount. The regulations increased the prescribed amount from £6 per week to £12 per week with effect from 22 November 1982. The previous limit had been effective since the commencement of the allowance in 1976 and the increase to £12 per week was in line with inflation.

# I.  Right to work

*(article 23 of the Universal Declaration;
article 6 of the International Covenant on Economic,
Social and Cultural Rights)*[9]

The Open Tech Programme was launched in the autumn of 1982 with the aim of offering additional opportunities to meet the training and retraining needs of adults at technician and supervisory levels of skill, through a range of collaborative projects over an initial four-year period. The Programme will be employment-led and consist

---

[9] *Ibid.* (E/1984/7/Add.20).

of a limited number of major operational projects concerned with the production of open-learning materials and the setting up of open-learning systems. Other projects will be commissioned in areas such as staff training needs to provide support for those participating.

Central responsibility for Careers Service Training rests with the Local Government Training Board (LGTB) under the direction of its Careers Service Training Council (CSTC) which includes representatives of the Careers Service Branch. In June 1982 the first meeting of a review group set up by LGTB was held to review all aspects of initial training for careers officers. The review group will make recommendations to CSTC on any changes which are felt to be required to the core training objectives; the assessment procedure; and the content of the probationary year which forms part of the course leading to the award of the Diploma in Careers Guidance—the professional qualifications which all newly appointed careers officers are required to have or obtain. At the regional level, staff of the Department of Employment also participate in the work of the Local Government Training Boards Regional In-Service Training Committees for Careers Service staff. (Similar arrangements apply in Wales and Scotland.)

In July 1982 the Department of Employment published a report of a systematic assessment of 680 vocational guidance interviews undertaken by careers officers during 1980/1981, entitled *Vocational Guidance Interviews*. This report indicated that where there was a careers education programme in schools more progress was made in the interviews, and the close involvement of careers officers in those programmes helped to make the subsequent interviewing more effective.

The Careers Service is currently being encouraged to improve its relationships with employers. The Careers Service Branch commissioned a research project into the local links between the Careers Service and employers. (The report, entitled *Careers Service Liaison with Employers*, was published in October 1982.) Continuing consideration is being given to further implementation of the report's recommendations.

## J. Right to just and favourable conditions of work

*(article 23 of the Universal Declaration;*
*article 7 of the International Covenant on Economic,*
*Social and Cultural Rights)*[10]

Enforcement of the Health and Safety at Work Act 1974 and its relevant statutory provisions rests principally with inspectorates within the Health and Safety Executive.

The Health and Safety Executive and the local authorities established the Local Authority Unit (LAU). The aim of the Unit is to give increased attention to the preparation of published guidance on standards covering workplaces for which the local authorities have enforcement responsibility. In the course of its work, the Unit is building up close working relationships with national organizations representing employers and employees in these sectors.

---

[10] *Ibid.* (E/1984/7/Add.20).

## K.  Trade union rights

*(article 23 (4) of the Universal Declaration;*
*article 22 of the International Covenant on Civil and Political Rights)*[11]

Individual employees have the right under the 1978 Act not be unfairly dismissed for being members of an independent trade union or for proposing to become members or for taking part or proposing to take part at an appropriate time in the activities of an independent trade union. In relation to this right, an "appropriate time" means a time which is outside the employee's working hours or a time within his working hours at which, in accordance with arrangements agreed with, or consent given by, his employer, it is permissible for him to take part in those activities. Any person dismissed in contravention of these rights will have been unfairly dismissed and an industrial tribunal can order the employer to re-employ the employee concerned where this is practicable or to pay him compensation. In order both to deter employers from making such dismissals and to provide adequate compensation should such dismissals nevertheless take place, the 1982 Employment Act has set compensation in such cases at substantially higher levels than in most other cases of unfair dismissal.

The Employment Act 1982 has (in amending the 1978 Act) further increased the protection for non-union employees working in a closed shop as well as re-enacting the closed shop dismissal provisions of the 1980 Act. In particular, the 1982 Act provides that the dismissal of an employee for not being a member of a trade union, or for refusing to join one, is automatically unfair where the closed shop agreement concerned is not "approved".

If an employee is unfairly dismissed from either an "approved" or an "unapproved" closed shop for not being a member of a trade union, or for refusing to join one, an industrial tribunal can order the employer to re-employ the employee concerned where this is practicable or to pay him compensation. As a result of the 1982 Act, compensation in such cases is set at the same levels as in cases of unfair dismissal in connection with trade-union membership or activities, i.e., at substantially higher levels than in most other cases of unfair dismissal.

---

[11] *Ibid.* (CCPR/C/32/Add.5).

# UNITED REPUBLIC OF TANZANIA

**Realization of economic rights**
*(article 22 of the Universal Declaration;*
*article 5 of the International Convention on the Elimination*
*of All Forms of Racial Discrimination)*[1]

The recent Co-operative Societies Act 1982 provides for the economic organization of both urban and rural population; under co-operatives which stem from the Ujamaa villages as the primary economic units in the country, for the implementation of the policy of socialism and self-reliance.

---

[1] Report submitted by State (CERD/C/75/Add.10).

# VENEZUELA

**Elimination of racial discrimination; development and protection of certain racial groups or individuals belonging to them**

*(articles 2 and 26 of the Universal Declaration;
article 2 of the International Convention on the Elimination
of All Forms of Racial Discrimination)*[1]

The basic legal instrument governing the system of intercultural education is Decree No. 283 of 20 September 1979, which provides, *inter alia*:

*"Article 1.* Without prejudice to the knowledge proper to the national culture, a system of intercultural bilingual education so designed as to be adapted to the socio-cultural characteristics of each of the relevant ethnic groups shall gradually be introduced in the educational establishments situated in areas inhabited by indigenous persons.

*"Article 2.* The cultural standards, rhythm of life and environmental conditions peculiar to each community must be taken into account in designing study programmes, selecting teaching materials and formulating norms of operation. The teaching staff must have training adjusted to the requirements of this type of education."

In connection with the implementation of Decree No. 283, Ministry of Education Decision No. 83 of 15 March 1982 authorizing the use of the alphabets in the intercultural educational establishments was promulgated.

---

[1] Report submitted by State (CERD/C/118/Add.24).

# YUGOSLAVIA

## A. Condemnation of racial segregation and *apartheid*

*(articles 1 and 2 of the Universal Declaration;*
*article V of the International Convention on the Suppression*
*and Punishment of the Crime of* Apartheid)[1]

In 1982, 61 persons were sentenced for provoking national, racial or religious intolerance, hatred or discord (art. 134 of the Criminal Code of Yugoslavia).

## B. Protection of human rights and fundamental freedoms

*(article 2 of the Universal Declaration;*
*article 2 of the International Covenant on Civil and Political Rights)[2]*

The questions regarding the realization and protection of the rights and freedoms of working people and citizens, in addition to being considered by a number of the organs of socio-political communities, socio-political and social organizations, self-managed organizations and communities, were dealt with by the Assembly of the Socialist Federal Republic of Yugoslavia in 1982.

## C. Right to social security

*(article 22 of the Universal Declaration;*
*article 9 of the International Covenant on Economic, Social and Cultural Rights)[3]*

A new law on basic rights deriving from pension and invalidity insurance was passed (*Official Gazette* of the Socialist Federal Republic of Yugoslavia, No. 23/82). The procedure of harmonizing republican and provincial laws on pension and invalidity insurance with the new federal law is under way.

## D. Right to just and favourable conditions of work

*(article 23 (1) of the Universal Declaration;*
*article 7 of the International Covenant on Economic, Social and Cultural Rights)[4]*

In January 1982, the Socialist Republic of Bosnia and Herzegovina passed the new Law on Guaranteed Personal Income (*Official Gazette* of the Socialist

---

[1] Report submitted by State (E/CN.4/1985/26/Add.2).
[2] *Ibid.* (CCPR/C/28/Add.1).
[3] *Ibid.* (E/1984/7/Add.10).
[4] *Ibid.* (E/1984/7/Add.10).

Republics of Bosnia and Herzegovina, No. 5/82). By the entry into force of this new law, articles 74 to 80 of the Labour Relations Act ceased to apply. The new law stipulates that the guaranteed monthly personal income for work performed in the course of full hours of work shall be calculated as follows: (*a*) for the period January-June of the current year, 70 per cent of the average monthly advance payment of the personal income earned by the worker concerned in the period July-December of the previous year; and (*b*) in the period July-December of the current year, 70 per cent of the average monthly advance payment earned by the worker concerned in the period January-June of the current year. The minimum guaranteed personal income so determined may neither be lower than 60 per cent of the average monthly personal income realized in the economy of the commune in the preceding six months nor may it exceed the triple guaranteed lowest personal income. The communal assembly (i.e., workers in a basic organization) may fix a higher guaranteed personal income provided they have secured appropriate funds.

The Socialist Republic of Slovenia passed the Law on Guaranteed Personal Income and the Payment of Personal Income in Organizations of Associated Labour Operating with a Loss ("Uradni List SRS" (*Official Gazette* of the Socialist Republic of Slovenia, No. 7/82)). By the entry into force of this law, the following ceased to apply: the Lowest Personal Income Act ("Uradni List SRS", Nos. 17/73 and 27/79) and articles 111 and 112 of the Labour Relations Act ("Uradni List SRS", Nos. 24/77, 30/78, 27/82, 40/82 and 11/83). The funds for guaranteed personal income are fixed by law and amount to 80 per cent of the average monthly funds earmarked for personal income in the basic organization concerned in the previous quarter. Guaranteed personal income for individual workers is determined by the self-management general enactment of the basic organization. This statutory provision enables the application of the basic criteria for the distribution of resources for personal income and the payment of guaranteed personal income as well. The law also explicitly stipulates that the level of guaranteed personal income of workers, when they are performing their working duties in full hours of work, may not be lower than the amount necessary to cover the minimum cost of living (art. 8, para. 3). In accordance with article 15 of the law, the minimum cost of living is established and monitored by the Statistics Institute of the Socialist Republic of Slovenia and published twice a year in "Uradni List SRS" (i.e., in May and September).

In the Socialist Republic of Serbia, the law amending the Law on Labour Relations ("Uradni List SRS", No. 24/82) stipulates that the guaranteed personal income shall amount to 60 per cent of the average personal income of workers in the economy of the commune concerned in the previous year (previously it amounted to 55 per cent).

More intensive work has been undertaken to amend the republican and provincial laws on health and safety at work, the labour inspection acts and other relevant regulations. According to an agreement reached in 1981 with respect to issues that needed to be regulated in a uniform way by republican and provincial laws on health and safety at work and on labour inspection with a view to ensuring uniform basic rights of workers in the field of health and safety at work and a uniform Yugoslav market, as well as with a view to harmonizing certain provisions of those laws with the provisions of the respective ILO Conventions, the laws on health and safety at work have been amended in the Socialist Republic of Croatia and the Socialist

Autonomous Province of Vojvodina, while the Socialist Republic of Croatia passed a law on labour inspection.

In the course of 1982, a considerable number of technical regulations and Yugoslav standards have been adopted specifying technical standards and standardizing certain products and means of labour that affect employment safety and health.

# Section B.  Trust and Non-Self-Governing Territories

## A.  TRUST TERRITORIES

### Trust Territory of the Pacific Islands

In its annual report for the period 1 October 1981 to 30 September 1982,[1] the Administering Authority (the United States of America) stated that the constitutional Governments functioning in the federated States of Micronesia, the Marshall Islands, the Northern Mariana Islands and Palau had continued to consolidate their operations, to assume greater responsibilities for their internal affairs and to expand co-operative arrangements with regional and international organizations. It also reaffirmed its previously stated policy that the people of Micronesia would, following a thorough political education programme, have the opportunity to choose their future political status from a range of options which included independence.

In its report[2] the 1982 United Nations Visiting Mission noted that the 13 years of negotiations between the United States and the Trust Territory of the Pacific Islands had been concluded with the signing of the compact and its subsidiary agreements by the United States and the Marshall Islands on 30 May 1982, Palau on 26 August and the federated States of Micronesia on 1 October.

The Special Committee on the Situation with regard to the Implementation of the Declaration on the Granting of Independence to Colonial Countries and Peoples discussed the situation in the Trust Territory at its 1215th to 1217th, and 1228th meetings between 5 August and 20 September 1982. On 10 August the Special Committee adopted a text of conclusions and recommendations in which, *inter alia*, it reaffirmed the inalienable right of the people of the Trust Territory to self-determination and independence; called again upon the Administering Authority to ensure that its representative be present at meetings of the Committee; took note of developments that had taken place in the Trust Territory; urged the Administering Authority to continue to take effective measures to safeguard and to guarantee, in co-operation with the authorities of the Trust Territory, the right of the people of Micronesia to own and to dispose freely of the natural resources of the Trust Territory and to establish and maintain control of their future development.

On 20 September 1982 the Special Committee decided to authorize its Rapporteur to reformulate its conclusions and recommendations, which had been

---

[1] T/1853.

[2] *Official Records of the Trusteeship Council, Fiftieth Session, Supplement No. 2* (T/1850).

adopted on 10 August, into a draft resolution to be submitted to the General Assembly for consideration by the Fourth Committee.[3]

On 16 November 1982 the Fourth Committee decided to adopt its Chairman's suggestion that the Committee decide not to take any action at the present stage on the draft resolution submitted by the Special Committee.[4]

## B. NON-SELF-GOVERNING TERRITORIES

### 1. American Samoa

On 5 August 1982 the Special Committee adopted the report of its Sub-Committee on Small Territories concerning American Samoa and approved its conclusions and recommendations.[5]

On 16 September 1982 the Special Committee decided to submit a draft resolution on the question of American Samoa for consideration by the Fourth Committee of the General Assembly.

The draft was adopted on 23 November 1982 as resolution 37/20, in which the Assembly, *inter alia*, approved the chapter of the Special Committee's report on American Samoa; called upon the Government of the United States of America, as the administering Power, to take all necessary steps to expedite the process of decolonization of the Territory; recommended that the Chief Justice and Associate Justices should be appointed by the Governor and approved by the Legislature, and that the recommendation of the second temporary Political Status Commission for a change in the judicial system should be acted upon; reaffirmed the responsibility of the administering Power, under the Charter, for the economic and social development of the Territory.

### 2. Anguilla

In October 1981, the House of Assembly of Anguilla had approved the enactment of a new Constitution for the Territory. An order-in-council was subsequently issued enabling the new Constitution to come into effect on 1 April 1982.[6]

The Special Committee considered the question of Anguilla on 20 August 1982, and decided to transmit the relevant documentation to the General Assembly.[7]

By its decision 37/419 of 23 November 1982, the Assembly decided to defer until its thirty-eighth session consideration of the question of Anguilla.

---

[3] *Official Records of the General Assembly, Thirty-seventh Session, Supplement No. 23* (A/37/23/Rev.1), chap. XIX.

[4] A/37/621 and Corr.1.

[5] A/37/23/Rev.1, chap. XVII.

[6] A/AC.109/713.

[7] A/37/23/Rev.1, chap. XXVII.

## 3. Bermuda

The Special Committee considered the question of Bermuda on 5 August and 16 September 1982. On 5 August, it adopted the report of its Sub-Committee on Small Territories concerning Bermuda and endorsed its conclusions and recommendations.

On 16 September 1982 the Special Committee decided to submit a draft resolution on the question of Bermuda for consideration by the Fourth Committee of the General Assembly.[8]

The draft was adopted on 23 November 1982 as resolution 37/22 in which the Assembly, *inter alia*, approved the chapter of the Special Committee's report on Bermuda; urged the administering Power to continue to take all necessary steps to ensure the full and speedy implementation of General Assembly resolution 1514 (XV) containing the Declaration on the Granting of Independence to Colonial Countries and Peoples; strongly urged the administering Power to make every effort to diversify the economy of Bermuda; reiterated its call upon the administering Power to expedite the process of "bermudanization" in the Territory.

## 4. British Virgin Islands

The Special Committee considered the question of the British Virgin Islands on 28 June and 16 September 1982. On 28 June it adopted the report of its Sub-Committee on Small Territories concerning this Territory and endorsed its conclusions and recommendations.

On 16 September the Special Committee decided to submit a draft resolution on the question of the British Virgin Islands for consideration by the Fourth Committee of the General Assembly.[9]

The draft was adopted on 23 November 1982 as resolution 37/23 in which the Assembly, *inter alia*, approved the chapter of the report of the Special Committee relating to the British Virgin Islands; reaffirmed that it is ultimately for the people of the British Virgin Islands themselves to determine their future political status; called upon the administering Power to take all necessary steps to ensure the full and speedy attainment of the objectives of decolonization.

## 5. Brunei

Two bills passed by the Legislative Council in January 1982 provided the framework necessary for the establishment of foreign consulates in Brunei. The Diplomatic Privileges Bill and the Diplomatic and Consular Relations Bill put into effect international agreements governing diplomatic affairs.[10]

The Special Committee considered the question of Brunei on 20 August 1982. It decided to transmit the relevant documentation to the General Assembly.[11]

---

[8] *Ibid.*, chap. XX.

[9] *Ibid.*, chap. XXI.

[10] A/AC.109/714.

[11] A/37/23/Rev.1, chap. XII.

By its decision 37/417 of 23 November 1982, the Assembly decided to defer until its thirty-eighth session consideration of the question of Brunei.

## 6. Cayman Islands

The Special Committee considered the question of the Cayman Islands on 28 June and 16 September 1982. On 28 June it adopted the report of its Sub-Committee on Small Territories containing an account of its consideration of the Territory and endorsed its conclusions and recommendations.

On 16 September 1982, the Special Committee decided to submit a draft resolution on the Cayman Islands for consideration by the Fourth Committee of the General Assembly.[12]

The draft was adopted on 23 November 1982 as resolution 37/24 in which the General Assembly, *inter alia*, approved the chapter of the report of the Special Committee on the Cayman Islands; reaffirmed the importance of fostering an awareness among the people of the Territory of the possibilities open to them in the exercise of their right to self-determination; urged the administering Power to safeguard the inalienable right of the people of the Territory to the enjoyment of their natural resources.

## 7. Cocos (Keeling) Islands

The Special Committee considered the question of the Cocos (Keeling) Islands on 5 August and 16 September 1982.

On 5 August the Special Committee adopted the report of its Sub-Committee on Small Territories containing an account of its consideration of the Territory, and approved the draft consensus adopted therein.

On 16 September 1982 the Special Committee submitted a draft consensus for consideration by the Fourth Committee of the General Assembly.[13]

The draft was adopted on 23 November 1982 as decision 37/413 in which the General Assembly, *inter alia*, noted the positive and continuing commitment of the administering Power to the political, social and economic advancement of the people of the Territory so that they might be able, as quickly as possible, to exercise fully their inalienable rights.

In a letter dated 1 December 1982, addressed to the Chairman of the Special Committee,[14] the Permanent Representative of Australia to the United Nations stated that "the Australian Government will be in contact with the United Nations at a later stage should the Cocos community confirm that it wishes to proceed with an act of self-determination".[15]

---

[12] *Ibid.*, chap. XXII.
[13] *Ibid.*, chap. XIII.
[14] A/AC.109/723.
[15] A/AC.109/730.

## 8. East Timor

East Timor participated in the general election held in Indonesia on 4 May 1982. According to official figures, Golkar, the Indonesian governing party, won all four seats at stake in the Territory.[16]

The Special Committee considered the question of East Timor on 1 July and 20 August 1982.

On 20 August the Special Committee decided to transmit the relevant documentation to the General Assembly.[17]

By its resolution 37/30 of 23 November 1982, the General Assembly, *inter alia*, requested the Secretary-General to initiate consultations with all parties directly concerned with a view to exploring avenues for achieving a comprehensive settlement of the problem and to report thereon to the General Assembly at its thirty-eighth session.

## 9. Falkland Islands (Malvinas)

On 26 and 27 February 1982 a meeting at ministerial level was held in New York between Argentina and the United Kingdom on the question of the Falkland Islands (Malvinas). According to the press release issued after the talks "The two sides reaffirmed their resolve to find a solution to the sovereignty dispute and considered in detail an Argentine proposal for procedures to make better progress in this sense."

In a letter dated 1 April 1982, the Permanent Representative of Argentina to the United Nations notified the President of the Security Council of "the situation of grave tension existing between the Argentine Republic and the United Kingdom of Great Britain and Northern Ireland".

In a letter of the same date, the Permanent Representative of the United Kingdom stated that his Government had "good reason to believe that the armed forces of the Republic of Argentina are about to invade the Falklands Islands", and requested an immediate meeting of the Security Council.

The 2345th meeting of the Security Council was held on the same day. During that meeting statements were made by the two parties setting out their views on the incidents up to that date (S/PV.2345). The President issued a statement on behalf of the Council expressing its concern "about the tension in the region of the Falkland Islands (Malvinas)" and calling upon the Governments of Argentina and the United Kingdom to exercise the utmost restraint at this time.

By a letter of 2 April, the Permanent Representative of the United Kingdom notified the President of the Security Council that Argentine forces were at that time invading the Falkland Islands (Malvinas) and requested an immediate meeting of the Security Council.

On 3 April the Security Council adopted resolution 502 (1982), by which it demanded an immediate cessation of hostilities and an immediate withdrawal of all

---

[16] A/AC.109/715.

[17] A/37/23/Rev.1, chap. X.

Argentine forces from the islands and called on the two Governments to seek a diplomatic solution to their differences.

On 5 May the President of the Security Council issued a statement expressing deep concern at the situation in the region and at the loss of lives.

On 21 May 1982 the Security Council took up the "Question concerning the situation in the region of the Falkland Islands (Islas Malvinas)". On 26 May it adopted unanimously resolution 505 (1982), by which, *inter alia*, it reaffirmed its resolution 502 (1982), urged the parties to co-operate fully with the Secretary-General in his mission of good offices, and requested the Secretary-General to contact the parties with a view to negotiating acceptable terms for a cease-fire.

On 3 June 1982 the Security Council continued its consideration of the situation.

On 14 June, at Port Stanley, Argentine forces in the Falkland Islands (Malvinas) surrendered to the United Kingdom forces after a *de facto* cease-fire had occurred some hours earlier. In a letter dated 17 June 1982, addressed to the President of the Security Council, the Chargé d'affaires a.i. of the Permanent Mission of Argentina to the United Nations transmitted communiqué No. 166 of 16 June 1982, confirming the *de facto* cease-fire in the area of Port Stanley.[18]

The Special Committee considered the question of the Falkland Islands between 29 April and 20 August 1982.

On 20 August 1982 the Special Committee decided to transmit the relevant documentation to the General Assembly.[19]

By its resolution 37/9 adopted on 4 November 1982, the General Assembly, *inter alia*, requested the Governments of Argentina and the United Kingdom to resume negotiations in order to find as soon as possible a peaceful solution to the sovereignty dispute relating to the question of the Falkland Islands (Malvinas); requested the Secretary-General to undertake a renewed mission of good offices in order to assist the parties in complying with the above request; and requested the Secretary-General to report to the Assembly at its thirty-eighth session on the progress made in the implementation of the present resolution.

By its decision 37/404 of 3 November 1982, the Assembly took note of the report of the Fourth Committee on the question.[20]

### 10.  Gibraltar

Following a meeting in London on 8 January 1982, the two Governments of Spain and the United Kingdom announced that they had agreed to meet in Lisbon on 20 April 1982 to begin talks on the future of the Territory, and that Spain would reopen the frontier with Gibraltar on the same date.

On 8 April, however, both Governments issued a statement indicating their agreement on the postponing of the arrangements for such negotiations.

---

[18] A/AC.109/712 and Add.1.

[19] A/37/23/Rev.1.

[20] A/37/592.

On 21 June 1982 the Secretary of State for Foreign and Commonwealth Affairs of the United Kingdom and the Minister for External Affairs of Spain issued a statement in which they stated, *inter alia*, their determination to keep alive the process opened by the Lisbon Agreement of 10 April 1980, in the spirit of the letters exchanged in London on 8 January 1982, and added that a new date for their meeting would be fixed in due course.[21]

The Special Committee considered the question of Gibraltar on 20 August 1982, and decided to transmit the relevant documentation to the General Assembly.[22]

By its decision 37/412 of 23 November 1982 the General Assembly, noting the recent developments, decided to urge both Governments to make possible the initiation of the negotiations as envisaged in the consensus adopted by the Assembly on 14 December 1979, with the object of reaching a lasting solution to the problem of Gibraltar in the light of the relevant resolutions of the Assembly and in the spirit of the Charter of the United Nations.

Following a decision taken at the first cabinet meeting of the new Socialist Government of Spain, the border between Gibraltar and Spain, which had been closed by Spain in 1969, was reopened on 15 December 1982 for "humanitarian reasons". Since July 1982 a limited number of border crossings by special permits had been allowed. Spain had also authorized Spanish workers in Gibraltar with voter registration certificates to participate in Spain's general elections of 28 October 1982.

The reopening of the border was accompanied by a number of restrictions. The crossings were limited to pedestrian traffic of Spaniards, Gibraltarians and British subjects living in the colony, thereby excluding Moroccan and Portuguese workers living in Gibraltar as well as tourists. No more than one crossing a day in either direction was authorized. Spain intended to keep the gates open 24 hours a day. These restrictions were ill received by the Government of Gibraltar, which in turn decided to close the border from 1 a.m. to 6 a.m. each day. However, the Foreign and Commonwealth Office overruled that decision and the gates have remained open around the clock.[23]

## 11.  Guam

On 30 January 1982 the Guam Commission on Self-Determination and the Guam Election Commission conducted a referendum on the political status of the Territory in which the voters were asked which of seven alternatives they preferred as "the ultimate goal of the Territory of Guam". The choices were: (*a*) statehood; (*b*) independence; (*c*) free association; (*d*) the status of incorporated Territory; (*e*) Commonwealth status; (*f*) the *status quo*; or (*g*) other. Commonwealth as a status choice received 4,914 votes (49.5 per cent), just short of the 4,965 votes needed to make an absolute majority. Statehood came in a distant second and the *status quo* was the third choice. Existing law required that a run-off election between Commonwealth status and statehood be held by 31 March 1982. Bill 645, which postponed the run-off until 4 September, was signed into law on 10 March 1982. In the run-off vote

---

[21] A/AC.109/708.

[22] A/37/23/Rev.1, chap. XI.

[23] A/AC.109/741.

held on 4 September 1982, the people of Guam voted three-to-one for Commonwealth status in association with the United States.[24]

The Special Committee considered the question of Guam between 1 July and 16 September 1982.

On 5 August the Special Committee adopted the report of its Sub-Committee on Small Territories concerning Guam and endorsed its conclusions and recommendations.

On 16 September 1982 the Special Committee decided to submit a draft resolution on Guam for consideration by the Fourth Committee of the General Assembly.[25]

The draft was adopted as resolution 37/21 of 23 November 1982, in which the General Assembly, *inter alia*, approved the chapter of the report of the Special Committee relating to Guam; reaffirmed its strong conviction that the administering Power must ensure that military bases and installations do not hinder the population of the Territory from exercising its right to self-determination and independence; urged the administering Power to continue to take effective measures to safeguard and guarantee the right of the people of Guam to their natural resources and to establish and maintain control over their future development; urged the administering Power to strengthen its efforts to develop and promote the language and culture of the Chamorro people, who comprise more than half of the population of the Territory.

## 12. Montserrat

In response to an invitation from the Government of the United Kingdom, the Special Committee dispatched a Visiting Mission to Montserrat in August 1982. The Visiting Mission also held consultations with representatives of the administrative Power in London on 7 September 1982.

The Visiting Mission held discussions on the future status of the Territory with the Governor, the elected representatives and the general public while in the Territory, and with officials of the administering Power in London. From the meetings held in the Territory, the Mission gained the impression that although the population as a whole regarded independence as inevitable, in the current circumstances, the people did not feel that the Territory was ready to accede to independence. The Mission recommended, *inter alia*, that political education should be intensified so that the people might be made fully aware of the implications of their choice in the exercise of their right to self-determination and independence.[26]

The Special Committee considered the question of Montserrat between 28 June and 8 November 1982.

On 28 June the Special Committee adopted the report of its Sub-Committee on Small Territories containing an account of its consideration of the Territory and endorsed its conclusions and recommendations.

---

[24] A/AC.109/735.

[25] A/37/23/Rev.1, chap. XVIII.

[26] A/AC.109/726.

On 8 November the Special Committee, having considered the report of the Visiting Mission,[27] decided to adopt it and to endorse the conclusions and recommendations contained therein. It submitted a draft resolution to the General Assembly for its consideration.[28]

The draft was adopted on 23 November as resolution 37/27, in which the General Assembly, *inter alia*, approved the chapter of the report of the Special Committee on Montserrat, approved also the report of the United Nations Visiting Mission to Montserrat, and called upon the administering Power to take the necessary measures to promote the political, economic and social development of Montserrat and, in co-operation with the Government of Montserrat, to launch programmes of political education so that the people might be fully informed of the options available to them in the exercise of their right to self-determination and independence.

## 13. Namibia

The foreign ministers of the front-line States and Kenya, a representative of Nigeria and the President of the South West African Peoples' Organization (SWAPO) met for talks at Dar-es-Salaam (Tanzania). In a communiqué of 4 May 1982 they reiterated their total support for SWAPO and its continuing struggle for the independence of Namibia and endorsed the proposal previously conveyed by SWAPO to the Western Five, that all outstanding issues should be discussed together in a comprehensive manner in order to resolve them as a package. Such negotiations should ideally take place in a Geneva-type conference under the auspices of the United Nations.[29]

The Special Committee considered the question of Namibia between 16 and 20 August 1982. On 20 August the Special Committee adopted a draft consensus prepared on the basis of the latest developments concerning the Territory, as well as the views expressed by the President of the United Nations Council for Namibia, by members of the Committee and by the representative of SWAPO during the course of the Committee's discussion on the item. In this consensus the Special Committee, *inter alia*, reaffirmed the inalienable right of the people of Namibia to self-determination, freedom and national independence in a united Namibia, reaffirmed that Namibia is the direct responsibility of the United Nations until self-determination and national independence are achieved in the Territory, and strongly condemned South Africa's continued illegal occupation of Namibia.[30]

## 14. Pitcairn

The Special Committee considered the question of Pitcairn on 28 June and 16 September 1982.

---

[27] A/AC.109/722.

[28] A/37/23/Rev.1, chap. XXVIII.

[29] A/AC.109/699.

[30] A/37/23/Rev.1, chap. VIII.

On 28 June the Special Committee adopted the report of its Sub-Committee on Small Territories containing an account of its consideration of the Territory and approved the draft consensus contained therein.

On 16 September the Special Committee decided to submit a draft consensus for consideration by the Fourth Committee of the General Assembly.[31]

The draft was adopted as decision 37/415 of 23 November 1982, in which the General Assembly, *inter alia*, called once again upon the administering Power (the United Kingdom) to continue to take the necessary measures to safeguard the interests of the people of Pitcairn.

## 15. St. Helena

In May 1982 the representative of the United Kingdom informed the Special Committee's Sub-Committee on Small Territories that his Government would look favourably on any request for change in the present constitutional status of St. Helena if the people of the Territory so desired.[32]

The Special Committee considered the question of St. Helena on 28 June and 16 September 1982.

On 28 June the Special Committee adopted the report of its Sub-Committee on Small Territories containing an account of its consideration of the Territory and approved the draft consensus contained therein.

On 16 September the Special Committee decided to submit a draft consensus for consideration by the Fourth Committee of the General Assembly.[33]

The draft was adopted as decision 37/416 of 23 November 1982, in which the General Assembly, *inter alia*, noted the commitment of the Government of the United Kingdom to respect the wishes of the Territory, and urged the administering Power to continue to take all necessary steps to ensure the speedy implementation of the Declaration on the Granting of Independence to Colonial Countries and Peoples in respect to that Territory.

## 16. St. Kitts-Nevis

Premier Simmonds indicated in early 1982 that his Government was preparing proposals for constitutional advancement in view of the "significant progress" which had been made in various areas of economic development since the February 1980 general election.[34]

The Special Committee considered the question of St. Kitts-Nevis on 20 August 1982. It decided to transmit the relevant documentation to the General Assembly.[35]

By its decision 37/418 of 23 November 1982, the Assembly decided to defer until its thirty-eighth session consideration of the question of St. Kitts-Nevis.

---

[31] *Ibid.*, chap. XV.

[32] A/AC.109/734.

[33] A/37/23/Rev.1, chap. XVI.

[34] A/AC.109/711.

[35] A/37/23/Rev.1, chap. XXVI.

## 17. Tokelau

The Special Committee considered the question of Tokelau on 28 June and 16 September 1982.

On 28 June the Special Committee adopted the report of its Sub-Committee on Small Territories containing an account of its consideration of Tokelau, and approved the draft consensus contained therein.

On 16 September 1982 the Special Committee decided to submit a draft consensus for consideration by the Fourth Committee of the General Assembly.[36]

The draft was adopted as decision 37/414 of 23 November 1982, in which the General Assembly, *inter alia*, noted with appreciation the willingness of the administering Power (New Zealand) to maintain its close co-operation with the United Nations in the exercise of its responsibility towards Tokelau; it noted that the people of the Territory had expressed the view that, for the time being, they did not wish to review the nature of the existing relationship between Tokelau and New Zealand; it welcomed the assurances of the administering Power that it would continue to be guided solely by the wishes of the people of Tokelau as to the future status of the Territory.

## 18. Turks and Caicos Islands

The Special Committee considered the question of the Turks and Caicos Islands on 5 August and 16 September 1982.

On 5 August the Special Committee adopted the report of its Sub-Committee on Small Territories containing an account of its consideration of the Territory and endorsed its conclusions and recommendations.

On 16 September 1982 the Special Committee decided to submit a draft resolution for consideration by the Fourth Committee of the General Assembly.[37]

This draft was adopted as resolution 37/25 of 23 November 1982, in which the General Assembly, *inter alia*, approved the chapter of the report of the Special Committee relating to the Turks and Caicos Islands; reiterated that it is the obligation of the administering Power to create such conditions in the Territory as will enable its people to exercise freely their inalienable right to self-determination and independence; reaffirmed its strong conviction that the administering Power must ensure that military bases and installations did not hinder the people of the Territory from exercising their right to self-determination and independence and urged the United Kingdom to comply fully with the relevant United Nations resolutions relating to military bases and installations in colonial and Non-Self-Governing Territories.

---

[36] *Ibid.*, chap. XIV.
[37] *Ibid.*, chap. XXIII.

## 19. United States Virgin Islands

The question of the Territory's relationship with the United States continues to be explored. At a meeting held on St. Croix on 25 January 1982, the Status Commission decided to seek public participation in the formulation of a decision on a status for negotiation with the federal Government. It was further decided that public involvement should start with a public education and review campaign on the basis of information about the Commission, its function, its process and some general sketches on status options.[38]

The Special Committee considered the question of the United States Virgin Islands on 5 August and 16 September 1982.

On 5 August the Special Committee adopted the report of its Sub-Committee on Small Territories containing information on the latest developments concerning the Territory, and endorsed its conclusions and recommendations.

On 16 September 1982 the Special Committee decided to submit a draft resolution for consideration by the Fourth Committee of the General Assembly.[39]

This draft was adopted as resolution 37/26 of 23 November 1982, in which the General Assembly, *inter alia*, approved the chapter of the report of the Special Committee relating to the United States Virgin Islands; called upon the administering Power, taking into account the freely expressed wishes of the people of the United States Virgin Islands, to take all necessary steps to expedite the process of decolonization; called upon the administering Power to facilitate the work of the recently established Status Commission and to ensure that the people are fully informed of the discussions concerning the future political status of the Territory; urged the administering Power to expedite the passage of legislation currently before the Congress of the United States of America concerning the problem of aliens in the Territory.

## 20. Western Sahara

The Implementation Committee of the Organization of African Unity charged with organizing a referendum in Western Sahara held two meetings in February 1982, at the conclusion of which it issued a two-part decision on the question of Western Sahara. In the first part of its decision the Committee decided, *inter alia*, that a comprehensive cease-fire would come into force on a date to be fixed by the Committee. It called on the parties to the conflict to extend full co-operation to the peace-keeping force and/or observer group and to respect and adhere scrupulously to the terms of the cease-fire. In the second part of its decision, the Implementation Committee set down the modalities and organizational framework for the referendum in Western Sahara.[40]

The Special Committee considered the question of Western Sahara on 1 July and 20 August 1982. On 20 August it decided to transmit the relevant documentation to the General Assembly.[41]

---

[38] A/AC.109/697.

[39] A/37/23/Rev.1, chap. XXIV.

[40] A/AC.109/695.

[41] A/37/23/Rev.1, chap. IX.

In its resolution 37/28 of 23 November 1982, the General Assembly, *inter alia*, appealed to the two parties to the dispute to enter into negotiations with a view to achieving a cease-fire; reaffirmed the determination of the United Nations to co-operate fully with the Organization of African Unity in the fair and impartial organization of the referendum; requested, to that end, the Secretary-General to take the necessary steps to ensure that the United Nations participates effectively in the organization and conduct of the referendum.

By its decision 37/411 of 23 November 1982, the Assembly decided to request the Secretary-General to give assistance, in consultation and co-operation with the Organization of African Unity, to the Implementation Committee in the discharge of its mandate relating to the question of Western Sahara and to report thereon to the General Assembly and the Security Council as appropriate.

# PART II

# ACTIVITIES OF THE SUPERVISORY BODIES

# Section A. Practice of the supervisory bodies

## A. Committee on the Elimination of Racial Discrimination

### INTRODUCTION

The Committee on the Elimination of Racial Discrimination held two regular sessions in 1982. The twenty-fifth session (549th-574th meetings) was held from 1 to 19 March 1982 at the United Nations Office at Geneva; and the twenty-sixth session (575th-597th meetings) was held from 2 to 20 August 1982 at United Nations Headquarters, New York.[1]

In accordance with decision 2 (VI) of 21 August 1972 of the Committee concerning co-operation with the International Labour Organisation (ILO) and the United Nations Educational, Scientific and Cultural Organization (UNESCO), representatives of both organizations attended the twenty-fifth and twenty-sixth sessions of the Committee.[2]

The documents submitted by UNESCO (CERD/C/69 and Add.1) in response to the Committee's invitation were considered by the Committee at its twenty-fifth session under the item of its agenda entitled "Implementation of article 7 of the Convention", culminating in the adoption by the Committee of additional general guidelines.

At the twenty-sixth session, the report of the ILO Committee of Experts on the Application of Conventions and Recommendations, submitted to the sixty-eighth session of the International Labour Conference, was made available to the members of the Committee on the Elimination of Racial Discrimination in accordance with arrangements for co-operation between the two Committees. The Committee took note with appreciation of the report of the Committee of Experts, in particular of those sections which dealt with the application of the 1958 Convention (No. 111) concerning discrimination in respect of employment and occupation as well as other information in the report relevant to its activities.[3]

### 1. IMPLEMENTATION OF ARTICLE 7 OF THE CONVENTION

This item, included on the agenda of the twenty-fifth session of the Committee in accordance with a decision taken at its twenty-third session, was considered at the

---

[1] Report of the Committee on the Elimination of Racial Discrimination, *Official Records of the General Assembly, Thirty-seventh Session, Supplement No. 18* (A/37/18), para. 3.

[2] *Ibid.*, para. 16.

[3] *Ibid.*, paras. 18-19.

570th and 571st meetings, held on 16 and 17 March 1982. For its consideration of the item, the Committee had before it two documents (CERD/C/69 and Add.1), one entitled "Preliminary reflections of UNESCO concerning the implementation of the provisions of article 7 of the International Convention on the Elimination of All Forms of Racial Discrimination" and the other entitled "Implementation of article 7 of the Convention: draft guidelines proposed by UNESCO", both submitted in response to decision 2 (XIX) of the Committee, inviting UNESCO to transmit to it suggestions for the preparation of general guidelines with a view to assisting States parties in the implementation of article 7 of the Convention. The Committee also had before it draft guidelines and recommendations submitted in an informal working paper by its Special Rapporteur, as well as suggestions submitted by two of its members.

The representative of UNESCO informed the Committee of his organization's activities in relation to article 7 of the Convention during the period 1980-1981.

Members of the Committee expressed their appreciation to UNESCO for the contribution it had made to its work which deserved war recognition. However, they were of the opinion that the draft guidelines proposed by UNESCO were very complex and that most States parties to the Convention would be unable to reply to a questionnaire as suggested by UNESCO or would refuse to answer all such questions. Moreover, the questionnaire exceeded the Committee's mandate which was not to dictate what measures States parties should take to implement article 7 of the Convention, but to appraise the moves made to that end when it considered the reports submitted by States parties.

Members of the Committee agreed that an informal working group composed of four or five members, including the Rapporteur of the Committee, should be appointed to prepare a text for additional guidelines concerning the implementation of article 7, for consideration by the Committee at a later stage.

At the 571st meeting of the Committee, one of the members of the working group introduced the draft additional guidelines for the implementation of article 7 of the Convention proposed by the working group.

The Committee adopted the text proposed by the Working Group, as amended during the discussion, as the additional guidelines of the Committee for the implementation of article 7 of the Convention.[4] The text as adopted appears in decision 2 (XXV), which is reproduced in the annex to the present *Yearbook*, p. 275.

### 2. CONSIDERATION OF REPORTS, COMMENTS AND INFORMATION SUBMITTED BY STATES PARTIES UNDER ARTICLE 9 OF THE CONVENTION

#### (a) *Status of submission of reports by States parties; action taken by the Committee to ensure submission of reports*

At its twenty-fifth session the Committee discussed in some detail the issues of non-submission of reports by States parties in accordance with their obligation under article 9 of the Convention, and took the following decisions:

---

[4] *Ibid.*, paras. 31-37.

(i) In accordance with rule 66, paragraph 1, of its provisional rules of procedure, the Committee requested the Secretary-General to send appropriate reminders to States parties whose reports were due before the closing date of its twenty-fifth session, but had not yet been received, requesting them to submit their reports by 30 June 1982.

(ii) At its 569th meeting, on 15 March 1982, the Committee authorized its Chairman to address personal letters to the Governments of Guyana, Liberia and Togo, which have not submitted any report at all since the entry into force of the Convention in respect to their States, requesting them to submit their overdue reports in one consolidated document by 30 June 1982 for consideration by the Committee at its twenty-sixth session. By the closing date of the twenty-sixth session of the Committee no report had been received from those States.

(iii) At the same meeting, the Committee adopted its General Recommendation VI (CERD/C/94) in which it invited the General Assembly to take note of the situation and to use its authority in order to ensure that the Committee could more effectively fulfil its obligations under the Convention. The full text of General Recommendation VI is reproduced below in part II, section B, as decision 1 (XXV), p. 194.

Acting under rule 67, paragraph 1, of its provisional rules of procedure, the Committee requested the Secretary-General to transmit the text of its General Recommendation VI to the States parties for comments in accordance with article 9, paragraph 2, of the Convention. As of 20 August 1982, comments had been received from the following States parties: Cyprus, France, Italy, Mexico, Republic of Korea and Yugoslavia.[5]

### (b) *Consideration of reports*

At its twenty-fifth and twenty-sixth sessions, the Committee examined the reports submitted by the following 40 States parties under article 9 of the Convention:[6]

| State party | Type of report | Document symbol | Meetings at which considered | Date of consideration | Summary of consideration contained in the report (A/37/18), paragraphs: |
|---|---|---|---|---|---|
| Gambia | Initial | CERD/C/61/Add.3 | 550 | 2/3/82 | 61-72 |
| Gabon | Initial | CERD/C/71/Add.1 | 550 | 2/3/82 | 73-75 |
| Tonga | Fourth/ Fifth | CERD/C/75/Add.3 | 551 | 2/3/82 | 76-79 |
| Malta | Fourth/ Fifth | CERD/C/65/Add.5 | 552 | 3/3/82 | 80-90 |
| United Arab Emirates | Fourth | CERD/C/74/Add.1 | 552 | 3/3/82 | 91-98 |
| Fiji | Fourth | CERD/C/64/Add.4 | 553 | 3/3/82 | 99-105 |
| Nepal | Fifth | CERD/C/65/Add.6 | 553 | 3/3/82 | 106-111 |
| Haiti | Third/ Fourth | CERD/C/64/Add.5 | 554 | 4/3/82 | 112-122 |

[5] *Ibid.*, para. 45.

[6] *Ibid.*, para. 57.

| State party | Type of report | Document symbol | Meetings at which considered | Date of consideration | Summary of consideration contained in the report (A/37/18), paragraphs: |
|---|---|---|---|---|---|
| Australia........ | Third | CERD/C/63/Add.3 | 555-556 | 4-5/3/82 | 123-134 |
| Cape Verde..... | Initial | CERD/C/61/Add.5 | 557 | 5/3/82 | 135-141 |
| Barbados ....... | Third/ Fourth/ Fifth | CERD/C/75/Add.7 | 557 | 5/3/82 | 142-150 |
| Qatar ........... | Third | CERD/C/73/Add.1 | 557 | 5/3/82 | 151-157 |
| Panama ......... | Seventh | CERD/C/91/Add.1 | 558-559 | 8/3/82 | 158-166 |
| Mauritius ....... | Fourth/ Fifth | CERD/C/75/Add.8 | 559-560 | 8-9/3/82 | 167-181 |
| Austria .......... | Fifth | CERD/C/75/Add.9 | 560-561 | 8-9/3/82 | 182-194 |
| Ethiopia......... | Third | CERD/C/73/Add.2 | 561 | 9/3/82 | 195-203 |
| Ecuador......... | Seventh | CERD/C/91/Add.2 | 562 | 10/3/82 | 204-213 |
| Kuwait .......... | Seventh | CERD/C/91/Add.3 | 563 | 10/3/82 | 214-222 |
| Iceland .......... | Seventh | CERD/C/91/Add.4 | 563 | 10/3/82 | 223-228 |
| Republic of Korea......... | Second | CERD/C/86/Add.1 | 564 | 11/3/82 | 229-237 |
| Hungary ........ | Seventh | CERD/C/91/Add.5 | 564-565 | 11/3/82 | 238-248 |
| Jordan........... | Third/ Fourth | CERD/C/74/Add.2 | 565 | 11/3/82 | 249-255 |
| Norway ......... | Sixth | CERD/C/76/Add.2 | 565-566 | 11-12/3/82 | 256-264 |
| Greece........... | Sixth | CERD/C/76/Add.1 | 576-577 | 3/8/82 | 265-276 |
| Spain ........... | Seventh | CERD/C/91/Add.6 | 577 | 3/8/82 | 277-287 |
| Philippines ..... | Seventh | CERD/C/91/Add.7 and 12 | 577-578 | 3-4/8/82 | 288-295 |
| Argentina....... | Seventh | CERD/C/91/Add.8 | 578-579 | 4/8/82 | 296-304 |
| Uruguay ........ | Seventh | CERD/C/91/Add.9 | 579 | 4/8/82 | 305-316 |
| Romania........ | Sixth | CERD/C/76/Add.3 | 579-580 | 4-5/8/82 | 317-328 |
| Israel............. | Second | CERD/C/86/Add.2 | 580 | 5/8/82 | 329-340 |
| Sudan........... | Initial/ Second/ Third | CERD/C/87/Add.1 | 580-581 | 5/8/82 | 341-351 |
| Mongolia ....... | Seventh | CERD/C/91/Add.10 | 581 | 5/8/82 | 352-358 |
| Mexico .......... | Fourth | CERD/C/88/Add.1 | 582-583 | 6/8/82 | 359-369 |
| German Democratic Republic.............. | Fifth | CERD/C/89/Add.1 | 583 | 6/8/82 | 370-381 |
| Czechoslovakia | Seventh | CERD/C/91/Add.14 | 584 | 9/8/82 | 382-395 |
| Egypt ........... | Seventh | CERD/C/91/Add.15 | 584-585 | 9/8/82 | 396-403 |
| Finland.......... | Sixth | CERD/C/76/Add.4 | 585 | 9/8/82 | 404-413 |
| Holy See ........ | Seventh | CERD/C/91/Add.17 | 586 | 10/8/82 | 414-419 |
| USSR ............ | Seventh | CERD/C/91/Add.18 | 586-587 | 10/8/82 | 420-434 |
| Costa Rica...... | Seventh | CERD/C/91/Add.11 and 13 | 587 | 10/8/82 | 435-447 |

3. Consideration of petitions, reports and other information relating to Trust and Non-Self-Governing Territories and to all other Territories to which General Assembly resolution 1514 (XV) applies, in conformity with article 15 of the Convention

Article 15, paragraph 2, of the Convention reads as follows:

"(*a*)   The Committee established under article 8, paragraph 1, of this Convention shall receive copies of the petitions from, and submit expressions of opinion and recommendations on these petitions to, the bodies of the United Nations which deal with matters directly related to the principles and objectives of this Convention in their consideration of petitions from the inhabitants of Trust and Non-Self-Governing Territories and all other Territories to which General Assembly resolution 1514 (XV) applies, relating to matters covered by this Convention which are before these bodies.

"(*b*)   The Committee shall receive from the competent bodies of the United Nations copies of the reports concerning the legislative, judicial, administrative or other measures directly related to the principles and objectives of this Convention applied by the administering Powers within the Territories mentioned in subparagraph (*a*) of this paragraph, and shall express opinions and make recommendations to these bodies."

Article 15, paragraph 3, states:

"The Committee shall include in its report to the General Assembly a summary of the petitions and reports it has received from United Nations bodies, and the expressions of opinion and recommendations of the Committee relating to the said petitions and reports."

The Committee considered this item at its 567th meeting (twenty-fifth session), on 12 March 1982, and at its 594th meeting (twenty-sixth session), on 17 August 1982.[7]

The opinions and recommendations of the Committee based on its consideration of copies of reports and other information submitted to it in 1982 under article 15 of the Convention, as adopted by the Committee at its 594th meeting, on 17 August 1982, appear below in part II, section B, of the present *Yearbook*, p. 190.

4. Decade for Action to Combat Racism and Racial Discrimination

During the year under review, the Committee considered this item at its 551st, 557th, 558th, 572nd and 573rd meetings (twenty-fifth session), on 2, 5, 8, 17 and 18 March 1982, and at its 589th to 592nd meetings (twenty-sixth session), on 13 and 16 August 1982.[8]

---

[7] *Ibid.*, para. 448.

[8] *Ibid.*, paras. 459-477.

## 5. Meetings of the Committee scheduled for 1983 and 1984

The Committee considered this item at its 574th meeting (twenty-fifth session), on 19 March 1982, and at its 593rd and 595th meetings (twenty-sixth session), on 17 and 19 August 1982.[9]

A number of decisions were taken by the Committee at its twenty-sixth session in connection with the dates and the venue of its sessions to be held in 1983 and 1984.

At its 595th meeting, on 19 August 1982, the Committee considered a draft decision proposed by one of its members in connection with the venue of its twenty-eighth session. The draft decision, as amended during the discussion, was adopted by the Committee unanimously. For the text, see part II, section B, decision 1 (XXVI),[10] p. 195.

## B. Human Rights Committee

### Introduction

The Human Rights Committee held three sessions in 1982: the fifteenth session (334th to 359th meetings) was held at United Nations Headquarters, New York, from 22 March to 9 April 1982; the sixteenth session (360th to 382nd meetings) was held at the United Nations Office at Geneva from 12 to 30 July 1982, and the seventeenth session (383rd to 409th meetings) was held at the United Nations Office at Geneva from 11 to 29 October 1982.[11]

In accordance with rule 89 of its provisional rules of procedure, the Committee established working groups to meet before its fifteenth, sixteenth and seventeenth sessions in order to make recommendations to the Committee regarding communications under the Optional Protocol.[12]

Under rule 62 of its provisional rules of procedure, the Committee established working groups to meet before its fifteenth and sixteenth sessions with a view to making recommendations on the duties and functions of the Committee under article 40 of the Covenant and related matters.[13]

---

[9] *Ibid.*, paras. 479-482.

[10] *Ibid.*, paras. 483-484.

[11] Reports of the Human Rights Committee, *Official Records of the General Assembly, Thirty-seventh Session, Supplement No. 40* (A/37/40), para. 4; *ibid., Thirty-eighth Session, Supplement No. 40* (A/38/40), para. 4.

[12] A/37/40, para. 7; A/38/40, para. 11.

[13] A/37/40, para. 11.

1. Consideration of reports submitted by States parties under article 40
of the Covenant

### (a) *Consideration of reports*

The initial reports submitted by Rwanda, Guyana, Uruguay, and the report submitted by the Islamic Republic of Iran were considered by the Committee at its fifteenth and sixteenth sessions:

| State party | Type of report | Document symbol | Meetings at which considered | Date of consideration | Summary of consideration contained in the report (A/37/40), paragraphs: |
|---|---|---|---|---|---|
| Rwanda ......... | Initial | CCPR/C/1/Add.54 | 345, 346, 348 | 30-31/3/82 | 214-248 |
| Guyana.......... | Initial | CCPR/C/4/Add.6 | 353, 354, 357 | 5 and 7/4/82 | 249-264 |
| Uruguay ........ | Initial | CCPR/C/1/Add.57 | 355-357, 359 | 6-8/4/82 | 265-297 |
| Iran (Islamic Rep. of) ...... | Initial | CCPR/C/1/Add.58 | 364-366, 368 | 15, 16 and 19/7/82 | 298-335 |

The initial reports submitted by Mexico, Iceland and Australia were considered by the Committee at its seventeenth session:

| State party | Type of report | Document symbol | Meetings at which considered | Date of consideration | Summary of consideration contained in the report (A/38/40), paragraphs: |
|---|---|---|---|---|---|
| Mexico .......... | Initial | CCPR/C/22/Add.1 | 386, 387, 404 | 13 and 26/10/82 | 60-98 |
| Iceland .......... | Initial | CCPR/C/10/Add.4 | 391, 392, 395 | 18 and 20/10/82 | 99-134 |
| Australia........ | Initial | CCPR/C/14/Add.1 | 401-403, 407, 408 | 25-26/10 and 2/11/82 | 135-177 |

### (b) *Question of the reports and general comments of the Committee*

At the fifteenth session, members of the Committee exchanged views on whether, in order to encourage States parties to submit supplementary reports, to amend the Committee's decision on periodicity to the effect that the Committee would, if appropriate, defer the date for the submission of the State party's next periodic report in the case where that State party submitted a supplementary report following the examination of its initial report or of any subsequent report. And, if so, whether the amendment should provide for a time-limit within which such supplementary report had to be submitted in order that the State party concerned would benefit from the extension of the period during which its subsequent report had to be submitted. A draft compromise amendment was subsequently circulated between members of the Committee which read as follows:

"In cases where a State party submits a supplementary report within one year, or such other period as the Committee may decide, following the examination of its initial report or of any subsequent periodic report and the supplementary report is examined at a meeting with representatives of the reporting State, the Committee will, if appropriate, defer the date for the submission of the State party's next periodic report."

At its sixteenth session, the Committee decided to adopt the proposed additional paragraph. The full text of the Decision on periodicity as amended appears in part II, section B, of the present *Yearbook*, p. 196.

Members of the Committee exchanged views on what some of them called the general problem of derogation and notification under article 4 of the Covenant and its relation to the reporting system and the obligations of both the States parties and the Committee under the Covenant, particularly article 40.

Members of the Committee agreed to defer for further consideration the question of derogations and notifications under article 4 of the Covenant and other questions raised during the discussion in relation to the reporting system and the obligations of States parties under article 40.

The Committee was informed that the general comments adopted by the Committee at its thirteenth session had been transmitted to all States parties by a note verbale dated 18 September 1981.

At its sixteenth session, the Committee considered the draft general comments as prepared before and during the fifteenth and sixteenth sessions by its working group and adopted a number of general comments relating to articles 6, 7, 9 and 10 of the Covenant (see part II, section B, of the present *Yearbook*, p. 196-261).[14]

At its seventeenth session, the Committee resumed briefly the consideration of the general problem of derogations and notifications under article 4 of the Covenant and its relation to the reporting system and the obligation of both the States parties and the Committee under the Covenant, particularly article 40, which it had begun at its sixteenth session.[15] A draft proposal in connection with article 40 (1) (*b*) of the Covenant was submitted for the Committee's consideration at a later stage.

### 2. Consideration of communications under the Optional Protocol

Under the Optional Protocol to the International Covenant on Civil and Political Rights, individuals who claim that any of their rights enumerated in the Covenant have been violated and who have exhausted all available domestic remedies may submit written communications to the Human Rights Committee for consideration. Twenty-seven of the 70 States which have acceded to or ratified the Covenant have accepted the competence of the Committee for dealing with individual complaints by ratifying or acceding to the Optional Protocol. These States

---

[14] *Ibid.*, paras. 338-346.
[15] A/38/40, para. 374.

are Barbados, Canada, the Central African Republic, Colombia, Costa Rica, Denmark, the Dominican Republic, Ecuador, Finland, Iceland, Italy, Jamaica, Madagascar, Mauritius, the Netherlands, Nicaragua, Norway, Panama, Peru, Saint Vincent and the Grenadines, Senegal, Suriname, Sweden, Trinidad and Tobago, Uruguay, Venezuela and Zaire. No communication can be received by the Committee if it concerns a State party to the Covenant which is not also a party to the Optional Protocol.

Consideration of communications under the Optional Protocol takes place in closed meetings (article 5 (3) of the Optional Protocol). All documents pertaining to the work of the Committee under the Optional Protocol (submission from the parties and other working documents of the Committee) are confidential. The texts of final decisions of the Committee, consisting of views adopted under article 5 (4) of the Optional Protocol, are however made public. This may also apply to such other decisions which the Committee decides to make public.

In carrying out its work under the Optional Protocol, the Committee is assisted by Working Groups on Communications, consisting of not more than five of its members, which submit recommendations to the Committee on the actions to be taken at the various stages in the consideration of each case. A working group may also decide on its own to request additional information or observations from the parties on questions relevant to the admissibility of a communication. The Committee has also designated individual members to act as special rapporteurs in a number of cases. The special rapporteurs place their recommendations before the Committee for consideration.

Since the Committee started its work under the Optional Protocol at its second session in 1977, 124 communications have been placed before it for consideration (102 of these were placed before the Committee from its second to its thirteenth session; 22 further communications have been placed before the Committee at its fourteenth, fifteenth and sixteenth sessions). During these six years some 249 formal decisions have been adopted. A publication intended to contain a selection of these decisions, in a suitable edited form, is in preparation.

The status of the 124 communications placed before the Human Rights Committee for consideration, so far, is as follows:

(a) Concluded by views under article 5 (4) of the Optional Protocol............    32

(b) Concluded in other manner (inadmissible, discontinued, suspended or withdrawn)........................................................................    40

(c) Declared admissible, not yet concluded..........................................    21

(d) Pending at pre-admissibility stage (18 thereof transmitted to the State party under rule 91 of the Committee's provisional rules of procedure) ...    31[16]

At its fifteenth session, held from 22 March to 8 April 1982, the Human Rights Committee, or its Working Group on Communications, examined 42 communications submitted to the Committee under the Optional Protocol. The Committee concluded consideration of nine cases by adopting its views thereon. These are cases Nos. R.2/10 (*Alberto Altesor* v. *Uruguay*); R.7/30 (*Eduardo Bleier* v. *Uruguay*); R.11/45 (*Pedro Pablo Camargo on behalf of the husband of María Fanny Suarez de*

---

[16] A/37/40, paras. 347-351.

*Guerrero* v. *Colombia*); R.12/50 (*Gordon C. Van Duzen* v. *Canada*); R.13/57 (*Vidal Martins* v. *Uruguay*); R.14/61 (*Leo R. Hertzberg et al.* v. *Finland*); R.15/64 (*Consuelo Salgar de Montejo* v. *Colombia*); R.17/70 (*Mirta Cubas Simones* v. *Uruguay*); and R.18/73 (*Mario Teti Izquierdo* v. *Uruguay*). Seven communications were declared admissible and one inadmissible. Decisions were taken in six cases under rule 91 of the Committee's provisional rules of procedure requesting information on questions of admissibility from one or both of the parties. Secretariat action was requested in the remaining 19 cases (10 of which concern in substance the same matter, submitted individually by 10 alleged victims), mainly for the collection of further information from the authors to allow further consideration by the Committee.

At its sixteenth session, held from 12 to 30 July 1982, the Human Rights Committee, or its Working Group on Communications, examined 24 communications submitted to the Committee under the Optional Protocol. The Committee concluded consideration of two cases by adopting its views thereon. These are, cases Nos. R.6/25 (*Carmen Améndola Massiotti and Graciela Baritussio* v. *Uruguay*) and R.11/46 (*Orlando Fals Borda et al.* v. *Colombia*). No communication was declared admissible but three inadmissible. Decisions were taken in six cases under rule 91 of the Committee's provisional rules of procedure, requesting information on questions of admissibility from one or both of the parties. Secretariat action was requested in the remaining 13 cases (some of which concern in substance the same matter, submitted individually by several alleged victims), mainly for the collection of further information from the authors to allow further consideration by the Committee.[17]

At its seventeenth session, held from 11 to 29 October 1982, the Human Rights Committee, or its Working Group on Communications, examined 31 communications submitted to the Committee under the Optional Protocol. The Committee concluded consideration of three cases by adopting its views thereon. These are cases Nos. 55/1979 (*Alexander MacIsaac* v. *Canada*), 66/1980 (*David Alberto Cámpora Schweizer* v. *Uruguay*) and 84/1981 (*Guillermo Ignacio Dermit Barbato and Hugo Haroldo Dermit Barbato* v. *Uruguay*). In one case an interim decision was taken. Five communications were declared admissible and one inadmissible. Decisions were taken in four cases under rule 91 of the Committee's provisional rules of procedure, requesting information on questions of admissibility from one or both of the parties. Consideration of four cases was suspended. Secretariat action was requested in the remaining 13 cases, mainly for the purpose of obtaining additional information from the authors to allow further consideration by the Committee.[18]

*Question of action subsequent to the adoption of the Committee's views under the Optional Protocol or to a decision declaring a communication to be inadmissible*

At the seventeenth session, the Chairman of the Committee invited the members to express their views on the question raised by the Chairman of the Working Group on Communications, namely, the reconsideration of the Committee's decisions, at the request either of the authors of communications or of the States parties con-

---

[17] *Ibid.*, paras. 353-354.
[18] A/38/40, para. 384.

cerned and the "follow-up" action which the Committee could take to ensure that its views were respected by States parties.

Some members were of the opinion that nothing in the Covenant and the Optional Protocol, which were the legal basis for the Committee's functions and limits, empowered the Committee to reconsider its views on communications or to ensure their implementation; that the Committee could have no inherent powers that had not been given to it explicitly by States parties and that it therefore had no competence to initiate the review of a case already concluded; that there was nothing in the Optional Protocol to prevent an individual from submitting a further communication if he was not satisfied with the Committee's views, or if he considered that there were facts or evidence to which attention should be drawn, and the question would then become one of admissibility of the new communication; that the Committee was a *sui generis* body, with no judicial powers and that the implementation of its views was left to the good will of the State party concerned; that the question of the monitoring of the implementation of those views in the absence of a clear legal mandate to that effect, might even be contrary to Article 2, paragraph 7, of the Charter of the United Nations relating to non-interference by the United Nations in the internal affairs of States; that States parties could, if they so wish, use the amendment procedure under article 11 of the Protocol, an easy matter at the current stage, when there were only 28 States parties to the Protocol; that if the Committee took it upon itself to change procedures for which explicit ratification was required, its action could be taken as a warning to States to think twice before ratifying the Optional Protocol, since there was no prediction what additional obligations and procedures the Committee would attach to that instrument; and that no useful progress could be made in trying to press States to do what they were not obliged to do.

The majority of members, however, pointed out that the Committee could not let its work under the Optional Protocol degenerate into an exercise of futility; that due consideration had to be paid to both the letter and spirit of the Covenant, and that where the Committee believed that certain appropriate action was reasonably open to it, or was not expressly prohibited, the Committee should take it and that the Optional Protocol allowed considerable latitude for interpretation since many issues were not specifically covered by its provisions. Several such issues were cited, as well as decisions and steps taken previously by the Committee, but which could not be traced back directly to the Covenant or the Optional Protocol. Considering that the Optional Protocol did not provide for the principle of *res judicata* as far as the Committee's decisions were concerned, and that the Committee's provisional rules of procedure allowed for a review of a decision on admissibility, reconsideration of a communication should be possible, but only as an exception, not as a rule; that it should primarily be based on new facts, although legal arguments adduced at a later stage could not be entirely excluded; that a new rule to that effect may not be desirable at the present stage, but that if one was ultimately to be drawn it should be an enabling rule whose effect would be to impose limitations and to discourage abuses. As to the question of whether the Committee was entitled to monitor the implementation of its decisions under the Optional Protocol, it was pointed out that, whereas the Committee had no executive powers enabling it to enforce its views, it could nevertheless do something to bring redress, or end continued violations, of the victim's rights after transmission of its views to the State party concerned. Moreover, it was clear from the preamble of the Protocol and article 2 (3) of the Covenant that the States parties intended the Covenant to be implemented. When a victim was clearly within the jurisdiction of a State and not in direct communication with the Committee, the Committee should indicate in its views that he might avail himself of certain remedies and the Committee should request the State party to communicate the entire decision to the victim and should also be requested to inform the Committee of any developments.

It was recalled that at the fifteenth session, the Committee decided that in the letter of transmittal accompanying the Committee's views, the State party would be requested to inform the Committee of the action it had taken on the particular case and it was pointed out that the decision had been taken to the satisfaction of all members and that it could be assumed that the decision had been implemented and applied to all views adopted by the Committee.[19]

## C. Sessional Working Group on the Implementation of the International Covenant on Economic, Social and Cultural Rights

### 1. ORGANIZATIONAL MATTERS

The 1982 session of the Sessional Working Group (of Governmental Experts) on the Implementation of the International Covenant on Economic, Social and Cultural Rights, established in accordance with Economic and Social Council resolution 1988 (LX) of 11 May 1976 and its decision 1978/10 of 3 May 1978, was held at United Nations Headquarters from 5 to 23 April 1982.[20]

The following specialized agencies were represented: the Food and Agriculture Organization of the United Nations, the International Labour Organisation, the United Nations Educational, Scientific and Cultural Organization and the World Health Organization.[21]

### 2. CONSIDERATION OF REPORTS SUBMITTED IN ACCORDANCE WITH ECONOMIC AND SOCIAL COUNCIL RESOLUTION 1988 (LX) BY STATES PARTIES CONCERNING RIGHTS COVERED BY ARTICLES 6 TO 9, 10 TO 12 AND 13 TO 15 OF THE COVENANT

The Sessional Working Group considered the reports submitted by States parties concerning rights covered by articles 6 to 9 of the Covenant at its 1st to 5th meetings, from 5 to 7 April; articles 10 to 12 at its 5th to 9th meetings, from 7 to 12 April; and articles 13 to 15 at its 9th to 21st meetings, from 12 to 21 April.

On each report, the Working Group heard introductory statements by a representative or representatives of the State party whose report was being considered. Comments were then made on the report and introductory statements and

---

[19] *Ibid.*, paras. 391-394.

[20] Report of the Sessional Working Group on the Implementation of the International Covenant on Economic, Social and Cultural Rights (E/1982/56), paras. 1 and 2.

[21] *Ibid.*, para. 5.

questions were posed to the representative or representatives of the State party by members of the Working Group.

The representatives of specialized agencies concerned made general statements on matters relating to their field of competence at the end of the discussion by the Working Group of the report of each State party.

The representative or representatives submitting the report then replied to the questions raised during the consideration of the report.

### Reports submitted by States parties concerning rights covered by articles 6 to 9 of the Covenant

| Report | Date(s) considered | Discussion contained in document |
|---|---|---|
| United Kingdom of Great Britain and Northern Ireland (E/1978/8/Add.30) | 5 April 1982 | E/1982/WG.1/SR.1 |
| Canada (E/1978/8/Add.32) | 5 April 1982 | E/1982/WG.1/SR.1 and 2 |
| Barbados (E/1978/8/Add.33) | 6 April 1982 | E/1982/WG.1/SR.3 |
| Italy (E/1978/8/Add.34) | 6 and 7 April 1982 | E/1982/WG.1/SR.3 and 4 |
| Yugoslavia (E/1978/8/Add.35) | 7 April 1982 | E/1982/WG.1/SR.4 and 5 |

### Reports submitted by States parties concerning rights covered by articles 10 to 12 of the Covenant

| Report | Date(s) considered | Discussion contained in document |
|---|---|---|
| Panama (E/1980/6/Add.20 and 23) | 7 April 1982 | E/1982/WG.1/SR.5 |
| Ukrainian Soviet Socialist Republic (E/1980/6/Add.24) | 7 and 8 April 1982 | E/1982/WG.1/SR.5 and 6 |
| Barbados (E/1980/6/Add.27) | 8 April 1982 | E/1982/WG.1/SR.6 and 7 |
| Spain (E/1980/6/Add.28) | 8 April 1982 | E/1982/WG.1/SR.7 |
| Bulgaria (E/1980/6/Add.29) | 12 April 1982 | E/1982/WG.1/SR.8 |

### Reports submitted by States parties concerning rights covered by articles 13 to 15 of the Covenant

| Report | Date(s) considered | Discussion contained in document |
|---|---|---|
| Byelorussian Soviet Socialist Republic (E/1982/3/Add.3) | 12 and 13 April 1982 | E/1982/WG.1/SR.9 and 10 |
| Ukrainian Soviet Socialist Republic (E/1982/3/Add.4) | 14 April 1982 | E/1982/WG.1/SR.11 and 12 |
| Union of Soviet Socialist Republics (E/1982/3/Add.1) | 14 April 1982 | E/1982/WG.1/SR.11 and 12 |
| Japan (E/1982/3/Add.7) | 14 April 1982 | E/1982/WG.1/SR.12 and 13 |
| Australia (E/1982/3/Add.9) | 15 April 1982 | E/1982/WG.1/SR.13 and 14 |
| Hungary (E/1982/3/Add.10) | 15 April 1982 | E/1982/WG.1/SR.14 |
| Mexico (E/1982/3/Add.8) | 15 April 1982 | E/1982/WG.1/SR.14 and 15 |
| Mongolia (E/1982/3/Add.11) | 16 April 1982 | E/1982/WG.1/SR.15 and 16 |

| Report | Date(s) considered | Discussion contained in document |
|--------|--------------------|----------------------------------|
| Norway (E/1982/3/Add.12) | 16 April 1982 | E/1982/WG.1/SR.16 |
| Romania (E/1982/3/Add.13) | 19 April 1982 | E/1982/WG.1/SR.17 and 18 |
| Federal Republic of Germany (E/1982/3/Add.14) | 19 April 1982 | E/1982/WG.1/SR.17 and 18 |
| Sweden (E/1982/3/Add.2) | 20 April 1982 | E/1982/WG.1/SR.19 and 20 |
| United Kingdom of Great Britain and Northern Ireland (E/1982/3/Add.16) | 20 and 21 April 1982 | E/1982/WG.1/SR.19, 20 and 21[22] |

### 3. Issues arising from the consideration of reports of States parties to the Covenant

In its consideration of the reports, the Sessional Working Group observed that some of the laws, especially those in the social security field, had become too complicated, to the point where it might be difficult for the ordinary beneficiary to understand them. For this reason, the beneficiary is, therefore, at a great disadvantage in trying to discover what his or her entitlements are, and how to obtain them.

With a view to further improving the quality of reports submitted under the relevant articles of the Covenant, the Working Group recommends that:

(a) Up-to-date statistics which reflect the real degree of implementing the relevant articles of the Covenant should be reflected in the reports.

(b) The question of co-ordination between central and local authorities should be explained in a clear manner in the reports, as necessary.

(c) The question of equal treatment for women, vis-à-vis men, for activities covered by the Covenant, should be paid attention to.

(d) Even although most of the States parties say that their laws are in accordance with the Covenant, it would be useful to indicate where any divergencies exist.

(e) Timely submission of reports of States parties to the Covenant is desirable.

(f) The circulation of documents in the official languages of the Working Group in accordance with the six-week rule is important.

(g) To the fullest extent possible, reports should conform to the guidelines provided by the Secretary-General in documents E/1978/8, E/1980/6 and E/1982/3.[23]

---

[22] *Ibid.*, paras. 11-15.

[23] *Ibid.*, paras. 19-20.

## D. Group of Three Established under the Convention on the Suppression and Punishment of the Crime of *Apartheid*

### 1. Organization of the session

The Group held its fifth (1982) session at the United Nations Office at Geneva from 25 to 29 January 1982.[24]

### 2. Consideration of reports submitted by States parties under article VII of the Convention

The Group undertook the examination of the following reports: report of Barbados (E/CN.4/1505/Add.1); third report of the United Arab Emirates (E/CN.4/1505/Add.2); report of Mexico (E/CN.4/1505/Add.3); second report of Qatar (E/CN.4/1505/Add.4); second report of Iraq (E/CN.4/1505/Add.5); third report of Hungary (E/CN.4/1505/Add.6); report of Mongolia (E/CN.4/1505/Add.7); third report of the German Democratic Republic (E/CN.4/1505/Add.8); third report of the Union of Soviet Socialist Republics (E/CN.4/1505/Add.9); and third report of the Syrian Arab Republic (E/CN.4/1505/Add.10).

The Group undertook the examination of each report in the presence of the representatives of the reporting States who had been invited to attend the meetings of the Group in accordance with the recommendation made by the Group at its 1979 session, with the exception of the report of Barbados which was considered without the participation of a representative.[2]

A summary of the consideration of the reports by the Group can be found in paragraphs 11 to 20 of its report (E/CN.4/1507).

---

[24] Report of the Group of Three Established under the Convention (E/CN.4/1507), para. 6.

[25] *Ibid.*, para. 10.

# Section B. Relevant decisions, general recommendations, comments and observations of the supervisory bodies

## A. Committee on the Elimination of Racial Discrimination

1. CONSIDERATION OF PETITIONS, REPORTS AND OTHER INFORMATION RELATING TO TRUST AND NON-SELF-GOVERNING TERRITORIES AND TO ALL OTHER TERRITORIES TO WHICH GENERAL ASSEMBLY RESOLUTION 1514 (XV) APPLIES, IN CONFORMITY WITH ARTICLE 15 OF THE CONVENTION

The opinions and recommendations of the Committee based on its consideration of copies of reports and other information submitted to it under article 15 of the Convention as adopted by the Committee at its 594th meeting, on 17 August 1982, are as follows:

"*The Committee on the Elimination of Racial Discrimination,*

"*Having examined* the information contained in the documents relating to Trust and Non-Self-Governing Territories and to all other Territories to which General Assembly resolution 1514 (XV) of 14 December 1960 applies, transmitted to it by the Trusteeship Council and the Special Committee on the Situation with regard to the Implementation of the Declaration on the Granting of Independence to Colonial Countries and Peoples in accordance with the provisions of paragraph 2 of article 15 of the International Convention on the Elimination of All Forms of Racial Discrimination,

"*Wishes* to draw the attention of the General Assembly, the Trusteeship Council and Special Committee to the following opinions and recommendations in conformity with its obligations under article 15 of the Convention.

## "GENERAL

"With regard to the Territories considered by the Committee, the Committee wishes to reiterate its regret that, despite its repeated requests, no information directly relevant to the princibles and objectives of the Convention has been forthcoming and that no positive response to its requests for information has been received. The Committee, therefore, finds it difficult to discharge fully its obligations under article 15 of the Convention.

## "A. African Territories

### "1. *Namibia*

"(1) The Committee, having examined the working papers listed below,[1] reiterates its grave concern over the continuing and growing exacerbation of racial discrimination in the Territory, particularly in its most inhuman form, *apartheid*.

"(2) Pending the attainment by Namibia of its full and legitimate sovereignty, the Committee reiterates its request to the United Nations, which is already involved in the search for an equitable, peaceful and internationally acceptable settlement under its auspices, to use every possible means to prevent the South African régime from pursuing its policy of *apartheid* and to ensure the speedy exercise by the people of Namibia of their right to self-determination and the attainment of independence of the Territory of Namibia, including Walvis Bay.

"(3) The Committee strongly deplores the fact that the South African régime continues to defy the decisions and resolutions of the United Nations, in particular Security Council resolution 439 (1978) of 13 November 1978, by further intensifying its efforts to enhance the executive and legislative powers of the illegal local administration to convey the impression that the Territory had become internally self-governing, and determined to ignore completely the claims of the vast majority of the population, who are demanding the total abolition of *apartheid* and the exercise of their right to self-determination leading to genuine majority rule.

"(4) The Committee suggests again to the General Assembly to urge the South African régime to take full account of its resolutions and of the relevant decisions of the Security Council and to implement as soon as possible the proposals for a peaceful settlement through, *inter alia*, the initiation of a cease-fire, the withdrawal of South African military forces and the organization of free and fair elections under United Nations supervision reflecting the will of the Namibian population in the exercise of its right to self-determination.

"(5) The Committee believes that, with a view to attaining this ultimate objective, the South African régime should be urged and, if necessary, compelled to put an end to its intimidation and harassment of the black population; to the repressive measures against SWAPO and its supporters and the arrest of such nationalists; to the conscription of African men; to the intensification of its illegal military occupation by, *inter alia*, the displacement of Namibians from their homes and the establishment of new bases; and to the

---

[1] Adopted at the 594th meeting, on 17 August 1982. With regard to these Territories, the following documents were submitted to the Committee:

A/AC.109/695 (Western Sahara);

A/AC.109/699 (Namibia);

A/AC.109/702 (Activities of foreign economic and other interests in Namibia);

A/AC.109/704 (Military activities and arrangements by colonial Powers in Namibia).

exploitation and rapid depletion of the resources of the Territory and of its economic zone and continental sea-bed, dominated by foreign interests and the white minority to the detriment of the African majority, which is deprived of all benefits under the existing system. The South African régime should also be prevented from continuing its acquisition of new arms and armaments in defiance of the decisions of the Security Council, and from the development of a nuclear capability which poses a constant threat to international peace and security and especially to the front-line States.

### "2.  Western Sahara

"The Committee, taking into account the situation in the Western Sahara, welcomes and supports the efforts made by the Organization of African Unity and its Implementation Committee with a view to promoting a just and definitive solution to the question; endorses the resolutions of the United Nations reaffirming the inalienable right of the people of the Western Sahara to self-determination in full co-operation with the Organization of African Unity.

### "B.   PACIFIC AND INDIAN OCEAN TERRITORIES[2]

"The Committee notes that the economic and administrative set-up in the Pacific and Indian Ocean Territories, in particular the presence of a considerable number of non-indigenous persons, as well as the composition of the indigenous population might lead to situations where racial discrimination could occur for various reasons. The Committee therefore finds the absolute lack of pertinent information all the more deplorable.

---

[2] Adopted at the 594th meeting, on 17 August 1982. With regard to these Territories, the following documents were submitted to the Committee:

A/36/23 (Part VII), chap. XXVII (Tokelau);

A/36/23 (Part VII), chap. XXVIII (American Samoa);

A/AC.109/679 and Add.1 (Report of the United Nations Visiting Mission to American Samoa, 1981);

A/AC.109/680 (Report of the United Nations Visiting Mission to Tokelau, 1981);

A/AC.109/684 (Pitcairn);

A/AC.109/689 (Tokelau);

A/AC.109/691 (American Samoa);

A/AC.109/693 (Cocos (Keeling) Islands);

A/AC.109/694 (Guam);

A/AC.109/698 (Military activities and arrangements by colonial Powers in Guam);

A/AC.109/700 (Trust Territory of the Pacific Islands);

T/L.1228 and Add.1-3 (Outline of conditions in the Trust Territory of the Pacific Islands);

T/1837, Report of the Government of the United States of America on the administration of the Trust Territory of the Pacific Islands for the period from 1 October 1980 to 30 September 1981.

"C. ATLANTIC OCEAN AND CARIBBEAN TERRITORIES, INCLUDING GIBRALTAR[3]

## "1. *British Virgin Islands*

"The Committee notes that in the field of public service, efforts have been made to replace expatriate workers by local employees. However, since a large percentage of the general labour force continues to be filled by non-locals, the Committee recommends that the Territorial Government should intensify its training of the locals to replace expatriates.

## "2. *Bermuda*

"The Committee once again expresses its wish to be provided with information regarding constitutional provisions, new laws and measures which embody the principle of non-discrimination and the protection and exercise of human rights. In addition, the Committee would like to be informed of measures taken by the administering Power to effectively expedite the process of its "bermudanization" in public service and the labour force.

## "3. *Turks and Caicos Islands*

"The Committee emphasizes the need to provide the necessary assistance to the training of qualified local personnel in the skills essential to the development of the various sectors of the society of the Territory.

## "4. *Cayman Islands*

"The Committee takes note of the information contained in the working paper and, in particular, the Government's policy, which has resulted in the employment of a growing number of Caymanians. The Committee expressed the wish to be given information on additional measures for the advancement of this process, and on any other specific measures for the protection and enjoyment of human rights.

---

[3] Adopted at the 594th meeting, on 17 August 1982. With regard to these Territories, the following documents were submitted to the Committee:

A/36/23 (Part V), chap. XXIV (Falkland Islands (Malvinas));
A/AC.109/670 (Falkland Islands (Malvinas));
A/AC.109/682 (British Virgin Islands);
A/AC.109/683 (Bermuda);
A/AC.109/685 (Turks and Caicos Islands);
A/AC.109/686 (Montserrat);
A/AC.109/688 (Cayman Islands);
A/AC.109/690 (Activities of foreign economic and other interests in Bermuda);
A/AC.109/692 (St. Helena);
A/AC.109/696 (Military activities and arrangements by colonial Powers in Bermuda, Turks and Caicos Islands and United States Virgin Islands);
A/AC.109/697 (United States Virgin Islands);
A/AC.109/701 (Activities of foreign economic and other interests in Turks and Caicos Islands);
A/AC.109/703 (Activities of foreign economic and other interests in Cayman Islands).

## "5. *St. Helena*

"The Committee once again reiterates its expression of serious concern that trade between the Territory and South Africa continues, and expresses the hope that the administering Power would promptly take the appropriate measures in compliance with the pertinent resolutions of the United Nations.

## "6. *The United States Virgin Islands*

"The Committee once again reiterates its requests for detailed information on the ethnic composition of the population of the islands and wishes to be informed also of the constitutional provisions and other measures relevant to the protection of human rights."

## 2. Decisions adopted by the Committee at its twenty-fifth and twenty-sixth sessions

### A. *Twenty-fifth session*

#### "1 (XXV).   *General Recommendation VI*[4]

"*The Committee on the Elimination of Racial Discrimination,*

"*Recognizing* the fact that an impressive number of States has ratified, or acceded to, the International Convention on the Elimination of All Forms of Racial Discrimination,

"*Bearing in mind*, however, that ratification alone does not enable the control system set up by the Convention to function effectively,

"*Recalling* that article 9 of the Convention obliges States parties to submit initial and periodic reports on the measures that give effect to the provisions of the Convention,

"*Stating* that at present no less than 89 reports are overdue from 62 States, that 42 of those reports are overdue from 15 States, each with two or more outstanding reports, and that four initial reports which were due between 1973 and 1978 have not been received,

"*Noting with regret* that neither reminders sent through the Secretary-General to States parties nor the inclusion of the relevant information in the annual reports to the General Assembly has had the desired effect, in all cases,

"*Invites* the General Assembly:

"(*a*) To take note of the situation,

"(*b*) To use its authority in order to ensure that the Committee could more effectively fulfil its obligations under the Convention."

*569th meeting*
*15 March 1982*

---

[4] Report of the Committee on the Elimination of Racial Discrimination, *Official Records of the General Assembly, Thirty-seventh Session, Supplement No. 18* (A/37/18), chap. IX A.

## B. *Twenty-sixth session*

### "*1 (XXVI). Question of venue of the twenty-eighth session*[5]

"*The Committee on the Elimination of Racial Discrimination,*

"*Having considered* the agenda item entitled 'Decade for Action to Combat Racism and Racial Discrimination' and the contribution of the Committee to the Second World Conference to Combat Racism and Racial Discrimination, as well as the agenda item entitled 'Meetings of the Committee in 1983 and 1984',

"*Bearing in mind* General Assembly resolution 35/40 of 25 November 1980 in which the Assembly, among other things, requested the Secretary-General to make appropriate arrangements for the Committee to hold, as part of the activities within the Programme for the Decade, one session in a developing country, and Assembly resolution 36/12 of 28 October 1981 in which the Assembly reiterated the same request,

"*Taking note* of Economic and Social Council resolution 1982/32 of 5 May 1982 in which the Council, among other things, requested the Secretary-General to consult with the Government of the Philippines concerning arrangements for holding the Second World Conference to Combat Racism and Racial Discrimination at Manila from 1 to 12 August 1983, on the basis of the financial formula contained in General Assembly resolution 31/78 of 13 December 1976,

"*Convinced* that the holding of the twenty-eighth session of the Committee on the Elimination of Racial Discrimination at Manila, in conjunction with the Second World Conference to Combat Racism and Racial Discrimination, will be of immense value to the World Conference itself and will also represent a useful and significant contribution of the Committee to the attainment of the goals and objectives of the Decade,

"1.   *Requests* the Secretary-General, in consultation with the Government of the Philippines, to explore the possibility of arranging for the twenty-eighth session of the Committee to be held at Manila from 11 to 29 July 1983, immediately prior to the holding of the World Conference;

"2.   *Recommends* that the General Assembly consider extending the same formula under Assembly resolution 31/78 of 13 December 1976 to cover also the expenses of the holding of the twenty-eighth session of the Committee at Manila with a view to enabling the Government of the Philippines to act as host to the session."

*595th meeting*
*19 August 1982*

---

[5] *Ibid.,* chap. IX B.

## B. Human Rights Committee

### 1. DECISION ON PERIODICITY[6]

1. Under article 40 of the Covenant, States parties have undertaken to submit reports to the Human Rights Committee:

(a) Within one year of the entry into force of the Covenant for the State party concerned (initial reports);

(b) Thereafter, whenever the Committee so requests (subsequent reports).

2. In accordance with article 40, paragraph 1 (b), the Human Rights Committee requests:

(a) States parties which have submitted their initial reports or additional information relating to their initial reports before the end of the thirteenth session to submit subsequent reports every five years from the consideration of their initial report or their additional information;

(b) Other States parties to submit subsequent reports to the Committee every five years from the date when their initial report was due.

This is without prejudice to the power of the Committee, under article 40, paragraph 1 (b), of the Covenant, to request a subsequent report whenever it deems appropriate.

3. In such cases where a State party submits additional information within one year, or such other period as the Committee may decide, following the examination of its initial report or of any subsequent periodic report and the additional information is examined at a meeting with representatives of the reporting State, the Committee will, if appropriate, defer the date for the submission of the State party's next periodic report.

### 2. GENERAL COMMENTS UNDER ARTICLE 40, PARAGRAPH 4, OF THE COVENANT[7]

*General comment 6 (16) (article 6)*

1. The right to life enunciated in article 6 of the Covenant has been dealt with in all State reports. It is the supreme right from which no derogation is permitted even in time of public emergency which threatens the life of the nation (article 4). However, the Committee has noted that quite often the information given concerning article 6 has been limited to only one or other aspect of this right. It is a right which should not be interpreted narrowly.

2. The Committee observes that war and other acts of mass violence continue to be a scourge of humanity and take the lives of thousands of innocent human beings

---

[6] As amended by the Committee at its 380th meeting (sixteenth session) held on 28 July 1982. See *Official Records of the General Assembly, Thirty-seventh Session, Supplement No. 40* (A/37/40), annex IV.

[7] Adopted by the Committee at its 378th meeting (sixteenth session) held on 27 July 1982. See A/37/40, annex V.

every year. Under the Charter of the United Nations the threat or use of force by any State against another State, except in exercise of the inherent right of self-defence, is already prohibited. The Committee considers that States have the supreme duty to prevent wars, acts of genocide and other acts of mass violence causing arbitrary loss of life. Every effort they made to avert the danger of war, especially thermo-nuclear war, and to strengthen international peace and security would constitute the most important condition and guarantee for the safeguarding of the right to life. In this respect, the Committee notes, in particular, a connection between article 6 and article 20, which states that the law shall prohibit any propaganda for war (paragraph 1) or incitement to violence (paragraph 2) as therein described.

3. The protection against arbitrary deprivation of life which is explicitly re-quired by the third sentence of article 6 (1) is of paramount importance. The Com-mittee considers that States parties should take measures not only to prevent and punish deprivation of life by criminal acts, but also to prevent arbitrary killing by their own security forces. The deprivation of life by the authorities of the State is a matter of the utmost gravity. Therefore, the law must strictly control and limit the circumstances in which a person may be deprived of his life by such authorities.

4. States parties should also take specific and effective measures to prevent the disappearance of individuals, something which unfortunately has become all too fre-quent and leads too often to arbitrary deprivation of life. Furthermore, States should establish effective facilities and procedures to investigate thoroughly cases of missing and disappeared persons in circumstances which may involve a violation of the right to life.

5. Moreover, the Committee has noted that the right to life has been too often narrowly interpreted. The expression "inherent right to life" cannot properly be understood in a restrictive manner, and the protection of this right requires that States adopt positive measures. In this connection, the Committee considers that it would be desirable for States parties to take all possible measures to reduce infant mortality and to increase life expectancy, especially in adopting measures to eliminate malnutrition and epidemics.

6. While it follows from article 6 (2) to (6) that States parties are not obliged to abolish the death penalty totally, they are obliged to limit its use and, in particular, to abolish it for other than the "most serious crimes". Accordingly, they ought to consider reviewing their criminal laws in this light and, in any event, are obliged to restrict the application of the death penalty to the "most serious crimes". The article also refers generally to abolition in terms which strongly suggest (para. 2 (2) and (6)) that abolition is desirable. The Committee concludes that all measures of abolition should be considered as progress in the enjoyment of the right to life within the meaning of article 40, and should as such be reported to the Committee. The Com-mittee notes that a number of States have already abolished the death penalty or suspended its application. Nevertheless, States' reports show that progress made towards abolishing or limiting the application of the death penalty is quite inade-quate.

7. The Committee is of the opinion that the expression "most serious crimes" must be read restrictively to mean that the death penalty should be a quite excep-tional measure. It also follows from the express terms of article 6 that it can only be imposed in accordance with the law in force at the time of the commission of

the crime and not contrary to the Covenant. The procedural guarantees therein prescribed must be observed, including the right to a fair hearing by an independent tribunal, the presumption of innocence, the minimum guarantees for the defence, and the right to review by a higher tribunal. These rights are applicable in addition to the particular right to seek pardon or commutation of the sentence.

*General comment 7 (16) (article 7)*

1. In examining the reports of States parties, members of the Committee have often asked for further information under article 7 which prohibits, in the first place, torture or cruel, inhuman or degrading treatment or punishment. The Committee recalls that even in situations of public emergency such as are envisaged by article 4 (1) this provision is non-derogable under article 4 (2). Its purpose is to protect the integrity and dignity of the individual. The Committee notes that it is not sufficient for the implementation of this article to prohibit such treatment or punishment or to make it a crime. Most States have penal provisions which are applicable to cases of torture or similar practices. Because such cases nevertheless occur, it follows from article 7, read together with article 2 of the Covenant, that States must ensure an effective protection through some machinery of control. Complaints about ill-treatment must be investigated effectively by competent authorities. Those found guilty must be held responsible, and the alleged victims must themselves have effective remedies at their disposal, including the right to obtain compensation. Among the safeguards which may make control effective are provisions against detention incommunicado, granting, without prejudice to the investigation, persons such as doctors, lawyers and family members access to the detainess; provisions requiring that detainees should be held in places that are publicly recognized and that their names and places of detention should be entered in a central register available to persons concerned, such as relatives; provisions making confessions or other evidence obtained through torture or other treatment contrary to article 7 inadmissible in court; and measures of training and instruction of law enforcement officials not to apply such treatment.

2. As appears from the terms of this article, the scope of protection required goes far beyond torture as normally understood. It may not be necessary to draw sharp distinctions between the various prohibited forms of treatment or punishment. These distinctions depend on the kind, purpose and severity of the particular treatment. In the view of the Committee the prohibition must extend to corporal punishment, including excessive chastisement as an educational or disciplinary measure. Even such a measure as solitary confinement may, according to the circumstances, and especially when the person is kept incommunicado, be contrary to this article. Moreover, the article clearly protects not only persons arrested or imprisoned, but also pupils and patients in educational and medical institutions. Finally, it is also the duty of public authorities to ensure protection by the law against such treatment even when committed by persons acting outside or without any official authority. For all persons deprived of their liberty, the prohibition of treatment contrary to article 7 is supplemented by the positive requirement of article 10 (1) of the Covenant that they shall be treated with humanity and with respect for the inherent dignity of the human person.

3. In particular, the prohibition extends to medical or scientific experimentation without the free consent of the person concerned (article 7, second sentence).

The Committee notes that the reports of States parties have generally given little or no information on this point. It takes the view that at least in countries where science and medicine are highly developed, and even for peoples and areas outside their borders if affected by their experiments, more attention should be given to the possible need and means to ensure the observance of this provision. Special protection in regard to such experiments is necessary in the case of persons not capable of giving their consent.

### General comment 8 (16) (article 9)

1. Article 9 which deals with the right to liberty and security of persons has often been somewhat narrowly understood in reports by States parties, and they have therefore given incomplete information. The Committee points out that paragraph 1 is applicable to all deprivations of liberty, whether in criminal cases or in other cases such as, for example, mental illness, vagrancy, drug addiction, educational purposes, immigration control, etc. It is true that some of the provisions of article 9 (part of paragraph 2 and the whole of paragraph 3) are only applicable to persons against whom criminal charges are brought. But the rest, and in particular the important guarantees laid down in paragraph 4, i.e. the right to control by a court of the legality of the detention, applies to all persons deprived of their liberty by arrest or detention. Furthermore, States parties have in accordance with article 2 (3) also to ensure that an effective remedy is provided in other cases in which an individual claims to be deprived of his liberty in violation of the Covenant.

2. Paragraph 3 of the article 9 requires that in criminal cases any person arrested or detained has to be brought "promptly" before a judge or other officer authorized by law to exercise judicial power. More precise time-limits are fixed by law in most States parties and, in the view of the Committee, delays must not exceed a few days. Many States have given insufficient information about the actual practices in this respect.

3. Another matter is the total length of detention pending trial. In certain categories of criminal cases in some countries this matter has caused some concern within the Committee, and members have questioned whether their practices have been in conformity with the entitlement "to trial within a reasonable time or to release" under paragraph 3. Pre-trial detention should be an exception and as short as possible. The Committee would welcome information concerning mechanisms existing and measures taken with a view to reducing the duration of such detention.

4. Also if so-called preventive detention is used, for reasons of public security, it must be controlled by these same provisions, i.e. it must not be arbitrary, and must be based on grounds and procedures established by law (paragraph 1), information available (paragraph 4) as well as compensation in the case of a breach (paragraph 5). And if, in addition, criminal charges are brought in such cases, the full protection of article 9 (2) and (3), as well as article 14, must also be granted.

### General comment 9 (16) (article 10)

1. Article 10, paragraph 1, of the Covenant provides that all persons deprived of their liberty shall be treated with humanity and with respect for the inherent dignity of the human person. However, by no means all the reports submitted by States

parties have contained information on the way in which this paragraph of the article is being implemented. The Committee is of the opinion that it would be desirable for the reports of States parties to contain specific information on the legal measures designed to protect that right. The Committee also considers that reports should indicate the concrete measures being taken by the competent State organs to monitor the mandatory implementation of national legislation concerning the humane treatment and respect for the human dignity of all persons deprived of their liberty that paragraph 1 requires.

2. The Committee notes in particular that paragraph 1 of this article is generally applicable to persons deprived of their liberty, whereas paragraph 2 deals with accused as distinct from convicted persons, and paragraph 3 with convicted persons only. This structure quite often is not reflected in the reports, which mainly have related to accused and convicted persons. The wording of paragraph 1, its context —especially its proximity to article 9, paragraph 1, which also deals with all deprivations of liberty—and its purpose support a broad application of the principle expressed in that provision. Moreover, the Committee recalls that this article supplements article 7 as regards the treatment of all persons deprived of their liberty.

3. The humane treatment and the respect for the dignity of all persons deprived of their liberty is a basic standard of universal application which cannot depend entirely on material resources. While the Committee is aware that in other respects the modalities and conditions of detention may vary with the available resources, they must always be applied without discrimination, as required by article 2(1).

4. Ultimate responsibility for the observance of this principle rests with the State as regards all institutions where persons are lawfully held against their will, not only in prisons but also, for example, hospitals, detention camps or correctional institutions.

5. Subparagraph 2 (*a*) of the article provides that, save in exceptional circumstances, accused persons shall be segregated from convicted persons and shall receive separate treatment appropriate to their status as unconvicted persons. Some reports have failed to pay proper attention to this direct requirement of the Covenant and, as a result, to provide adequate information on the way in which the treatment of accused persons differs from that of convicted persons. Such information should be included in future reports.

6. Subparagraph 2 (*b*) of the article calls, *inter alia*, for accused juvenile persons to be separated from adults. The information in reports shows that a number of States are not taking sufficient account of the fact that this is an unconditional requirement of the Covenant. It is the Committee's opinion that, as is clear from the text of the Covenant, deviation from States parties' obligations under subparagraph 2 (*b*) cannot be justified by any consideration whatsoever.

7. In a number of cases, the information appearing in reports with respect to paragraph 3 of the article has contained no concrete mention either of legislative or of administrative measures or of practical steps to promote the reformation and social rehabilitation of prisoners, by, for example, education, vocational training and useful work. Allowing visits, in particular by family members, is normally also such a measure which is required for reasons of humanity. There are also similar lacunae in the reports of certain States with respect to information concerning juv-

enile offenders, who must be segregated from adults and given treatment appropriate to their age and legal status.

8. The Committee further notes that the principles of humane treatment and respect for human dignity set out in paragraph 1 are the basis for the more specific and limited obligations of States in the field of criminal justice set out in paragraphs 2 and 3 of article 10. The segregation of accused persons from convicted ones is required in order to emphasize their statuts as unconvicted persons who are at the same time protected by the presumption of innocence stated in article 14, paragraph 2. The aim of these provisions is to protect the groups mentioned, and the requirements contained therein should be seen in that light. Thus, for example, the segregation and treatment of juvenile offenders should be provided for in such a way that it promotes their reformation and social rehabilitation.

3. VIEWS OF THE HUMAN RIGHTS COMMITTEE UNDER ARTICLE 5, PARAGRAPH 4, OF THE OPTIONAL PROTOCOL TO THE INTERNATIONAL COVENANT ON CIVIL AND POLITICAL RIGHTS

During its sessions held in 1982, having concluded its consideration of a number of communications submitted to it under the Optional Protocol, and having taken into account all written information made available to it by the authors of the communications and by the States parties concerned, the Human Rights Committee adopted views and decisions under article 5, paragraph 4, of the Optional Protocol. A detailed account of views and decisions adopted can be found in annexes IX to XX of the Committee's report to the General Assembly at its thirty seventh session[8] and annexes VII to IX of its report to the Assembly at its thirty-eighth session.[9]

## C. Sessional Working Group on the Implementation of the International Covenant on Economic, Social and Cultural Rights

RECOMMENDATIONS OF THE SESSIONAL WORKING GROUP[10]

The Sessional Working Group recommends to the Council the adoption of the following draft decisions:

"DRAFT DECISION I

"**Provisional agenda for 1983 of the Sessional Working Group (of Governmental Experts) on the Implementation of the International Covenant on Economic, Social and Cultural Rights**

"The Economic and Social Council approves the provisional agenda for 1983 of the Sessional Working Group (of Governmental Experts) on the Im-

---

[8] *Official Records of the General Assembly, Thirty-seventh Session, Supplement No. 40* (A/37/40).

[9] *Ibid., Thirty-eighth Session, Supplement No. 40* (A/38/40).

[10] Report of the Sessional Working Group on the Implementation of the International Covenant on Economic, Social and Cultural Rights (E/1982/56), para. 25.

plementation of the International Covenant on Economic, Social and Cultural Rights set out below.

"1.  Consideration of reports submitted in accordance with Council resolution 1988 (LX) by States parties to the Covenant concerning rights covered by articles 6 to 9.

*Documentation*

Syrian Arab Republic (E/1978/8/Add.25 and 31).

"2.  Consideration of reports submitted in accordance with Council resolution 1988 (LX) by States parties to the Covenant concerning rights covered by articles 10 to 12.

*Documentation*

"3.  Consideration of reports submitted in accordance with Council resolution 1988 (LX) by States parties to the Covenant concerning rights covered by articles 13 to 15.

*Documentation*

Guyana (E/1982/3/Add.5)

Libyan Arab Jamahiriya (E/1982/3/Add.6)

German Democratic Republic (E/1982/3/Add.15).

"4.  Consideration of the report of the Sessional Working Group (of Governmental Experts) on the Implementation of the International Covenant on Economic, Social and Cultural Rights."

"Draft decision II

"Bureau for 1983 of the Sessional Working Group (of Governmental Experts) on the Implementation of the International Covenant on Economic, Social and Cultural Rights

"The Economic and Social Council decides that the Bureau for 1983 of the Sessional Working Group (of Governmental Experts) on the Implementation of the International Covenant on Economic, Social and Cultural Rights shall be constituted as follows:

"*Chairman:* Asian States;

"*Vice-Chairmen:* African States, Eastern European States, Latin American States;

"*Rapporteur:* Western European and other States."

## D. Group of Three Established under the Convention on the Suppression and Punishment of the Crime of *Apartheid*

CONCLUSIONS AND RECOMMENDATIONS OF THE FIFTH (1982) SESSION
OF THE GROUP OF THREE[11]

The Group of Three expressed its appreciation to the representatives of the reporting States for their presence at its meetings and for their participation in its work. The practice of inviting representatives of States parties to the International Convention on the Suppression and Punishment of the Crime of *Apartheid* to be present at its meetings when reports were submitted by their Governments proved once again to be a useful and constructive contribution to its work and should be continued in the future.

The Group commends those States parties which have submitted periodic reports and urges those States parties which have not yet done so to submit their reports as required under article VII of the Convention as soon as possible. The Group reiterates its recommendation that the general guidelines (E/CN.4/1286, annex) regarding the form and contents of reports should be fully taken into account by all States parties when preparing their reports.

The Group expresses concern at the fact that only 65 States have, as at 31 December 1981, become parties to the Convention. Being convinced that the ratification of, or accession to, the Convention on a universal basis and the implementation of its provisions are necessary for its effectiveness, the Group recommends once again to the Commission on Human Rights that it should urge all States which have not yet done'so to ratify or to accede to the Convention without delay.

The Group calls upon States parties to provide in their reports full information on the legislative, judicial and administrative measures they have adopted to give effect to the provisions of article IV of the Convention, or on the difficulties which they may have encountered in the implementation of that article.

The Group wishes once again to invite States parties, through the Commission on Human Rights, to submit their views on the interim study (E/CN.4/1426) prepared by the *Ad Hoc* Working Group of Experts on southern Africa in accordance with Commission resolution 12 (XXXVI) concerning ways and means of ensuring the implementation of international instruments such as the International Convention on the Suppression and Punishment of the Crime of *Apartheid*.

The Group wishes to appeal once again to States parties, through the Commission on Human Rights, to strengthen their co-operation at the international level to implement fully in accordance with the Charter of the United Nations the decisions taken by the Security Council and other competent organs of the United Nations aimed at the prevention, suppression and punishment of the crime of *apartheid*, in accordance with article VI of the Convention.

---

[11] Report of the Group of Three Established under the Convention (E/CN.4/1507), paras. 21-29.

The Group wishes to draw attention to the importance of strengthening the assistance given to the national liberation movements in southern Africa.

The Group wishes once again to draw the attention of States parties, through the Commission on Human Rights, to the desirability of disseminating more information about the Convention, the implementation of its provisions by States parties as well as the work of the Group of Three established under article IX of the Convention. It also recommends that the progressive list of individuals, organizations, institutions and representatives of States deemed responsible for crimes enumerated in article II of the Convention, be brought to the attention of all States parties to the Convention, and all States Members of the United Nations in accordance with General Assembly resolution 36/13 of 28 October 1981, and be given the widest publicity.

The Group wishes to request, through the Commission on Human Rights, the international organizations, organs and bodies of the United Nations system to intensify their activities aimed at publicizing and disseminating materials concerning problems of racial discrimination in general and *apartheid* in particular.

## E.  Relevant decisions and resolutions of parent bodies

### 1.  COMMISSION ON HUMAN RIGHTS

At its thirty-eighth session in 1982, the Commission on Human Rights adopted the following resolutions and decisions with regard to the International Convention on the Suppression and Punishment of the Crime of *Apartheid* and the International Covenants on Human Rights:

*Resolution 1982/10 of 25 February 1982 on the "Implementation of the International Convention on the Suppression and Punishment of the Crime of Apartheid":*[12]

"*The Commission on Human Rights,*

"*Recalling* its resolutions 10 (XXXV) of 5 March 1979, 13 (XXXVI) of 26 February 1980 and 6 (XXXVII) of 23 February 1981,

"*Recalling* its resolution 7 (XXXIV) of 22 February 1978, in which it called on States parties to the International Convention on the Suppression and Punishment of the Crime of *Apartheid* to submit, in accordance with article VII of the Convention, their first report not later than two years after becoming parties to the Convention and their periodic reports at two-year intervals,

"*Having considered* the report of the Group of Three members of the Commission appointed under article IX of the International Convention on the Suppression and Punishment of the Crime of *Apartheid,*

---

[12] *Official Records of the Economic and Social Council, 1982, Supplement No. 2* (E/1982/12), chap. XXVI, sect. A.

"*Reaffirming* its conviction that wider ratification of, or accession to, the Convention will contribute significantly to the eradication of the crime of *apartheid*,

"1.   *Takes note* with appreciation of the report of the Group of Three and in particular the conclusions and recommendations contained in it;

"2.   *Commends* those States parties that have submitted periodic reports and urges those States parties that have not yet done so to submit their reports as soon as possible, in accordance with article VII of the Convention;

"3.   *Again calls upon* States which have not yet done so to ratify or accede to the Convention without delay;

"4.   *Recommends* once again that all States parties should take full account of the general guidelines laid down by the Group of Three in 1978 for the submission of reports;

"5.   *Again requests* the Secretary-General to invite the States parties to submit their views and comments on the interim study prepared by the *Ad Hoc* Working Group of Experts on southern Africa in accordance with Commission resolution 12 (XXXVI);

"6.   *Calls once again* on States parties to strengthen their co-operation at the national and international levels in order to implement fully the decisions taken by the Security Council and other competent United Nations bodies with a view to the prevention, suppression and punishment of the crime of *apartheid*, in accordance with article VI of the Convention and the Charter of the United Nations;

"7.   *Draws the attention* of States parties to the desirability of disseminating further information on the Convention, the implementation of its provisions and the work of the Group of Three established under article IX of the Convention;

"8.   *Decides* that the Group of Three shall meet for a period of not more than five days before the thirty-ninth session of the Commission to consider the reports submitted by States parties in accordance with article VII of the Convention."

**Resolution 1982/18 of 9 March 1982 on the "Status of the International Covenants on Human Rights":[13]**

"*The Commission on Human Rights,*

"*Mindful* that the International Covenants on Human Rights constitute the first all-embracing and legally binding international treaties in the field of human rights, and together with the Universal Declaration of Human Rights, form the heart of the International Bill of Human Rights,

"*Recalling* its resolution 16 (XXXVII) of 10 March 1981 and General Assembly resolution 36/58 of 25 November 1981,

---

[13] *Ibid.*

"*Recalling* its resolution 24 (XXXVII) of 11 March 1981 and Economic and Social Council resolution 1980/30 of 2 May 1980 on development of public information activities in the field of human rights,

"*Having considered* the report of the Secretary-General on the status of the International Covenant on Economic, Social and Cultural Rights, the International Covenant on Civil and Political Rights, and the Optional Protocol to the International Covenant on Civil and Political Rights,

"*Noting with appreciation* that, following the appeals of the General Assembly and the Commission, more Member States have acceded to the International Covenants on Human Rights,

"*Bearing in mind* the important responsibilities of the Economic and Social Council in the implementation of the International Covenant on Economic, Social and Cultural Rights,

"*Recognizing* the important role of the Human Rights Committee in the implementation of the International Covenant on Civil and Political Rights and the Optional Protocol thereto, as reflected in its report,

"1. *Reaffirms* the importance of the International Covenants on Human Rights as major parts of international efforts to promote universal respect for and observance of human rights and fundamental freedoms;

"2. *Takes due note* of Economic and Social Council decision 1981/162 of 8 May 1981 concerning the review of the composition, organization and administrative arrangements of the Sessional Working Group of Governmental Experts on the Implementation of the International Covenant on Economic, Social and Cultural Rights and looks forward to further results in this regard at the first regular session of the Council in 1982;

"3. *Appreciates* that the Human Rights Committee continues to strive for uniform standards in the implementation of the provisions of the International Covenant on Civil and Political Rights and the Optional Protocol thereto and takes note of the decisions of the Human Rights Committee on the question of periodicity and on guidelines regarding the form and content of reports from States parties under article 40, paragraph 1 (*b*), of the Covenant as well as the adoption by the Committee of general comments under article 40, paragraph 4, of the Covenant;

"4. *Urges* all States which have not yet done so to become parties to the International Covenant on Economic, Social and Cultural Rights and the International Covenant on Civil and Political Rights as well as to consider acceding to the Optional Protocol to the International Covenant on Civil and Political Rights;

"5. *Invites* the States parties to the International Covenant on Civil and Political Rights to consider making the declarations provided for in article 41 of the Covenant;

"6. *Emphasizes* the importance of the strictest compliance by States parties with their obligations under the International Covenant on Economic, Social and Cultural Rights, the International Covenant on Civil and Political Rights and, where applicable, the Optional Protocol thereto;

"7. *Welcomes* the measures taken by the Secretary-General to improve the publicity for the work of the Human Rights Committee and takes note of the General Assembly's request to the Secretary-General in resolution 36/58 to consider the more appropriate steps for the publication of the Committee's documentation and to report on this question to the General Assembly at its thirty-seventh session;

"8. *Takes note* of paragraph 14 of General Assembly resolution 36/58 in which the Assembly urges the Secretary-General to take all possible steps to ensure that the Division of Human Rights of the Secretariat is able to assist effectively the Human Rights Committee and the Economic and Social Council in the implementation of their respective functions under the International Covenants on Human Rights;

"9. *Encourages* all Governments to publish the texts of the International Covenant on Economic, Social and Cultural Rights, and the Optional Protocol to the International Covenant on Civil and Political Rights and to distribute them and make them known as widely as possible in their territories;

"10. *Requests* the Secretary-General to submit to the Commission on Human Rights, at its thirty-ninth session, a report on the status of the International Covenant on Economic, Social and Cultural Rights, the International Covenant on Civil and Political Rights and the Optional Protocol to the International Covenant on Civil and Political Rights, and to include in this report information on the work of the Economic and Social Council and its Working Group on the Implementation of the International Covenant on Economic, Social and Cultural Rights."

*Decision 1982/107 of 12 March 1982 on the "Composition of the Group of Three members of the Commission, who are also representatives of States parties to the International Convention on the Suppression and Punishment of the Crime of* Apartheid, *to consider reports submitted by States parties in accordance with article VII of the Convention":*[14]

"The Commission took note of the announcement by the Chairman that the representatives of Bulgaria, Mexico and Zaire would form the Group of Three members of the Commission, who are also representatives of States parties to the International Convention on the Suppression and Punishment of the Crime of *Apartheid*, to consider reports submitted by States parties in accordance with article VII of the Convention."

## 2. ECONOMIC AND SOCIAL COUNCIL

At its first regular session of 1982, the Economic and Social Council adopted the following resolution and decisions with regard to the International Covenant on Economic, Social and Cultural Rights:

---

[14] *Ibid.*, sect. B.

*Resolution 1982/33 of 6 May 1982 on the "Review of the composition, organization and administrative arrangements of the Sessional Working Group (of Governmental Experts) on the Implementation of the International Covenant on Economic, Social and Cultural Rights":*

"*The Economic and Social Council,*

"*Recalling* its resolution 1988 (LX) of 11 May 1976, by which it noted the important responsibilities placed upon the Economic and Social Council by the International Covenant on Economic, Social and Cultural Rights, in particular those resulting from articles 21 and 22 of the Covenant, and expressed its readiness to fulfil those responsibilities,

"*Recalling* its decision 1978/10 of 3 May 1978, by which it decided to establish a Sessional Working Group on the Implementation of the International Covenant on Economic, Social and Cultural Rights, for the purpose of assisting the Council in the consideration of reports submitted by States parties to the Covenant in accordance with Council resolution 1988 (LX), and determined the composition of the Working Group,

"*Recalling also* its resolution 1979/43 of 11 May 1979, by which it approved the methods of work of the Sessional Working Group, and its decision 1981/158 of 8 May 1981, by which it incorporated certain changes in, and modified the methods of work of, the Sessional Working Group,

"*Recalling further* its resolution 1980/24 of 2 May 1980, by which it noted that the Sessional Working Group, established in accordance with Council decision 1978/10, had encountered certain difficulties in discharging its responsibilities under the arrangements and requested the Secretary-General to solicit the views of members of the Council and all States parties to the Covenant on the future composition, organization and administrative arrangements of the Sessional Working Group and to submit a report thereon, together with any comments he might wish to make, to the Council at its organizational session for 1981, in order to assist the Council in reviewing its decision 1978/10,

"*Recalling* its decision 1981/162 of 8 May 1981, by which it decided to review the composition, organization and administrative arrangements of the Sessional Working Group at its first regular session of 1982,

"*Having considered* the report of the Sessional Working Group (of Governmental Experts) on the Implementation of the International Covenant on Economic, Social and Cultural Rights,

"*Decides* that:

"(*a*)　The Working Group established by Economic and Social Council decision 1978/10 and modified by Council decision 1981/158 shall be renamed "Sessional Working Group of Governmental Experts on the Implementation of the International Covenant on Economic, Social and Cultural Rights" (thereinafter referred to as "the Group of Experts");

"(*b*)　The fifteen members of the Group of Experts shall be elected by the Economic and Social Council from among the States parties to the International Covenant on Economic, Social and Cultural Rights, in accordance with the geographical distribution established by the Council in paragraph (*a*) of its decision 1978/10, under the following conditions:

"(i)  The members of the Group of Experts shall be elected for a term of three years and shall be eligible for re-election at the end of their terms;

"(ii)  One third of the membership of the Group of Experts, comprising one member from each regional group, shall be renewed each year;

"(iii)  The first elections shall take place during the resumed second regular session of 1982 of the Economic and Social Council and the confirmation of the experts designated by Member States to represent them in the Group of Experts shall take place at the organizational session for 1983 of the Council; immediately after the first elections, the President of the Council shall choose by lot the name of one member from each regional group whose term shall expire at the end of one year and the name of another member from each regional group whose term shall expire at the end of two years;

"(iv)  The terms of office of members elected to the Group of Experts shall begin on 1 January following their election and shall expire on 31 December following the election of members that are to succeed them as members of the Group of Experts;

"(v)  Subsequent elections shall take place each year during the first regular session of the Council;

"(vi)  Each Member State elected to the Group of Experts shall designate, in consultation with the Secretary-General and subject to confirmation by the Council, a qualified person to represent that Member State in the Group of Experts;

"(vii)  The person so designated by his or her Government shall be an expert with recognized competence in the field of human rights;

"(c)  The Group of Experts shall meet annually for a period of three weeks, beginning two weeks before the first regular session of the Council; the duration of each session may be extended by the Council at its organizational session, if required, taking into account the number of reports to be examined by the Group of Experts in the course of its following session;

"(d)  At the end of each of its sessions, the Group of Experts shall submit to the Economic and Social Council a report on its activities and shall make suggestions and recommendations of a general nature based on its consideration of reports submitted by States parties to the Covenant and by the specialized agencies, in order to assist the Council to fulfil, in particular, its responsibilities under articles 21 and 22 of the Covenant;

"(e)  The Secretary-General shall provide the Group of Experts with summary records of its proceedings; those summary records shall be made available to the Council at the same time as the report of the Group of Experts; the Secretary-General shall also provide the Group of Experts with appropriate conference facilities;

"(f)  The Economic and Social Council shall review the composition, organization and administrative arrangements of the Group of Experts at its first regular session of 1985, and subsequently every three years, taking into account the principle of equitable geographical distribution and the increase in the number of States parties to the Covenant;

"(*g*)   The procedures and methods of work established by the resolutions and decisions referred to in the preamble to the present resolution shall remain in force in so far as they are not modified by the present resolution."

*Decision 1982/118 of 3 May 1982 on the "Provisional agenda for 1983 of the Sessional Working Group (of Governmental Experts) on the Implementation of the International Covenant on Economic, Social and Cultural Rights":*

"At its 20th plenary meeting, on 3 May 1982, the Council approved the provisional agenda for 1983 of the Sessional Working Group (of Governmental Experts) on the Implementation of the International Covenant on Economic, Social and Cultural Rights set out below:

"PROVISIONAL AGENDA FOR 1983 OF THE SESSIONAL WORKING GROUP (OF GOVERN-MENTAL EXPERTS) ON THE IMPLEMENTATION OF THE INTERNATIONAL COVENANT ON ECONOMIC, SOCIAL AND CULTURAL RIGHTS

"1.  Consideration of reports submitted in accordance with Council resolution 1988 (LX) by States parties to the Covenant concerning rights covered by articles 6 to 9.

*Documentation*

Syrian Arab Republic (E/1978/8/Add.25 and 31)
Any other reports received by the Secretary-General.

"2.  Consideration of reports submitted in accordance with Council resolution 1988 (LX) by States parties to the Covenant concerning rights covered by articles 10 to 12.

*Documentation*

Reports received by Secretary-General.

"3.  Consideration of reports submitted in accordance with Council resolution 1988 (LX) by States parties to the Covenant concerning rights covered by articles 13 to 15.

*Documentation*

Guyana (E/1982/3/Add.5)
Libyan Arab Jamahiriya (E/1982/3/Add.6)
German Democratic Republic (E/1982/3/Add.15 and Corr.1)
Any other reports received by the Secretary-General.

"4.  Consideration of the report of the Sessional Working Group (of Governmental Experts) on the Implementation of the International Covenant on Economic, Social and Cultural Rights."

*Decision 1982/119 of 3 May 1982 on the "Bureau for 1983 of the Sessional Working Group (of Governmental Experts) on the Implementation of the International Covenant on Economic, Social and Cultural Rights":*

"At its 20th plenary meeting, on 3 May 1982, the Council decided that the Bureau for 1983 of the Sessional Working Group (of Governmental Experts) on the Implementation of the International Covenant on Economic, Social and Cultural Rights should be constituted as follows:

"*Chairman*: Asian States;

"*Vice-Chairmen*: African States, Eastern European States, Latin American States;

"*Rapporteur*: Western European and other States."

### 3. GENERAL ASSEMBLY

At its thirty-seventh session in 1982, the General Assembly adopted the following resolutions relating to the International Convention on the Elimination of All Forms of Racial Discrimination; the International Convention on the Suppression and Punishment of the Crime of *Apartheid*; and the International Covenants on Human Rights:

*Resolution 37/44 of 3 December 1982 on the "Report of the Committee on the Elimination of Racial Discrimination: General Recommendation VI":*

"*The General Assembly,*

"*Taking note* of decision 1 (XXV) of 15 March 1982 of the Committee on the Elimination of Racial Discrimination, entitled "General Recommendation VI",

"*Acknowledging* the burden which reporting obligations under international instruments places upon States parties, especially those with limited technical and administrative resources,

"*Convinced*, none the less, that the value of international conventions relies upon the full and conscientious implementation of the obligations undertaken upon ratification or accession,

"*Noting with concern* that many periodic reports due under article 9 of the International Convention on the Elimination of All Forms of Racial Discrimination are outstanding and that in some cases initial reports are several years overdue,

"1.  *Appeals* to all States parties to the International Convention on the Elimination of All Forms of Racial Discrimination to fulfil their obligations under article 9 of the Convention and to submit their reports within the appropriate time;

"2.  *Requests* the Secretary-General to invite the views and observations of States parties to the Convention on the causes of the situation described in General Recommendation VI of the Committee on the Elimination of Racial Discrimination and to submit an analysis of the replies received in a report to the General Assembly at its thirty-eighth session, together with such suggestions as he might wish to make with a view to improving the situation;

"3.  *Also requests* the Secretary-General, in preparing his report, to consider the situation described in General Recommendation VI of the Committee in the overall framework of reporting obligations that Member States have under the various human rights instruments in order to be able to take into account similar and related problems which may have arisen in compliance with such obligations;

"4.  *Further requests* the Secretary-General to submit his report, together with the records of the Secretary-General's consideration thereof, to the ninth meeting of the States parties to the Convention, to be held in 1984."

*Resolution 37/45 of 3 December 1982 on the "Status of the International Convention on the Elimination of All Forms of Racial Discrimination":*

"*The General Assembly,*

"*Recalling* its resolutions 3057 (XXVIII) of 2 November 1973, 3135 (XXVIII) of 14 December 1973, 3225 (XXIX) of 6 November 1974, 3381 (XXX) of 10 November 1975, 31/79 of 13 December 1976, 32/11 of 7 November 1977, 33/101 of 16 December 1978, 34/26 of 15 November 1979, 35/38 of 25 November 1980 and 36/11 of 28 October 1981,

"*Welcoming* the increase in the number of declarations made under article 14 of the Convention,

"1.  *Takes note* of the report of the Secretary-General on the status of the International Convention on the Elimination of All Forms of Racial Discrimination;

"2.  *Expresses its satisfaction* with the increase in the number of States which have ratified the Convention or acceded thereto;

"3.  *Reaffirms once again its conviction* that ratification of or accession to the Convention on a universal basis and implementation of its provisions are necessary for the realization of the objectives of the Decade for Action to Combat Racism and Racial Discrimination;

"4.  *Requests* States that have not yet become parties to the Convention to ratify it or accede thereto;

"5.  *Calls upon* States parties to the Convention to consider the possibility of making the declaration provided for in article 14 of Convention;

"6.  *Requests* the Secretary-General to continue to submit to the General Assembly annual reports concerning the status of the Convention, in accordance with general Assembly resolution 2106 A (XX) of 21 December 1965."

*Resolution 37/46 of 3 December 1982 on the "Report of the Committee on the Elimination of Racial Discrimination":*

"*The General Assembly,*

"*Recalling* its resolutions 36/12 of 28 October 1981 on the report of the Committee on the Elimination of Racial Discrimination and 37/45 of 3 December 1982 on the Status of the International Convention on the Elimination of All Forms of Racial Discrimination, as well as its other relevant resolutions on the implementation of the Programme for the Decade for Action to Combat Racism and Racial Discrimination,

"*Having considered* the report of the Committee on the Elimination of Racial Discrimination on its twenty-fifth and twenty-sixth sessions, submitted under article 9, paragraph 2, of the International Convention on the Elimination of All Forms of Racial Discrimination,

"*Emphasizing* the importance for the success of the struggle against all practices of racial discrimination, including vestiges and manifestations of racist ideologies wherever they exist, that all Member States be guided in their internal and foreign policy by the basic provisions of the Convention,

"*Mindful* of the obligation of all States parties to comply fully with the provisions of the Convention,

"*Welcoming* the continued co-operation of the Committee on the Elimination of Racial Discrimination with the competent specialized agencies, especially the United Nations Educational, Scientific and Cultural Organization and the International Labour Organisation, and with other United Nations bodies,

"*Noting* the decisions adopted and recommendations made by the Committee at its twenty-fifth and twenty-sixth sessions,

"1.   *Takes note with appreciation* of the report of the Committee on the Elimination of Racial Discrimination on its twenty-fifth and twenty-sixth sessions;

"2.   *Commends* the Committee for its contribution to the elimination of all forms of discrimination based on race, colour, descent or national or ethnic origin, wherever it exists;

"3.   *Strongly condemns* the policy of *apartheid* in South Africa and Namibia as the most abhorrent form of racial discrimination and urges all Member States to adopt effective political, economic and other measures in order to secure the elimination of that policy and to achieve full implementation of the relevant resolutions of the General Assembly, the Security Council and other United Nations bodies;

"4.   *Calls upon* the United Nations bodies concerned to ensure that the Committee is supplied with all relevant information on all the Territories to which General Assembly resolution 1514 (XV) of 14 December 1960 applies and urges the administering Powers to co-operate with these bodies by providing all necessary information in order to enable the Committee to discharge fully its responsibilities under article 15 of the International Convention on the Elimination of All Forms of Racial Discrimination;

"5.   *Commends* the Committee for its continuous endeavours towards the elimination of *apartheid*, racism and racial discrimination in southern Africa and the implementation of United Nations resolutions relating to the liberation and independence of Namibia;

"6.   *Takes note with satisfaction* of the efforts of the Committee aimed at securing the prosperity of national or ethnic minorities and indigenous populations through the implementation of the principles and provisions of the Convention;

"7.   *Expresses grave concern* at the Israeli policy of defiance of the basic principles and objectives of the Convention, as reflected in the report of the

Committee, and calls for the respect and preservation of the national and cultural identity of the Palestinian people;

"8. *Welcomes* the efforts of the Committee aimed at the elimination of all forms of discrimination against migrant workers and their families, the promotion of their rights on a non-discriminatory basis and the achievement of their full equality and of the possibility to preserve their cultural characteristics;

"9. *Commends* the States parties to the Convention on the measures taken to ensure within their jurisdiction the availability of appropriate recourse procedures for the victims of racial discrimination;

"10. *Calls upon* all Member States to adopt effective legislative, socio-economic and other necessary measures in order to ensure the elimination or prevention of discrimination based on race, colour, descent or national or ethnic origin;

"11. *Calls upon* the States parties to the Convention to protect fully, by the adoption of relevant legislative and other measures, the rights of national or ethnic minorities, as well as the rights of indigenous populations;

"12. *Reiterates its invitation* to the States parties to the Convention to furnish the Committee, in accordance with its general guidelines, with information on the implementation of the provisions of the Convention, including information on the demographic composition of their population and on their relations with the racist régime of South Africa;

"13. *Takes note with appreciation* of the Committee's contribution to the work of the Preparatory Sub-Committee for the Second World Conference to Combat Racism and Racial Discrimination and to the regional seminars held in implementation of the Programme for the Decade for Action to Combat Racism and Racial Discrimination;

"14. *Welcomes* the decision of the Committee to contribute to the Second World Conference by preparing a study on the implementation of articles 4 and 7 of the Convention and reiterates its request to the Committee to explore the possibility of also preparing for the Conference a study on the implementation of subparagraph (*e*) of article 5;

"15. *Takes note* of decision 1 (XXVI) of 19 August 1982 of the Committee on the Elimination of Racial Discrimination, in which the Committee requested the Secretary-General, in consultation with the Government of the Philippines, to explore the possibility of arranging for the twenty-eighth session of the Committee to be held at Manila immediately prior to the holding of the Second World Conference to Combat Racism and Racial Discrimination."

**Resolution 37/47 of 3 December 1982 on the "Status of the International Convention on the Suppression and Punishment of the Crime of Apartheid":**

"*The General Assembly,*

"*Recalling* its resolution 3068 (XXVIII) of 30 November 1973, by which it adopted and opened for signature and ratification the International Convention on the Suppression and Punishment of the Crime of *Apartheid*, and its subsequent resolutions on the status of the Convention,

"*Convinced* that the Declaration and the Programme of Action adopted by the World Conference to Combat Racism and Racial Discrimination, as well as the programme of activities to be undertaken during the second half of the Decade for Action to Combat Racism and Racial Discrimination, adopted by the General Assembly in its resolution 34/24 of 15 November 1979, and their full implementation will contribute to the final eradication of *apartheid* and all other forms of racism and racial discrimination,

"*Reaffirming its conviction* that *apartheid* constitutes a total negation of the purposes and principles of the Charter of the United Nations and is a gross violation of human rights and a crime against humanity, seriously threatening international peace and security,

"*Strongly condemning* South Africa's continued policy of *apartheid*, repression and "bantustanization" and its continued illegal occupation of Namibia, thereby perpetuating on Namibian territory its odious policy of *apartheid*, racial discrimination and fragmentation,

"*Gravely concerned* over the widespread torture and ill-treatment of political prisoners and trade unionists detained by the racist régime of South Africa, leading to the death in detention of many prisoners, including Neil Aggett, Tshifiwa Muofhe and Ernest Moabi Dipale,

"*Deeply concerned* about South Africa's repeated acts of aggression against sovereign African States, which constitute a manifest breach of international peace and security,

"*Condemning* the continued collaboration of certain States and transnational corporations with the racist régime of South Africa in the political, economic, military and other fields as an encouragement to the intensification of its odious policy of *apartheid*,

"*Underlining* that the strengthening of the existing mandatory arms embargo and the application of comprehensive mandatory economic sanctions under Chapter VII of the Charter of the United Nations are vital in order to compel the racist régime of South Africa to abandon its policy of *apartheid*,

"*Recalling* its resolutions 36/172 A to P of 17 December 1981, in particular resolution 36/172 B in which it proclaimed the year 1982 International Year of Mobilization for Sanctions against South Africa,

"*Stressing* the need to disseminate on a wider basis more information on the crimes committed by the racist régime of South Africa, taking into consideration the recommendation contained in the documents adopted by the International Seminar on Publicity and the Role of Mass Media in the International Mobilization against *Apartheid*, held at Berlin, German Democratic Republic, from 31 August to 2 September 1981,

"*Firmly convinced* that the legitimate struggle of the oppressed peoples in southern Africa against *apartheid*, racism and colonialism and for the effective implementation of their inalienable right to self-determination and independence demands more than ever all necessary support by the international community and, in particular, further action by the Security Council,

"*Commending* the work of the Preparatory Sub-Committee for the Second World Conference to Combat Racism and Racial Discrimination and the recommendations contained in its report to the Economic and Social Council,

"*Underlining* that ratification of and accession to the International Convention on the Suppression and Punishment of the Crime of *Apartheid* on a universal basis and the implementation of its provisions without any delay are necessary for its effectiveness and would be a useful contribution towards achieving the goals of the Decade for Action to Combat Racism and Racial Discrimination,

"1.    *Takes note* of the report of the Secretary-General on the status of the International Convention on the Suppression and Punishment of the Crime of *Apartheid*;

"2.    *Commends* those States parties to the Convention that have submitted their reports under article VII thereof, in particular those that have presented their second reports and appeals to those States parties that have not yet done so to submit their reports as soon as possible;

"3.    *Appeals once again* to those States that have not yet done so to ratify or to accede to the Convention without further delay;

"4.    *Appreciates* the constructive role played by the Group of Three of the Commission on Human Rights, established in accordance with article IX of the International Convention on the Suppression and Punishment of the Crime of *Apartheid*, in analysing the periodic reports of States and in publicizing the experience gained in the international struggle against the crime of *apartheid*;

"5.    *Requests* States parties to the Convention to take fully into account the guidelines prepared by the Group of Three;

"6.    *Calls upon* all States parties to the Convention to implement fully article IV thereof by adopting legislative, judicial and administrative measures to prosecute, bring to trial and punish, in accordance with their jurisdiction, persons responsible for, or accused of, the acts enumerated in article II of the Convention;

"7.    *Again calls upon* all States parties to the Convention and the competent United Nations organs to consider the conclusions and recommendations of the Group of Three contained in its reports and to submit their views and comments to the Secretary-General;

"8.    *Requests* the Commission on Human Rights to continue to undertake the functions set out in article X of the Convention and invites the Commission to intensify, in co-operation with the Special Committee against *Apartheid*, its efforts to compile periodically the progressive list of individuals, organizations, institutions and representatives of States deemed responsible for crimes enumerated in article II of the Convention, as well as of those against whom or which legal proceedings have been undertaken;

"9.    *Requests* the Commission on Human Rights to take into account General Assembly resolutions 33/23 of 29 November 1978 and 35/32 of 14 November 1980, as well as relevant documents of the Commission and its subsidiary organs reaffirming, *inter alia*, that States giving assistance to the racist régime of South Africa become accomplices in the inhuman practices of racial discrimination and *apartheid*;

"10.  *Calls upon* all States parties to the Convention and competent United Nations organs to continue to provide the Commission on Human Rights, through the Secretary-General, with information relevant to the periodic compilation of the above-mentioned list, as well as with information concerning the obstacles that prevent the effective suppression and punishment of the crime of *apartheid*;

"11.  *Requests* the Secretary-General to distribute the above-mentioned list among all States parties to the Convention and all Member States and to bring such facts to the attention of the public by all means of mass communications;

"12.  *Invites* the Special Committee against *Apartheid* and the Centre against *Apartheid* of the Secretariat to publicize the above-mentioned list and related particulars as widely as possible;

"13.  *Appeals* to all States, United Nations organs, specialized agencies and international and national non-governmental organizations to step up their activities in enhancing public awareness through denouncing the crimes committed by the racist régime of South Africa;

"14.  *Requests* the Secretary-General to intensify his efforts, through appropriate channels, to disseminate information on the Convention and its implementation with a view to further promoting ratification of or accession to the Convention;

"15.  *Calls upon* all States to participate actively in the Second World Conference to Combat Racism and Racial Discrimination, to be held in 1983, and to contribute to achieving effective results at that Conference;

"16.  *Requests* the Secretary-General to include in his next annual report under General Assembly resolution 3380 (XXX) of 10 November 1975 a special section concerning the implementation of the International Convention on the Suppression and Punishment of the Crime of *Apartheid*."

*Resolution 37/191 of 18 December 1982 on the "International Covenants on Human Rights":*

"*The General Assembly,*

"*Recalling* its resolutions 33/51 of 14 December 1978, 34/45 of 23 November 1979, 35/132 of 11 December 1980 and 36/58 of 25 November 1981,

"*Having noted* the report of the Secretary-General on the status of the International Covenant on Economic, Social and Cultural Rights, the International Covenant on Civil and Political Rights and the Optional Protocol to the International Covenant on Civil and Political Rights,

"*Noting with appreciation* that, following its appeal, more Member States have acceded to the International Covenants on Human Rights,

"*Bearing in mind* the important responsibilities of the Economic and Social Council in relation to the International Covenants on Human Rights,

"*Recognizing* the important role of the Human Rights Committee in the implementation of the International Covenant on Civil and Political Rights and the Optional Protocol thereto,

"*Taking into account* the useful work of the Sessional Working Group of Governmental Experts on the Implementation of the International Covenant on Economic, Social and Cultural Rights,

"*Taking note* of Economic and Social Council resolution 1980/30 of 2 May 1980 on the development of public information activities in the field of human rights and the report of the Secretary-General on publicity for the work of the Human Rights Committee,

"1.   *Notes with appreciation* the report of the Human Rights Committee on its fourteenth, fifteenth and sixteenth sessions, and expresses satisfaction at the serious and constructive manner in which the Committee is continuing to perform its functions;

"2.   *Expresses its appreciation* to those States parties to the International Covenant on Civil and Political Rights that have extended their co-operation to the Human Rights Committee in submitting their reports under article 40 of the Covenant and urges States parties that have not yet done so to submit their reports to the Committee as speedily as possible;

"3.   *Urges* those States parties to the International Covenant on Civil and Political Rights that have been requested by the Human Rights Committee to provide additional information to comply with that request;

"4.   *Commends* those States parties to the International Covenant on Economic, Social and Cultural Rights that have submitted their reports under article 16 of the Covenant and urges States that have not yet done so to submit their reports as soon as possible;

"5.   *Takes note* of Economic and Social Council resolution 1982/33 of 6 May 1982 concerning the review of the composition, organization and administrative arrangements of the Sessional Working Group of Governmental Experts on the Implementation of the International Covenant on Economic, Social and Cultural Rights;

"6.   *Emphasizes* the importance of States parties sending experts to present their reports under the International Covenants on Human Rights;

"7.   *Again invites* all States that have not yet done so to become parties to the International Covenant on Economic, Social and Cultural Rights and the International Covenant on Civil and Political Rights as well as to consider acceding to the Optional Protocol to the International Covenant on Civil and Political Rights;

"8.   *Invites* the States parties to the International Covenant on Civil and Political Rights to consider making the declaration provided for in article 41 of the Covenant;

"9.   *Appreciates* that the Human Rights Committee continues to strive for uniform standards in the implementation of the provisions of the International Covenant on Civil and Political Rights and of the Optional Protocol thereto;

"10.   *Emphasizes* the importance of strictest compliance by States parties with their obligations under the International Covenant on Civil and Political Rights and, where applicable, the Optional Protocol thereto;

"11.   *Requests* the Secretary-General to continue to keep the Human Rights Committee informed of the activities of the Commission on Human Rights, the Sub-Commission on Prevention of Discrimination and Protection of Minorities, the Committee on the Elimination of Racial Discrimination and the Committee on the Elimination of Discrimination against Women and also to transmit the annual reports of the Human Rights Committee to those bodies;

"12.   *Requests* the Secretary-General to submit to the General Assembly at its thirty-eighth session a report on the status of the International Covenant on Economic, Social and Cultural Rights, the International Covenant on Civil and Political Rights and the Optional Protocol to the International Covenant on Civil and Political Rights;

"13.   *Takes note with appreciation* of the request of the Human Rights Committee that its official records be made available annually in bound volumes—one volume to contain the summary records of public meetings of the Committee and a second volume to contain other public documents of the Committee, including reports of States parties under article 40 of the Covenant—and requests the Secretary-General to consider making, within existing resources, the arrangements which he deems most suitable and economical for publishing those annual volumes;

"14.   *Requests* the Secretary-General to continue to take all possible steps to ensure that the Centre for Human Rights of the Secretariat is able effectively to assist the Human Rights Committee and the Economic and Social Council in the implementation of their respective functions under the International Covenants on Human Rights, taking into account General Assembly resolutions 3534 (XXX) of 17 December 1975 and 31/93 of 14 December 1976."

# PART III

# INTERNATIONAL DEVELOPMENTS

# Section A.  United Nations organs

## Introduction

The United Nations organs whose work in the field of human rights is summarized here are: the General Assembly, the Economic and Social Council, the Commission on Human Rights and its Sub-Commission on Prevention of Discrimination and Protection of Minorities.

During the period under review, human rights matters were dealt with at various sessions of those organs as follows:

General Assembly, thirty-seventh session (21 September-21December 1982 and 10-13 May 1983);

Economic and Social Council, first regular session of 1982 (13 April-7 May 1982);

Commission on Human Rights, thirty-eighth session (1 February-12 March 1982);

Sub-Commission on Prevention of Discrimination and Protection of Minorities, thirty-fifth session (16 August-10 September 1982).


## A. Elimination of racial discrimination: Decade for Action to Combat Racism and Racial Discrimination

At its thirty-eighth session in February-March 1982, the Commission on Human Rights considered the question of the implementation of the Programme for the Decade. By its resolution 1982/11 of 25 February,[1] it recommended to the Preparatory Sub-Committee for the Second World Conference to Combat Racism and Racial Discrimination that the Second World Conference should pay particular attention of the findings of the seminars, round-tables and studies conducted during the second half of the Decade; it urged the appointment of a Secretary-General for the Conference, and decided that the Commission should be represented at the Conference by the Chairman of its thirty-ninth session.

During its first regular session in 1982, the Economic and Social Council, by its resolution 1982/31 of 5 May 1982, recommended to the General Assembly the adoption of a draft resolution concerning the implementation of the Programme for the Decade; by its resolution 1982/32 adopted on the same day, the Council approved the draft provisional agenda and the draft provisional rules of procedure of the Second World Conference.

---

[1] *Official Records of the Economic and Social Council, 1982, Supplement No. 2* (E/1982/12), chap. XXVI A.

In another resolution adopted on 4 May 1982, the Council expressed its expectation that non-governmental organizations in consultative status with the Economic and Social Council will take due account in their activities of relevant resolutions of the Council and the General Assembly condemning the policy of *apartheid* as practised by the Government of South Africa (Council resolution 1982/16).

By its decision 1982/120 of 4 May 1982, the Council requested the Secretary-General to take the necessary steps to organize the seminar for the region of the Economic and Social Commission for Asia and the Pacific under the Programme for the Decade at the headquarters of the Economic and Social Commission for Asia and the Pacific from 2 to 13 August 1982.

Consequently, the Secretary-General organized in Bangkok, Thailand, from 2 to 13 August 1982, a "Seminar on recourse procedures and other forms of protection available to victims of racial discrimination and activities to be undertaken at the national and regional levels, with specific reference to Asia and the Pacific". In its recommendations, the Seminar suggested various measures in order to achieve the goal of contributing to the realization of the objectives of the International Convention on the Elimination of All Forms of Racial Discrimination; it also recommended that the Second World Conference should consider all forms of social discrimination and give urgent consideration to the protection of the land rights of indigenous populations, and that more concentrated endeavours should be made to rid the world of the scourge of discrimination especially from areas in which it was so conspicuously manifest in the form of *apartheid* and genocide[2].

The General Assembly also considered the question of the implementation of the Programme for the Decade for Action to Combat Racism and Racial Discrimination at its thirty-seventh session. By its resolution 37/40 of 3 December 1982, the Assembly, *inter alia*, invited once again all Member States, United Nations organs, specialized agencies and other organizations concerned to strengthen and enlarge the scope of their activities in support of the objectives of the Programme for the Decade; it decided to consider the implementation of the Programme for the Decade as a matter of high priority at its thirty-eighth session.

By its resolution 37/41 adopted on the same day, the Assembly endorsed Economic and Social Council resolution 1982/32 which contained recommendations regarding the organization of the Second World Conference to Combat Racism and Racial Discrimination, and decided to convene the Conference at Geneva from 1 to 12 August 1983; it requested the Secretary-General, *inter alia*, to ensure the widest possible participation in the Conference and urged all States to co-operate with the Secretary-General of the Conference in the preparatory work and to report to the Assembly at its thirty-eighth session on the work of the Conference.

## B. Measures against ideologies and practices based on racial intolerance, hatred and terror

The question of measures to be taken against all totalitarian or other ideologies and practices, including Nazi, Fascist and neo-Fascist, based on racial or ethnic ex-

---

[2] ST/HR/SER.A/13.

clusiveness or intolerance, hatred, terror, systematic denial of human rights and fundamental freedoms, or which have such consequences, was considered by the Commission on Human Rights at its thirty-eighth session. By its decision 1982/105 of 11 March 1982,[3] the Commission decided to defer further discusison and action on the item to its thirty-ninth session.

For its consideration of the item, the Economic and Social Council at its first regular session of 1982 had before it a report prepared by the Secretary-General[4] in the light of the discussion in the Commission and on the basis of comments provided by States and international organizations. By its decision 1982/146 of 7 May 1982, the Council took note of the report of the Secretary-General and decided to transmit it to the General Assembly.

The report of the Secretary-General[5] was transmitted to the Assembly at its thirty-seventh session. By its resolution 37/179 of 17 December 1982 the Assembly, *inter alia*, invited Member States to adopt, as a matter of high priority, measures declaring punishable by law any dissemination of ideas based on racial superiority or hatred and of war propaganda, including Nazi, Fascist and neo-Fascist ideologies; appealed to States which have not yet done so to ratify or to accede to the relevant international instruments; called once again upon all States to provide the Secretary-General with their comments on this question; it also requested the Secretary-General to submit a report, through the Economic and Social Council, to the General Assembly at its thirty-eighth session in the light of the discussion to take place in the Commission on Human Rights and on the basis of comments provided by States and international organizations.

## C.  Elimination of all forms of religious intolerance

By its resolution 1982/41 of 11 May 1982,[6] the Commission on Human Rights requested the Secretary-General to disseminate widely, as a matter of priority and in as many languages as possible, the United Nations Declaration on the Elimination of All Forms of Intolerance and of Discrimination Based on Religion or Belief, proclaimed in General Assembly resolution 36/55 of 25 November 1981; it further requested the Secretary-General to issue, as soon as possible, a pamphlet containing the text of the Declaration in the six official languages of the United Nations, and to give the widest dissemination to this pamphlet.

The requests contained in this resolution were endorsed by the Economic and Social Council in its decision 1982/138 of 7 May 1982.

The Sub-Commission on Prevention of Discrimination and Protection of Minorities, in its resolution 1982/28 adopted on 10 September 1982,[7] requested the Secretary-General to submit all relevant and available information regarding the current dimensions of the problem of discrimination on grounds of religion or belief to

---

[3] E/1982/12, chap. XXVI B.

[4] A/37/188.

[5] A/37/188 and Corr.1 and Add.1.

[6] E/1982/12, chap. XXVI A.

[7] E/CN.4/1983/4, E/CN.4/Sub.2/1982/43, chap. XXI A.

its next session, and decided to consider at its thirty-sixth session in 1983 the question of the updating of the study entitled *Discrimination in the Matter of Religious Rights and Practices.*[8]

By its resolution 37/187 of 18 December 1982, the General Assembly endorsed Council decision 1982/138 and invited all Members to take necessary measures to ensure wide publicity for the Declaration; it requested the Secretary-General to bring the Declaration to the attention of appropriate specialized agencies and other appropriate United Nations bodies, for the consideration of measures to implement the Declaration, and to report to the Commission at its thirty-ninth session; it requested the Commission to report to it at its thirty-eighth session, through the Council, on measures to implement the Declaration.

## D.  Human rights of national, ethnic, religious and linguistic minorities

During the thirty-eighth session of the Commission on Human Rights, the informal working group established by the Commission continued its consideration of the revised consolidated text of the draft declaration on the rights of persons belonging to national, ethnic, religious and linguistic minorities,[9] and provisionally adopted the preamble of the draft declaration.

By its resolution 1982/38 of 11 March 1982,[10] the Commission decided to establish at its next session an open-ended working group to continue consideration of the revised draft declaration.

## E.  Studies relating to prevention of discrimination and protection of minorities

### 1.  STATUS OF THE INDIVIDUAL AND CONTEMPORARY INTERNATIONAL LAW

By its resolution 1982/35 adopted on 10 September 1982,[11] the Sub-Commission on Prevention of Discrimination and Protection of Minorities expressed its deep appreciation to the Special Rapporteur entrusted with the mandate of undertaking a study entitled *The Status of the Individual and Contemporary International Law* for the work she had accomplished so far in connection with his study; it also recommended to the Commission on Human Rights for adoption its draft resolution X[12] by which the Commission would recommend to the Economic and Social Council to adopt a resolution in which the Council would request the Special Rapporteur to continue her work with a view to submitting, if possible, her final report to the Sub-Commission at its thirty-sixth session.

---

[8] United Nations publication, Sales No. E.60.XVI.2.

[9] E/CN.4/Sub.2/L.734.

[10] E/1982/12, chap. XXVI A.

[11] E/CN.4/1983/4, E/CN.4/Sub.2/1982/43, chap. XXI A.

[12] E/CN.4/Sub.2/1982/43, chap. I A.

## 2. DISCRIMINATION IN THE ADMINISTRATION OF CRIMINAL JUSTICE

At its thirty-fifth session, the Sub-Commission on Prevention of Discrimination and Protection of Minorities had before it the final report of its Special Rapporteur on the study on discriminatory treatment of members of racial, ethnic, religious or linguistic groups at the various levels in the administration of criminal justice, such as police, military, administrative and judicial investigations, arrest, detention, trial and execution of sentences, including the ideologies or beliefs which contribute or lead to racism in the administration of justice[13]. By its resolution 1982/4 of 7 September 1982[14] the Sub-Commission expressed its thanks to the Special Rapporteur for his excellent work and decided to transmit the report to the Commission on Human Rights.

## 3. PREVENTION AND PUNISHMENT OF THE CRIME OF GENOCIDE

By its resolution 1982/2 of 7 September 1982,[15] the Sub-Commission recommended to the Commission for adoption draft resolution I[16] upon which the Commission would recommend to the Economic and Social Council to request the Sub-Commission to appoint one of its members as Special Rapporteur with the mandate to revise, as a whole, and update the *Study on the Question of the Prevention and Punishment of the Crime of Genocide*, and to request further the Sub-Commission to consider and submit the revised and updated study to the Commission on Human Rights at its fortieth session.

## 4. RIGHT OF EVERYONE TO LEAVE ANY COUNTRY

At its thirty-fifth session the Sub-Commission on Prevention of Discrimination and Protection of Minorities adopted, on 8 September 1982, resolution 1982/23,[17] in which it recalled the *Study of Discrimination in Respect of the Right of Everyone to Leave Any Country, Including His Own, and to Return to His Country,*[18] submitted to the Sub-Commission at its fifteenth session by the Special Rapporteur on that question, and the draft principles respecting this right, adopted by the Sub-Commission at the same session. By this resolution, the Sub-Commission requested the Special Rapporteur to prepare an analysis of current trends and developments in respect of the right of everyone to leave any country, including his own, and to return to his country, without discrimination or hindrance; it requested the Rapporteur to present to it at its thirty-seventh session recommendations for promoting and encouraging respect for and observance of this right.

---

[13] E/CN.4/Sub.2/1982/7.

[14] E/CN.4/1983/4, E/CN.4/Sub.2/1982/43, chap. XXI A.

[15] *Ibid.*

[16] E/CN.4/Sub.2/1982/43, chap. I A.

[17] E/CN.4/1983/4, E/CN.4/Sub.2/1982/43, chap. XXI A.

[18] United Nations publication, Sales No. E.64.XIV.2.

##### 5. Draft principles on the right and responsibility of individuals

In its resolution 1982/30 of 11 March 1982,[19] the Commission on Human Rights requested the Sub-Commission to prepare, for submission to the Commission at its fortieth session, a report containing principles on the right and responsibility of individuals, groups and organs of society to promote and protect human rights and fundamental freedoms and decided to undertake, at its fortieth session, on the basis of the Sub-Commission's report, work on a draft declaration on the right and responsibility of individuals, groups and organs of society to promote and protect human rights and fundamental freedoms.

At its thirty-fifth session the Sub-Commission by its resolution 1982/24 of 8 September 1982[20] requested one of its members to prepare draft principles on the right and responsibility of individuals, groups and organs of society to promote and protect universally-recognized human rights and fundamental freedoms, and to submit them to the Sub-Commission at its next session.

## F. Question of the violation of human rights

##### 1. Study of situations which reveal a consistent pattern of gross violations of human rights

At its thirty-eighth session the Commission on Human Rights adopted, in closed meetings, a number of decisions within the framework of Council resolution 1503 (XLVIII) entitled "Procedures for dealing with communications relating to violations of human rights and fundamental freedoms".

Prior to that session, a Working Group of five Commission members had met for one week to examine documents referred to the Commission by the Sub-Commission and submitted a confidential report on its work to the Commission.

By its decision 1982/103 of 5 March 1982,[21] further endorsed by Economic and Social Council decision 1982/140 of 7 May 1982, the Commission decided to set up a Working Group to meet one week prior to its next session to examine situations referred to it by the Sub-Commission, as well as situations which the Commission had decided to keep under review.

The Working Group on Communications established by the Sub-Commission held its eleventh session from 2 to 13 August 1982 and submitted a confidential report to the thirty-fifth session of the Sub-Commission.

By its resolution 1982/14 of 7 September 1982,[22] the Sub-Commission, *inter alia*, requested the Commission on Human Rights to adopt draft resolution VI,[23] by which the Commission would recommend to the Economic and Social

---

[19] E/1982/12, chap. XXVI A.

[20] E/CN.4/1983/4, E/CN.4/Sub.2/1982/43, chap. XXI A.

[21] E/1982/12, chap. XXVI B.

[22] E/CN.4/1983/4, E/CN.4/Sub.2/1982/43, chap. XXI A.

[23] E/CN.4/Sub.2/1982/43, chap. I A.

Council to authorize the Sub-Commission, in consultation with the Secretary-General and with the consent of the governmental authorities concerned, to make arrangements for one or more members of the Sub-Commission, following a decision by the Commission, to visit, with the approval of the Government concerned, any country as regards which the Commission has received reliably attested allegations of a gross and consistent pattern of violations of human rights and fundamental freedoms with a view to examining such situations at first hand and reporting thereon to the Sub-Commission at its next session.

In another resolution concerning *the effects of gross violations of human rights on international peace and security* (resolution 1982/11 of 7 September 1982)[24] the Sub-Commission recommended to the Commission for adoption draft resolution IV.[25] By that draft, the Commission would have recommended to the Economic and Social Council to decide to draw the attention of the Security Council and the General Assembly to the fact that in many instances such mass and flagrant violations of human rights resulted in threats to, or breaches of, international peace and security, and requested the Security Council to consider how such violations can be dealt with as effectively as possible. The Council would have requested the Assembly to invite the International Law Commission to take mass and flagrant violations of human rights and the comments on such violations made by the members of the Sub-Commission into account when elaborating the draft code of offences against the peace and security of mankind. It would also have requested the Sub-Commission to continue its consideration of the item entitled "The Effects of Gross Violations of Human Rights on International Peace and Security" with a view to preparing principles and, in particular, establishing criteria to govern situations which could be considered as constituting gross and flagrant violations of human rights, the effect of which had an impact on international peace and security.

By its resolution 37/200 of 18 December 1982 the General Assembly, *inter alia*, noted that mass and flagrant violations of human rights in one State might threaten the peace and development of neighbouring States, of a region or of the international community as a whole.

2. VIOLATIONS OF HUMAN RIGHTS IN SOUTHERN AFRICA: AD HOC WORKING GROUP OF EXPERTS OF THE COMMISSION ON HUMAN RIGHTS WITH RESPECT TO SOUTHERN AFRICA

At its thirty-eighth session in 1982 the Commission on Human Rights examined three reports submitted to it by the *Ad Hoc* Working Group of Experts on southern Africa; a progress report[26] dealing with new developments concerning policies and practices which violate human rights in South Africa and Namibia; a study on the effects of the policy of *apartheid* on black women and children in South Africa;[27] and a report on infringements of trade union rights in South Africa.[28]

---

[24] *Ibid.*, chap. XXI A.

[25] *Ibid.*, chap. I A.

[26] E/CN.4/1485.

[27] E/CN.4/1497.

[28] E/CN.4/1486.

By its resolution 1982/8 of 25 February,[29] the Commission requested the Group of Experts to continue to study the policies and practices which violate human rights in South Africa and Namibia and bring to the attention of the Chairman of the Commission particularly serious violations; it also requested the Secretary-General further to prepare a summary of the findings of the *Ad Hoc* Working Group of Experts contained in the progress report and to give these findings and the Commission's condemnation of them wide publicity.

Concerning trade union rights the Commission, in the above-mentioned resolution, expressed its profound indignation at the fact that international standards concerning trade union rights for black workers were violated in South Africa.

By its resolution 1982/9[30] adopted on the same day, the Commission requested the Group to continue to study, as a matter of priority, the policies and practices which violate human rights in Namibia; it also requested that South Africa allow the Group to make an on-the-spot investigation of living conditions in the prisons of South Africa and Namibia and of the treatment of prisoners in those countries.

By resolution 1982/16 also adopted on 25 February,[31] the Commission reaffirmed the inalienable right of the people of Namibia to independence, and declared that the illegal occupation of that territory by South Africa constitutes a threat to international peace and security; it also reaffirmed the legitimacy of the struggle of the oppressed people of South Africa by all available means, condemned the brutal repression in South Africa, the continued policy of "bantustanization" and all collaboration with the Government of South Africa; it also demanded the immediate release of all people detained and the full respect for their fundamental rights.

The Economic and Social Council, by its resolution 1982/40 of 7 May 1982, took note of the report of the Working Group of Experts on infringements of trade union rights in South Africa,[32] demanded the immediate recognition of the impeded exercise of freedom of association and trade union rights by the entire population of South Africa without discrimination of any kind, called once again for the immediate release of all imprisoned trade unionists, demanded the lifting of the ban on fund-raising drives by the Federation of South African Trade Unions and reiterated its demand for the cessation of all government and police interference in labour disputes. It requested the Group to continue to study the situation and, in discharge of its mandate, to consult with the International Labour Organisation and the Special Committee against *Apartheid*, as well as with international and African trade union confederations.

The General Assembly also considered the question of human rights violations in southern Africa at its thirty-seventh session. In its resolution 37/43 of 3 December 1982, it condemned the increasingly widespread massacres of innocent people including women and children. It also demanded the immediate release of children detained in Namibian and South African prisons.

---

[29] E/1982/12, chap. XXVI A.

[30] *Ibid.*

[31] *Ibid.*

[32] E/CN.4/1486.

The General Assembly also considered at that session the report of the Special Committee against *Apartheid*,[33] and adopted, on 9 December 1982, resolution 37/69 A condemning the *apartheid* régime for its brutal repression and indiscriminate torture and killings of workers, schoolchildren and other opponents of *apartheid*, and the imposition of death sentences on freedom fighters.

### 3. QUESTION OF THE VIOLATION OF HUMAN RIGHTS IN THE OCCUPIED ARAB TERRITORIES, INCLUDING PALESTINE

The Commission on Human Rights at its thirty-eighth session adopted a number of resolutions concerning the violation of human rights in the occupied Arab territories. By its resolution 1982/1 A of 11 February 1982[34] the Commission, *inter alia*, called on Israel to take immediate steps for the return of displaced Arab inhabitants to their homes and property in the occupied territories and to implement a number of pertinent Security Council resolutions; to release all Arabs detained or imprisoned as a result of their struggle for self-determination. It reiterated its call to all States, international organizations and specialized agencies not to recognize any changes carried out by Israel in the occupied territories and to desist from extending any aid which Israel might use in pursuing the policies of annexation and colonization of these territories. It requested the Secretary-General to make available to it at its thirty-ninth session all relevant information concerning detainees. The Commission, in this resolution, decided that a seminar on violations of human rights in the Palestinian and other Arab territories occupied by Israel be held at the United Nations Office at Geneva.

By resolution 1982/1 B of the same date,[35] the Commission reaffirmed that the Geneva Convention relative to the Protection of Civilian Persons in Time of War was applicable to all the occupied Arab territories; condemned Israel's failure to acknowledge the applicability of that Convention to the occupied territories; called upon Israel to respect the obligations arising from the Charter and other instruments and rules of international law, in particular the provisions of the Geneva Convention; it urged once more all States parties to that Convention to exert all efforts in order to ensure respect for the provisions thereof in the occupied territories; and requested the Secretary-General to bring the resolution to the attention of all Governments, United Nations organs and other concerned international, regional and nongovernmental bodies.

By its resolution 1982/2 also adopted on 11 February 1982,[36] the Commission condemned Israel's decision annexing, through the imposition of its laws, jurisdiction and administration, the Golan Syrian territory and declared that decision null and void. It determined that Israel's persistent defiance of the United Nations resolutions and authority and the systematic violations of human rights in the occupied Arab territories constituted a continuing threat to international peace and security,

---

[33] A/37/22.

[34] E/1982/12, chap. XXVI A.

[35] *Ibid.*

[36] *Ibid.*

and called upon all Member States to apply against Israel the measures referred to in several paragraphs of General Assembly resolution ES-9/1 of 5 February 1982.

By resolution 1982/3 of the same date,[37] the Commission, *inter alia*, reaffirmed the inalienable right of the Palestinian people to self-determination; expressed its strong opposition to all partial agreements and separate treaties; it strongly rejected the continuation of the negotiations on the question of "autonomy" within the framework of the "Camp David accords" and declared that these accords have no validity.

At its first regular session of 1982 the Economic and Social Council endorsed by its decision 1982/127, draft decision 1[38] of the Commission on Human Rights upon which a seminar on violations of human rights in the Palestinian and other Arab territories occupied by Israel should be held in Geneva.

Accordingly, the seminar was held from 29 November to 3 December 1982 at Geneva. The report of the seminar[39] contained a number of recommendations to the Commission on Human Rights, among which mention can be made of the following:
A conference of States Parties to the Geneva Conventions should be convened in order to study the ways and means of implementing the Geneva Convention of 1949 in the Palestinian and other Arab territories occupied by Israel.

States Parties to the Fourth Geneva Convention of 1949 should insist with Israel that it should strictly comply with the provisions of the Convention.

The international community should nominate a Protecting Power in order to scrutinize the situation in the occupied territories and to safeguard the interests and rights of the Palestinian people in these territories.

Impartial and objective investigations in the occupied territories should be made according to the procedure provided in article 149 of the Fourth Geneva Convention of 1949.

Member States should consider imposing sanctions upon Israel analogous to those imposed on South Africa.

An appeal should be made to the mass media for their co-operation and help to the Palestinians in achieving their goals.

The Sub-Commission on Prevention of Discrimination and Protection of Minorities also examined the question at its thirty-fifth session. By its resolution 1982/18 of 8 September 1982,[40] the Sub-Commission, *inter alia*, called on Israel to withdraw from all the occupied Palestinian and Syrian territories and urged the implementation of all relevant United Nations resolutions on the subject. It recommended the Commission on Human Rights and the Council urgently to take measures for the implementation of that resolution.

At its thirty-seventh session, the General Assembly had before it in connection with this question, the report of the Special Committee to Investigate Israeli Practices Affecting the Human Rights of the Population of the Occupied Territories.[41] In

---

[37] *Ibid.*

[38] E/1982/12, chap. I B.

[39] ST/HR/SER.A/14.

[40] E/CN.4/1983/4, E/CN.4/Sub.2/1982/43, chap. XXI A.

[41] A/37/485.

its resolution 37/88 A-G of 10 December 1982 the Assembly, *inter alia*, reaffirmed the applicability of the Geneva Convention relative to the Protection of Civilian Persons in Time of War to the Arab territories occupied by Israel since 1967 (resolution 37/88 A); determined that measures and actions taken by Israel in these territories with a view to changing their legal status have no legal validity (resolution 37/88 B); commended the Special Committee for its thoroughness and impartiality; declared that Israel's grave breaches of the 1949 Geneva Convention relative to the Protection of Civilian Persons in Time of War were war crimes and an affront to humanity; demanded that Israel desist forthwith from policies and practices affecting the human rights of the population of the occupied territories; requested the Special Committee to continue investigating Israeli policies and practices in these territories (resolution 37/88 C); demanded once more that the Government of Israel facilitate the immediate return of three expelled Palestinian leaders (resolution 37/88 D); strongly condemned Israel's persistence in changing the physical character, demographic composition, institutional structure and legal status of the occupied Syrian Arab Golan Heights (resolution 37/88 E); condemned Israeli policies and practices against Palestinian students and faculties in schools, universities and other educational institutions in the occupied Palestinian territories (resolution 37/88 F); and expressed deep concern that Israel had failed for two years to apprehend and prosecute the perpetrators of the assassination attempts against the Mayors of Nablus, Ramallah and Al Bireh (resolution 37/88 G).

### 4. Question of human rights in Chile

At its thirty-eighth session the Commission on Human Rights had before it the report of the Special Rapporteur on the situation of human rights in Chile, to the thirty-sixth session of the General Assembly,[42] as well as an additional report of the Special Rapporteur, bringing up to date the report to the General Assembly.[43]

By its resolution 1982/25 of 10 March 1982,[44] the Commission, *inter alia*, commended the Special Rapporteur for his report; it repeated its appeal to the Chilean authorities to put an end to the state of emergency, arbitrary detentions, physical or psychological intimidations and prosecution of persons who exercise their right to freedom of expression and opinion; it urged the Chilean authorities to respect the human rights of persons detained for political reasons, to guarantee the right to life and to prevent torture and other forms of cruel, inhuman or degrading treatment; to investigate the fate of persons who have disappeared for political reasons, and to restore fully trade union rights and civil and political rights and freedoms. It also decided to extend the mandate of the Special Rapporteur for one year. This decision to extend the Special Rapporteur's mandate, also contained in Commission draft decision 7[45] was further endorsed by the Economic and Social Council in its decision 1982/132 of 7 May 1982.

---

[42] A/36/594.

[43] E/CN.4/1484.

[44] E/1982/12, chap. XXVI A.

[45] *Ibid.*, chap. I B.

The Sub-Commission on Prevention of Discrimination and Protection of Minorities adopted at its thirty-fifth session on 8 September 1982 resolution 1982/19[46] by which it recommended to the Commission that it call upon the Chilean authorities to respect and promote human rights and to co-operate with the machinery of the United Nations system; and further recommended to the Commission that it maintain vigilance in relation to the evolution of human rights and fundamental liberties in Chile.

At its thirty-seventh session the General Assembly had before it the report of the Special Rapporteur on the human rights situation in Chile.[47] In its resolution 37/183 adopted on 17 December 1982, the Assembly reiterated its grave concern at the persistence of serious and systematic violations of human rights in Chile, and at the inefficacy of the recourse of *habeas corpus* and *amparo*; it urgently requested the Chilean authorities to respect and promote human rights in conformity with the obligations undertaken under various international instruments, and urged once more these authorities to investigate and clarify the fate of persons who have disappeared in Chile for political reasons; it further urged the Chilean authorities to restore the full enjoyment of trade union rights, to respect the right of Chilean nationals to live in and enter and leave Chilean territory freely, to put an end to arbitrary detentions and imprisonment in secret places and the practice of torture; it requested these authorities to respect fully the economic, social and cultural rights of the Chilean population in general and the indigenous population in particular.

## 5. OTHER MATTERS RELATING TO VIOLATIONS OF HUMAN RIGHTS

### Bolivia

At its thirty-eighth session, the Commission on Human Rights had before it a study by the Special Envoy[48] as well as the Government's comments,[49] prepared in accordance with resolution 34(XXXVII) adopted by the Commission on 11 March 1981.

By its resolution 1982/33 of 11 March 1982,[50] the Commission expressed its deep concern over the grave, massive and repeated violations of human rights which took place in Bolivia after 17 June 1980; it further expressed its satisfaction that an improvement in the human rights situation had taken place since 4 September 1981. It urged the Bolivian Government to take further practical measures to implement its stated resolve to ensure full respect for human rights and fundamental freedoms; it requested the Secretary-General to provide advisory services and other forms of appropriate assistance requested by the Government; it decided to extend the mandate of the Special Envoy for another year, and invited the Government to continue its active co-operation with the Special Envoy.

---

[46] E/CN.4/1984/4, E/CN.4/Sub.2/1982/43, chap. XXI A.

[47] A/37/564.

[48] E/CN.4/1500.

[49] E/CN.4/1500/Add.1.

[50] E/1982/12, chap. XXVI A.

Commission draft decision 12[51], extending for another year the mandate of the Special Envoy, was endorsed by the Economic and Social Council as decision 1982/137 of 7 May 1982.

## Cyprus

At its thirty-eighth session the Commission on Human Rights had before it a report by the Secretary-General,[52] referring to the action undertaken by the Working Group on Enforced or Involuntary Disappearances regarding disappearances in Cyprus, and to the efforts of the Secretary-General and his representatives with respect to the problem of missing persons in Cyprus.

By its decision 1982/102 of 11 March 1982,[53] the Commission postponed until its next session the debate on this question, it being understood that action required by previous resolutions of the Commission on this subject continue to remain operative, including the request to the Secretary-General to provide a report to the Commission regarding their implementation.

## East Timor

At its thirty-fifth session the Sub-Commission on Prevention of Discrimination and Protection of Minorities, by its resolution 1982/20 of 8 September 1982,[54] expressed grave concern at the suffering of all kinds inflicted on the people of East Timor by the failure to respect their right to self-determination; it noted with appreciation recent diplomatic efforts, in which the administering Power pledged itself to undertake broad initiatives with a view to ensuring the full and speedy decolonization of East Timor; it deplored the fact that the gravity of the situation of the people of East Timor was not being given sufficient attention by a large part of the international community; and recommended to the Commission on Human Rights the adoption of draft resolution VII[54] which reaffirmed the inalienable right of the people of East Timor to self-determination and independence; declared that the people of East Timor must be enabled freely to determine their own future; called upon all interested parties to co-operate fully with the United Nations with a view to guaranteeing the exercise of the right to self-determination by the people of East Timor; expressed its deepest concern at the suffering of that people; and called upon all parties concerned to facilitate the entry into the territory of international aid to alleviate the suffering of the people.

## El Salvador

At its thirty-eighth session the Commission on Human Rights had before it the report of the Special Representative on the situation of human rights in El Salvador.[55]

---

[51] *Ibid.*, chap. I B.
[52] E/CN.4/1982/8.
[53] E/1982/12, chap. XXVI B.
[54] E/CN.4/1983/4, E/CN.4/Sub.2/1982/43, chap. XXI A.
[55] E/CN.4/1502.

The main points dealt with in this report were: international and national legal rules applicable in El Salvador in the field of human rights and fundamental freedoms; the current political situation in El Salvador; the exercise of economic, social and cultural rights and the respect for civil and political rights in El Salvador; the situation of refugees and other displaced persons; and the situation with regard to compliance with the international rules of humanitarian law applicable in armed conflicts.

By its resolution 1982/23 adopted on 11 March 1982[56] the Commission, *inter alia*, strongly urged the Government of El Salvador to take the necessary steps to en- sure full respect of human rights and fundamental freedoms in the country, and decided to extend the mandate of the Special Representative for another year, re- questing him to present his report on further developments in the situation of human rights in El Salvador to the General Assembly at its thirty-seventh session and to the Commission on Human Rights at its thirty-ninth session.

By its decision 1982/134 adopted on 7 May 1982, the Economic and Social Council endorsed Commission decision 9[57] to extend for another year the mandate of the Special Representative and to request the Special Representative to submit his report on further developments in the situation of human rights in El Salvador to the General Assembly at its thirty-seventh session and to the Commission on Human Rights at its thirty-ninth session.

The Sub-Commission on Prevention of Discrimination and Protection of Minorities also considered the question at its thirty-fifth session. By its resolution 1982/26 adopted on 8 September 1982,[58] the Sub-Commission, *inter alia*, expressed its deep concern at the gravity of the situation in El Salvador and the continued viol- ation of human rights; recommended to the Government of El Salvador to apply the rules of international law, particularly article 3 of the Geneva Conventions of 1949, and requested the Secretary-General to inform the Sub-Commission at its next ses- sion of the action of the Special Representative and of the deliberations of the Com- mission on the matter as well as of any consideration which may be given to it by the General Assembly, the Economic and Social Council or the Security Council.

At its thirty-seventh session the General Assembly had before it an interim report[59] by the Special Representative. In its resolution 37/185 adopted on 17 December 1982, the Assembly, *inter alia*, expressed its deepest concern at the con- tinued violations of human rights in El Salvador, reiterated its appeal to the Govern- ment and other political forces in El Salvador to work together towards a com- prehensive negotiated political solution, reiterated its appeal to all States to abstain from intervening in the internal situation in El Salvador and to suspend all supplies of arms and any type of military assistance, strongly urged the Government of El Salvador to fulfil its obligations towards its citizens and to assume its international responsibilities in this regard; urged the judiciary of El Salvador to assume its obli- gation to uphold the rule of law and to prosecute and punish those found responsible for assassinations, acts of torture and other forms of cruel, inhuman or degrading

---

[56] E/1982/12, chap. XXVI A.

[57] *Ibid.*, chap. I B.

[58] E/CN.4/1983/4, E/CN.4/Sub.2/1982/43, chap. XXI A.

[59] A/37/611.

treatment, requested the Commission on Human Rights at its next session to continue to examine, as a matter of high priority, the situation in El Salvador, and decided to maintain the question under consideration at its thirty-eighth session.

### Guatemala

At its thirty-eighth session the Commission on Human Rights adopted, on 11 March 1982, resolution 1982/31[60] in which it expressed its profound concern at the continuing deterioration in the situation of human rights and fundamental freedoms in Guatemala and requested its Chairman to appoint a Special Rapporteur of the Commission to make a thorough study, based on all information which he may deem relevant, including any comments and information which the Government of Guatemala may wish to submit, and to report to the Commission at its thirty-ninth session.

The Commission's request to its Chairman to appoint a Special Rapporteur was further endorsed by Economic and Social Council decision 1982/135 of 7 May 1982.

At its thirty-fifth session the Sub-Commission on Prevention of Discrimination and Protection of Minorities, in its resolution 1982/17 adopted on 7 September 1982,[61] *inter alia*, expressed its profound concern at the deterioration in the situation in Guatemala; urged the Government of Guatemala to take the necessary steps to guarantee full respect for human rights and fundamental freedoms; welcomed with satisfaction the appointment of a Special Rapporteur and the assurance given to the Commission by the Government of Guatemala that it will co-operate in that area; requested the Secretary-General to inform the Sub-Commission, at its next session, of the results of the mission of the Commission's Special Rapporteur and of the work of the Commission on the topic, as well as any consideration that might be given thereto by the General Assembly and the Economic and Social Council.

The General Assembly also considered the matter at its thirty-seventh session and adopted, on 17 December 1982, resolution 37/184 in which, *inter alia*, it expressed its deep concern at the serious violations of human rights reported to be taking place in Guatemala; appealed to the Government of Guatemala to allow international humanitarian organizations to give their assistance to those displaced; appealed to all parties concerned to seek an end to all acts of violence; called upon Governments to refrain from supplying arms and other military assistance as long as serious human rights violations in Guatemala continue to be reported; invited the Government of Guatemala and other parties concerned to co-operate with the Special Rapporteur of the Commission on Human Rights.

### Islamic Republic of Iran

By its resolution 1982/27 of 11 March 1982,[62] the Commission on Human Rights expressed its deep concern at the continuing reports about grave violations of human rights and fundamental freedoms in Iran, such as summary and arbitrary executions; urged the Government of the Islamic Republic of Iran, as a State party to

---

[60] E/1982/12, chap. XXVI A.

[61] E/CN.4/1983/4, E/CN.4/Sub.2/1982/43, chap. XXI A.

[62] E/1982/12, chap. XXVI A.

the International Covenant on Civil and Political Rights, to respect and ensure to all individuals within its territory and subject to its jurisdiction the rights recognized in that Covenant; requested the Secretary-General to establish direct contacts with the Government of Iran on the human rights situation prevailing in that country and to continue his efforts to endeavour to ensure that the Baha'is are guaranteed full enjoyment of their human rights and fundamental freedoms; requested the Secretary-General to submit to the Commission at its next session a report compiled on the basis of all available information, including information on any direct contacts which he may have established with the Government of Iran concerning the general human rights situation prevailing in that country.

The Sub-Commission on Prevention of Discrimination and Protection of Minorities also considered the question at its thirty-fifth session. By its resolution 1982/25 adopted on 8 September 1982,[63] it *inter alia* expressed its concern at the reports of continued violations of human rights in Iran; it expressed the hope that the direct contacts the Commission requested the Secretary-General to establish with the Government of Iran would produce positive improvement in the human rights situation prevailing in that country; and it determined that the human rights situation in Iran was sufficiently serious to merit continuing scrutiny by all concerned United Nations bodies, including the Commission on Human Rights.

### Lebanon

In its resolution 1982/18 adopted on 8 September 1982,[64] the Sub-Commission on Prevention of Discrimination and Protection of Minorities, *inter alia*, recommended the Commission on Human Rights to condemn Israel for its invasion of Lebanon and for the indiscriminate bombardment and destruction of the Lebanese cities, and Palestinian refugee camps; to urge Israel to grant the status of prisoner of war to Lebanese and Palestinian combatants and to release all civilians detained by the Israeli army; to call on Israel to comply with Security Council resolutions 508 (1982) and 509 (1982) which ask for the unconditional and immediate withdrawal of Israeli invasion troops from Lebanon.

By its decision 1982/2 of 17 August 1982,[65] the Sub-Commission requested the Secretary-General to forward to the Chairman of the Commission on Human Rights for transmission to the Government of Israel a text in which it expressed its grave concern over the vast human suffering resulting from the invasion of Lebanon and the blockade and massive bombardment of Beirut, and its urgent wish that all military operations in Lebanon should stop immediately and that international humanitarian norms be respected. The text also mentioned the urgent call of the Sub-Commission for the full co-operation of Israel, and all other States and parties concerned, in the efforts of the United Nations, the ICRC and other humanitarian organizations seeking to ameliorate the tragic human suffering that was being caused by the Israeli invasion.

At its thirty-seventh session the General Assembly, in its resolution 37/43 of 3 December 1982, strongly condemned the Israeli aggression against Lebanon and

---

[63] E/CN.4/1983/4, E/CN.4/Sub.2/1982/43, chap. XXI A.

[64] E/CN.4/Sub.2/1982/43, chap. XXI A.

[65] *Ibid.*, chap. XXI B.

reiterated its support for the efforts undertaken to implement the resolutions of the Security Council, in particular those demanding the immediate and unconditional withdrawal of Israeli forces from Lebanese territory to internationally recognized boundaries and respect for the sovereignty and territorial integrity of Lebanon.

## Poland

At its thirty-eighth session, the Commission on Human Rights, in its resolution 1982/26[66] of 10 March 1982, *inter alia*, expressed deep concern at the continued reports of widespread violations of human rights and fundamental freedoms in Poland; it affirmed the right of the Polish people to pursue its political, economic, social and cultural development, free from outside interference; it emphasized the importance of the activities of the international and national humanitarian organizations operating in Poland; it decided to request the Secretary-General or a person designated by him to undertake a thorough study of the human rights situation in Poland and to present a comprehensive report to the Commission at its next session.

By its decision 1982/133 of 7 May 1982, the Economic and Social Council approved the Commission's decision to request the Secretary-General or a person designated by him to undertake a thorough study of the human rights situation in Poland.

By its decision 1982/11 adopted on 8 September 1982,[67] the Sub-Commission on Prevention of Discrimination and Protection of Minorities deferred until its thirty-sixth session consideration of a draft resolution concerning the human rights situation in Poland.

## Mass exoduses

At its thirty-eighth session, the Commission on Human Rights had before it the study on human rights and mass exoduses prepared by its Special Rapporteur.[68]

By its resolution 1982/32 adopted on 11 March 1982,[69] the Commission, *inter alia*, requested the Secretary-General to transmit the study to the General Assembly for consideration at its thirty-seventh session, and to bring it to the attention of the Group of Governmental Experts on International Co-operation to Avert New Flows of Refugees, established by the Assembly by its resolution 36/148 of 16 December 1981; it also requested the Special Rapporteur to explore further with interested Governments, the Secretary-General, United Nations agencies and specialized agencies, intergovernmental organizations and non-governmental organizations the study and the recommendations contained therein to convey their observations together with his comments to the General Assembly in the course of introducing his study and to remain available for consultations with the group of Governmental Experts as required.

By its decision 1982/136 of 7 May 1982, the Economic and Social Council endorsed Commission draft decision 11,[70] thus approving the Commission's request to

---

[66] E/1982/12, chap. XXVI A.

[67] E/CN.4/1983/4, E/CN.4/Sub.2/1982/43, chap. XXI B.

[68] E/CN.4/1503.

[69] E/1982/12, chap. XXVI A.

[70] *Ibid.*, chap. I B.

the Special Rapporteur to explore further with interested Governments and others his study and recommendations contained therein.

The General Assembly also considered the matter at its thirty-seventh session. In its resolution 37/186 adopted on 17 December 1982 the Assembly, *inter alia*, renewed the invitation extended in Commission resolution 1982/32 to Governments, United Nations agencies or departments concerned, and various agencies and organizations concerned to communicate their views on the study of the Special Rapporteur and the recommendations contained therein to the Secretary-General; requested the Secretary-General to ensure that the views expressed on the study and the recommendations contained therein by all interested parties are made available to the Commission at its thirty-ninth session and to the Group of Governmental Experts on International Co-operation to Avert New Flows of Refugees; and requested the Secretary-General to pursue his examination of the recommendations contained in the study and to report to the Assembly at its thirty-eighth session.

### Summary executions

In its resolution 1982/29 of 11 March 1982,[71] the Commission on Human Rights recommended its draft resolution II[72] for adoption by the Economic and Social Council.

Upon this draft resolution, further endorsed by Council resolution 1982/35 of 7 May 1982, the Economic and Social Council requested the Chairman of the Commission on Human Rights to appoint for one year a Special Rapporteur to submit a comprehensive report to the Commission at its next session on the occurrence and extent of the practice of summary or arbitrary executions together with his conclusions and recommendations.

At its thirty-fifth session the Sub-Commission on Prevention of Discrimination and Protection of Minorities, in its resolution 1982/13 adopted on 7 September 1982[73] recommended the Commission on Human Rights to examine the report of the Special Rapporteur to be submitted at its thirty-ninth session and to adopt effective measures to prevent the occurrence of summary or arbitrary executions.

By its resolution 37/182 adopted on 17 December 1982, the General Assembly requested the Commission on Human Rights at its thirty-ninth session, on the basis of the report of the Special Rapporteur, to make recommendations concerning appropriate action to combat and eventually eliminate the practice of summary or arbitrary executions.

### G.  Adverse consequences for the enjoyment of human rights of political, military, economic and other forms of assistance given to the colonial and racist régime in southern Africa

At its thirty-eighth session the Commission on Human Rights, having considered the updated report[74] prepared by the Special Rapporteur of the Sub-

---

[71] *Ibid.*, chap. XXVI A.

[72] *Ibid.*, chap. I A.

[73] E/CN.4/1983/4, E/CN.4/Sub.2/1982/43, chap. XXI A.

[74] E/CN.4/Sub.2/469 and Corr.1 and Add.1.

Commission on the adverse consequences of assistance to the racist régime in South Africa for the enjoyment of human rights, which contained an updated list of banks and firms giving assistance to the racist régime, reiterated, in its resolution 1982/12 of 25 February 1982[75] its request to all States which have not yet done so to take effective measures to end all forms of collaboration and assistance to the racist régime of South Africa; it called again upon all States, relevant specialized agencies, non-governmental and other organizations to continue to give wide publicity to the report of the Special Rapporteur; it welcomed the decision of the Sub-Commission to mandate the Special Rapporteur to continue to update the list, subject to annual review, and submit, through the Sub-Commission, the revised report to the Commission; it requested the Group of Three set up under the International Convention on the Suppression and Punishment of the Crime of *Apartheid* to examine whether the actions of transnational corporations which operate in South Africa come under the definition of the crime of *apartheid*, and whether or not some legal action could be taken under the Convention, and to report to the Commission.

The Commission's decision to mandate the Special Rapporteur to continue updating the list and submit the revised report to the Commission was further endorsed by Economic and Social Council decision 1982/128 adopted on 7 May 1982.

At its thirty-fifth session the Sub-Commission on Prevention of Discrimination and Protection of Minorities had before it a report[76] supplementing the information provided in previous reports by the Special Rapporteur. In its resolution 1982/16 of 7 September 1982,[77] the Sub-Commission mandated the Special Rapporteur to continue to update the list, subject to annual review; it also invited the Secretary-General to give the updated report the widest publicity and dissemination and to issue it as a United Nations publication.

The question was also considered by the General Assembly at its thirty-seventh session. By its resolution 37/39 of 3 December 1982, the Assembly, *inter alia*, affirmed that the updating of the report was of the greatest importance to the cause of fighting *apartheid* and should continue to be an activity in the ongoing work programme for 1982-1983; it called upon all States, specialized agencies and organizations concerned to give wide publicity to the revised report; it called upon the Governments of the countries where the banks and firms named and listed in the revised report are based to take effective action to put a stop to their trading, manufacturing and investing activities in South Africa and Namibia; and it urgently requested all specialized agencies, particularly the International Monetary Fund and the World Bank, to refrain from granting loans to the racist régime in South Africa.

## H.  The right of peoples to self-determination

At its thirty-eighth session, on 25 February 1982, the Commission on Human Rights adopted resolution 1982/16[78] by which it, *inter alia*, called upon all States to

---

[75] E/1982/12, chap. XXVI A.

[76] E/CN.4/Sub.2/1982/10.

[77] E/CN.4/1983/4, E/CN.4/Sub.2/1982/43, chap. XXI A.

[78] E/1982/12, chap. XXVI A.

implement fully and faithfully the resolutions of the United Nations, in particular General Assembly resolution 1514 (XV), and to take all the necessary steps to enable the dependent peoples of the territories concerned to exercise fully and without further delay their inalienable right to self-determination and independence; it re-affirmed the inalienable right of the people of Namibia to self-determination, freedom and national independence, and the legitimacy of the struggle of the op-pressed people of South Africa for the elimination of the *apartheid* system and the exercise of the right of self-determination by the people of South Africa as a whole; it called upon Governments to enact legislation declaring the recruitment, financing and training of mercenaries in their territory, and their transit through it, to be punishable offences, and prohibiting their nationals from serving as mercenaries, and to report on such legislation to the Secretary-General; it urged all States to con-tribute towards the early adoption of an international convention against the recruit-ment, use, financing and training of mercenaries.

The General Assembly also considered the question of the universal realization of the right of peoples to self-determination at its thirty-seventh session. By its resolution 37/42 of 3 December 1982, the Assembly, *inter alia*, declared its firm op-position to acts of foreign military intervention, aggression and occupation; it called upon those States responsible to cease immediately their military intervention and occupation of foreign countries and territories, and to cease all acts of repression, discrimination, exploitation and maltreatment, particularly the brutal and inhuman methods reportedly employed for the execution of these acts against the peoples con-cerned. By its resolution 37/43 adopted on the same day, the Assembly, *inter alia*, strongly condemned the continued violations of the human rights of the peoples still under colonial and foreign domination and alien subjugation, the continuation of the illegal occupation of Namibia, and South Africa's attempts to dismember its Ter-ritory, the perpetuation of the racist minority régime in southern Africa and the denial to the Palestinian people of their inalienable national rights; strongly con-demned those Governments that did not recognize the right to self-determination and independence of all peoples still under colonial and foreign domination and alien subjugation; demanded the immediate and unconditional release of all persons detained or imprisoned as a result of their struggle for self-determination and in-dependence; urged all States, specialized agencies and competent organizations of the United Nations system to do their utmost to ensure the full implementation of the Declaration on the Granting of Independence to Colonial Countries and Peoples and to intensify their efforts to support peoples under colonial, foreign and racist domination in their just struggle for self-determination and national independence.

The right of peoples to self-determination in specific parts of the world was also the subject of discussion in various organs during the year 1982:

### Afghanistan

By its resolution 1982/14 adopted on 25 February 1982,[79] the Commission on Human Rights, *inter alia*, called for the immediate withdrawal of the foreign troops from Afghanistan, and for a political settlement of the situation on the basis of the withdrawal of foreign troops; affirmed the right of the Afghan refugees to return to

---

[79] *Ibid.*, chap. XXVI A.

their homes in safety and honour; urged all concerned to work towards a settlement which would ensure that the Afghan people would determine their destiny free from outside interference and which would enable the Afghan refugees to return to their homes.

At its thirty-fifth session the Sub-Commission on Prevention of Discrimination and Protection of Minorities adopted on 8 September 1982, resolution 1982/21,[80] in which it expressed its solemn view that withdrawal of foreign troops from Afghanistan is essential for restoring human rights; it urged the Secretary-General, in the continuation of his efforts to seek a political settlement acceptable to the Afghan people, to widen his consultations to include representatives of all parties concerned, and invited him to bring to the attention of the Sub-Commission, at its next session, any reports that may be submitted to the General Assembly, or to any of its Committees, pertaining to the use of illegal weapons in Afghanistan or against the Afghan people.

### Democratic Kampuchea

By its resolution 1982/13 adopted on 25 February 1982,[81] the Commission on Human Rights, *inter alia*, reaffirmed that the primary violation of human rights in Democratic Kampuchea at present is the persistence of foreign occupation which prevents the people of Kampuchea from exercising their right to self-determination; it further called upon all parties concerned to join in the efforts to seek a comprehensive solution to the Kampuchean problems and to co-operate in the work of the *Ad Hoc* Committee on the International Conference on Kampuchea; it requested the Secretary-General to exercise his good offices in order to contribute to a comprehensive political settlement and the restoration of human rights in Kampuchea; it requested the Sub-Commission to examine the practices of the foreign forces which affect the human rights of the people of Kampuchea and which prevent the people of Kampuchea from exercising their right to self-determination, and to submit its report to the Commission at its thirty-ninth session; it also recommended that the Economic and Social Council consider the situation in Kampuchea at its first session in 1982.

By its decision 1982/143 of 7 May 1982, the Economic and Social Council endorsed resolution 1982/13 of the Commission; it also noted with appreciation the recent visit to the area of the Special Representative of the Secretary-General.

The Sub-Commission on Prevention of Discrimination and Protection of Minorities also considered the question of Kampuchea at its thirty-fifth session, and adopted in this connection resolution 1982/22 on 8 September 1982.[82] In this resolution, the Sub-Commission, *inter alia*, requested the Secretary-General to transmit to the Commission at its next session the material reviewed by one of its members concerning the practices of the foreign forces which affect the human rights of the people of Kampuchea; it invited the Commission to urge all concerned to take steps to ensure, following the withdrawal of foreign forces from Kampuchea, that the

---

[80] E/CN.4/1983/4, E/CN.4/Sub.2/1982/43, chap. XXI A.

[81] E/1982/12, chap. XXVI A.

[82] E/CN.4/1983/4, E/CN.4/Sub.2/1982/43, chap. XXI A.

Kampuchean people choose their own representatives to a constitutional assembly, that the assembly so chosen lay down the basic principles for a democratic Kampuchea, that all foreign States publicly declare their intention not to interfere with the internal political process in Kampuchea, that the right of all Kampuchean refugees to return be recognized, that the United Nations offer its expert services in the field of human rights and fundamental freedoms in Kampuchea; it also recommended that the Commission call for a pledge by all foreign States not to intervene with armed forces after the withdrawal of the foreign forces now in Kampuchea.

### Palestine

In its resolution 1982/3 adopted on 11 February 1982,[83] the Commission on Human Rights, *inter alia*, reaffirmed the inalienable right of the Palestinian people to self-determination without external interference and the establishment of a fully independent and sovereign State of Palestine, and to return to their homes and property; it also reaffirmed that the future of the Palestinian people can only be decided with its full participation in all efforts, through its representative, the Palestine Liberation Organization; it requested the Secretary-General to make available to the Commission and the Sub-Commission the reports, studies and publications prepared by the Special Unit on Palestinian Rights.

The Sub-Commission on Prevention of Discrimination and Protection of Minorities adopted at its thirty-fifth session, on 8 September 1982, resolution 1982/18[84] in which, *inter alia*, it called for the full exercise in Palestine of the inalienable rights of the Palestinian people to return to their homes and property, to self-determination without external interference and to establish their sovereign and independent State.

### Western Sahara

In its resolution 1982/15 adopted on 25 February 1982,[85] the Commission on Human Rights welcomed the decisions and resolutions of the Organization of African Unity and the United Nations to organize throughout the Territory of Western Sahara a free and fair referendum on self-determination; urged to that end the two parties to the conflict, Morocco and the Frente Polisario, to enter into direct negotiations with a view to concluding a cease-fire; and decided to follow closely the developments of the situation in Western Sahara.

## I. Question of the human rights of persons subjected to any form of detention or imprisonment

At its thirty-fifth session, the Sub-Commission on Prevention of Discrimination and Protection of Minorities decided, on 19 August 1982, by its decision 1982/4,[86] to

---

[83] E/1982/12, chap. XXVI A.

[84] E/CN.4/1983/4, E/CN.4/Sub.2/1982/43, chap. XXI A.

[85] E/1982/12, chap. XXVI A.

[86] E/CN.4/1983/4, E/CN.4/Sub.2/1982/43, chap. XXI B.

set up a sessional working group for the consideration of the question of the human rights of persons subjected to any form of detention or imprisonment.

In its report to the Sub-Commission,[87] the Working Group included recommendations concerning safeguards for detention and trial, as well as possible action by the United Nations in the cases of capital punishment and extra-judicial executions.

In its resolution 1982/10 adopted on 7 September 1982,[88] the Sub-Commission, *inter alia*, requested the Secretary-General to submit to the Sub-Commission, at its next session, a preliminary survey on maximum periods of detention; the Secretary General was further requested to invite Governments, United Nations bodies, and organizations concerned, to submit reliably attested information concerning the problem of arrest and detention on vague grounds or no grounds at all; the problem of pre-trial detention; the question of procedural guarantees for preventive detention especially under states of emergency, existing practices of incommunicado detention, the question of extraterritorial abduction, and the question of "suicides" in detention under suspicious circumstances; the Sub-Commission recommended that the United Nations should take strong and effective measures to prevent extra-judicial executions; it also decided that its Working Group on Detention or Imprisonment at its next sessional meeting should give special attention to hearing and receiving information, in accordance with existing rules and practices of the Sub-Commission, concerning the extent of, and facts relating to, torture or cruel, inhuman or degrading treatment or punishment, unless the Commission on Human Rights establishes a system for examining such information.

On 31 August 1982, the Sub-Commission adopted decision 1982/8,[89] by which it decided to express, through the Chairman of the Commission on Human Rights, its concern to the Government of Malawi regarding allegations of capital charge against Orton Chirwa and his wife. The Sub-Commission also urged a public enquiry into the circumstances of the arrest as well as a trial before the high court.

At the same session of the Sub-Commission, the Special Rapporteur presented her study of the implications for human rights of recent developments concerning situations known as states of siege or emergency.[90] It is pointed out in the study that guarantees provided by law are deviated from and states of emergency tend to become clandestine, permanent or even institutionalized. The effects are particularly damaging for persons detained on political grounds. In her recommendations, the Special Rapporteur proposed a number of measures with a view to strengthening the substantive guarantees provided by the international law on human rights.

In its resolution 1982/32 of 10 September 1982,[91] the Sub-Commission decided to transmit the study to the Commission and to draw the Commission's attention to the Special Rapporteur's conclusions and recommendations which the Sub-Commission whole-heartedly endorsed. The Sub-Commission also recommended its

---

[87] E/CN.4/Sub.2/1982/34 and Corr.1.

[88] E/CN.4/1983/4, E/CN.4/Sub.2/1982/43, chap. XXI A.

[89] *Ibid.*, chap. XXI B.

[90] E/CN.4/Sub.2/1982/15.

[91] E/CN.4/1983/4, E/CN.4/Sub.2/1982/43, chap. XXI A.

draft resolution VIII[92] for adoption to the Commission. Upon this draft, the Commission would, *inter alia*, recommend that the Economic and Social Council should authorize a closer study by the Sub-Commission on the advisability of strengthening or extending the inalienability of the rights enumerated in article 4, paragraph 2, of the International Covenant on Civil and Political Rights.

## J. Enforced or involuntary disappearances of persons

At its thirty-eighth session, the Commission on Human Rights adopted, on 10 March 1982, resolution 1982/24[93] by which it took note of the report of the Working Group established to examine questions relevant to enforced or involuntary disappearances of persons;[94] it decided to extend for one year the term of the working group's mandate, and requested the group to submit to the Commission at its 1983 session a report on its work, together with its conclusions and recommendations. The Sub-Commission was requested to continue studying the most effective means for eliminating enforced or involuntary disappearances, with a view to making general recommendations to the Commission at its thirty-ninth session.

At its thirty-fifth session the Sub-Commission, in its resolution 1982/5 of 7 September 1982,[95] *inter alia*, expressed its conviction to the Commission that, in view of the persistence of violations resulting from the many cases of disappearances of persons which are still occurring in the world, the extension of the mandate of the Working Group on Enforced or Involuntary Disappearances is indispensable; urged the Commission to give special attention to the protection of persons who actively seek the whereabouts of missing persons and who provide information on missing persons; it also recommended to the Commission to give careful consideration to measures which might be used to obtain more information on the whereabouts or fate of missing persons.

The General Assembly also considered the question at its thirty-seventh session and adopted, on 17 December 1982, resolution 37/180 in which it welcomed the Commission's decision to extend for one year the term of the mandate of the Working Group. The Assembly also adopted, on the same day, resolution 37/181 relating to missing persons in Cyprus, in which it invited the Working Group to follow developments and to recommend to the parties concerned ways and means of overcoming the pending procedural difficulties of the Committee on Missing Persons in Cyprus and, in co-operation with the Committee, to facilitate the effective implementation of its investigative work on the basis of the existing relevant agreements.

## K. Torture and other cruel, inhuman or degrading treatment or punishment

An open-ended Working Group of the Commission on Human Rights met prior to the Commission's thirty-eighth session to continue work on a draft convention

---

[92] E/CN.4/Sub.2/1982/43, chap. I A.

[93] E/1982/12, chap. XXVI A.

[94] E/CN.4/1492 and Add.1.

[95] E/CN.4/1983/4, E/CN.4/1982/43, chap. XXI A.

against torture and other cruel, inhuman or degrading treatment or punishment, and provisionally adopted three articles of the draft convention. In its resolution 1982/44 of 11 March 1982,[96] the Commission recommended that the Economic and Social Council should adopt draft resolution V,[97] authorizing a meeting of the Working Group prior to the Commission's thirty-ninth session. The Economic and Social Council endorsed this draft by its resolution 1982/38 of 3 May 1982.

By its resolution 1982/43 of 11 March 1982,[98] the Commission called upon all Governments in a position to do so to respond favourably to requests for contributions to the United Nations Voluntary Fund for Victims of Torture.

By its resolution 1982/10 of 7 September 1982,[99] the Sub-Commission on Prevention of Discrimination and Protection of Minorities decided that the Working Group on Detention or Imprisonment at its next sessional meeting should give special attention to information concerning torture or cruel, inhuman or degrading treatment or punishment, unless the Commission established a system for examining such information. It further decided that the hearing and receipt of such information should be conducted on an annual basis, except in respect of States that would become parties to a convention against torture.

At its thirty-seventh session the General Assembly, in its resolution 37/193 adopted on 18 December 1982, welcomed the authorization by the Economic and Social Council of a meeting of an open-ended Working Group of the Commission on Human Rights to complete the work on a draft convention against torture.

As regards the issue of capital punishment, the Sub-Commission, in its resolution 1982/10 of 7 September 1982,[100] recommended that the United Nations should communicate with Governments in an attempt to avert or postpone the carrying out of capital punishment immediately after sentencing without allowing the person sentenced time or opportunity for appeal.

At its thirty-seventh session the General Assembly had before it a report[101] submitted by the Secretary-General on comments and observations sent by Member States on the idea of elaborating a draft of a second optional protocol to the International Covenant on Civil and Political Rights, aiming at the abolition of the death penalty. By its resolution 37/192 adopted on 18 December 1982, the Assembly requested the Commission on Human Rights to consider elaborating such a draft, and to report to the Assembly at its thirty-ninth session.

## L.  Draft code of medical ethics

In its resolution 37/194 of 18 December 1982, the General Assembly adopted the Principles of Medical Ethics relevant to the role of health personnel, particularly

---

[96] E/1982/12, chap. XXVI A.

[97] *Ibid.*, chap. I A.

[98] *Ibid.*, chap. XXVI A.

[99] E/CN.4/1983/4, E/CN.4/1982/43, chap. XXI A.

[100] E/CN.4/1983/4, E/CN.4/Sub.2/1982/43, chap. XXI A.

[101] A/37/407 and Add.1.

physicians, in the protection of prisoners and detainees against torture and other cruel, inhuman or degrading treatment or punishment. The Assembly called upon all Governments to give the Principles of Medical Ethics the widest possible distribution and invited all relevant organizations to bring those Principles to the attention of the widest possible group of individuals, especially those active in the medical and paramedical field.

## M. Slavery and the slave trade

By its resolution 1982/20 of 10 March 1982,[102] the Commission on Human Rights decided, pursuant to an invitation by the Government of Mauritania, to authorize the Sub-Commission to send a delegation to visit Mauritania in order to study the situation and ascertain the country's needs. The Commission also requested the Secretary-General to transmit the statements submitted by the Working Group on Slavery at its seventh session by several non-governmental organizations, containing allegations on slavery-like practices in certain countries, together with the relevant parts and recommendations of the report of the Working Group, to the Governments of those countries for information and observations, and to the intergovernmental organizations and agencies mentioned by the Working Group on its recommendations; it also requested the Secretary-General to call upon States parties to the Conventions related to slavery to submit regular reports on the situation in their countries, and to call upon other States, organizations concerned, relevant agencies of the United Nations and INTERPOL to supply relevant information to the Working Group on Slavery; the Commission appealed to Member States to ratify the Convention for the Suppression of the Traffic in Persons and of the Exploitation of the Prostitution of Others of 1949, or to implement its provisions effectively if they have already ratified it; to undertake concerted action against all enterprises promoting prostitution and traffic in persons; to intensify research into the economic, social and other causes of prostitution and pimping and to promote the social reintegration of victims of prostitution and traffic in persons.

Pursuant to draft decision 4 of the Commission on Human Rights,[103] the Economic and Social Council, in its decision 1982/129 of 7 May 1982, authorized the Sub-Commission to send a delegation to visit Mauritania in order to study the situation and ascertain the country's needs with regard to the question of slavery and the slave trade.

By its decision 1982/7 of 27 August 1982,[104] the Sub-Commission authorized its Chairman to appoint two of the Sub-Commission members to study the situation and ascertain Mauritania's needs with regard to the question of slavery and the slave trade.

At its thirty-fifth session the Sub-Commission had before it, in connection with the question of slavery a final report[105] by its Special Rapporteur entitled "Updating

---

[102] E/1982/12, chap. XXVI A.

[103] *Ibid.*, chap. I B.

[104] E/CN.4/1983/4, E/CN.4/Sub.2/1982/43, chap. XXI B.

[105] E/CN.4/Sub.2/1982/20 and Add.1.

of the Report of Slavery Submitted to the Sub-Commission in 1966''. The report contained an introduction and four parts: part I, containing the definition of slavery and slavery-like practices; part II, dealing with action taken at the national level to abolish and prevent slavery and the slave trade; part III, giving account of action taken at the international level in the field of slavery; and part IV, containing conclusions and recommendations of the Special Rapporteur. By its resolution 1982/9 adopted on 7 September 1982,[106] the Sub-Commission decided to transmit the report to the Commission at its thirty-ninth session, and to the competent United Nations organs, and to request those bodies to submit their comments to the Secretary-General for transmission to the Special Rapporteur; it also recommended to the Commission for adoption draft resolution III[107] upon which the Commission would recommend to the Economic and Social Council that the report be printed and given the widest possible distribution.

The Sub-Commission also considered, during its thirty-fifth session, the report of the Working Group on Slavery,[108] which held its eighth session in Geneva from 9 to 12 August 1982. By its resolution 1982/15 of 7 September 1982[109] the Sub-Commission, *inter alia*, suggested that the United Nations and its agencies should actively offer Member States co-ordinated assistance to eliminate conditions conducive to slavery and slavery-like situations; it suggested that organizations and agencies concerned should inform all meetings of the Working Group about inclusion in their technical assistance programmes of activities designed to eliminate slavery-type problems; it considered that the persons known as slavery experts should be more closely involved in the work done on slavery by the bodies concerned. By the same resolution, the Sub-Commission urged that the study on debt bondage should be undertaken without further delay; that the study on traffic in persons and prostitution[110] should be updated; that a report on the causes and implications of the sale of children should be prepared; it also requested two of its members to carry out and present a study on all aspects of the problem of female sexual mutilation.

## N.  Rights of the child

### 1.  QUESTION OF A CONVENTION ON THE RIGHTS OF THE CHILD

A pre-sessional Working Group on the draft convention on the rights of the child was held prior to the thirty-eighth session of the Commission on Human Rights. By its resolution 1982/39 of 11 March 1982[111] the Commission decided to continue at its next session its work on the draft. In its draft resolution IV[112] the Commission recommended to the Economic and Social Council that it authorize a

---

[106] E/CN.4/1983/4, E/CN.4/Sub.2/1982/43, chap. XXI A.

[107] E/CN.4/Sub.2/1982/43, chap. I A.

[108] E/CN.4/Sub.2/1982/21 and Corr.1.

[109] E/CN.4/1983/4, E/CN.4/Sub.2/1982/43, chap. XXI A.

[110] ST/SOA/SD/8.

[111] E/1982/12, chap. XXVI A.

[112] *Ibid.*, chap. I A.

one-week session of the Group prior to the 1983 session of the Commission. This recommendation was endorsed by Council resolution 1982/37 of 7 May 1982.

By its resolution 37/190 of 18 December 1982, the General Assembly, *inter alia*, requested the Commission to give the highest priority at its next session to completing the draft convention.

## 2. EXPLOITATION OF CHILD LABOUR

At its thirty-eighth session in 1982, the Commission on Human Rights had before it the study of the Special Rapporteur on the *Exploitation of Child Labour*.[113] In its resolution 1982/21, adopted on 10 March 1982,[114] the Commission recommended to the Economic and Social Council that the study be printed and given the widest possible distribution, and invited the Sub-Commission to present to the Council, through the Commission, a concrete programme of action to combat violations of human rights through the exploitation of child labour.

The Economic and Social Council, by its decision 1982/130 of 7 May 1982, endorsed the Commission's recommendation that the study should be printed and widely distributed.

At its thirty-fifth session the Sub-Commission on Prevention of Discrimination and Protection of Minorities decided, by its resolution 1982/33 of 10 September 1982,[115] to submit to the Commission for its consideration the recommendations of the Special Rapporteur, for a programme of action.

## 3. PARENTAL KIDNAPPING

By its resolution 1982/39 of 7 May 1982, the Economic and Social Council called the attention of States to the proliferation of cases of removal and retention of children, and invited them to co-operate actively with a view to preventing the occurrence of such cases and to solving them speedily. The Council also requested the Secretary-General to consult with Governments on this problem and report to the Commission at its thirty-ninth session.

## O. Human rights of disabled persons

By its resolution 1982/1 of 7 September 1982,[116] the Sub-Commission on Prevention of Discrimination and Protection of Minorities, *inter alia*, recommended that Governments give consideration to difficulties encountered by disabled persons in the enjoyment of human rights as well as to the need to strengthen procedures designed to permit them to bring allegations of violations of their rights to the ap-

---

[113] E/CN.4/Sub.2/479/Rev.1.

[114] E/1982/12, chap. XXVI A.

[115] E/CN.4/1983/4, E/CN.4/Sub.2/1982/43, chap. XXI A.

[116] *Ibid.*

propriate body or to the attention of the Government, and requested the Secretary-General to invite the view of Governments, specialized agencies and relevant organizations on ways and means for promoting the enjoyment of human rights by disabled persons. The Secretary-General was further requested to transmit to the Sub-Commission at its next session information received and to include in his report information drawn from the relevant reports of the Advisory Committee for the International Year of Disabled Persons as well as, if possible, comments received from the Advisory Committee itself.

### P. International legal protection of the human rights of individuals who are not citizens of the country in which they live

The open-ended Working Group established under General Assembly resolution 36/165 for the purpose of concluding the elaboration of a draft declaration on the human rights of individuals who are not citizens of the country in which they live continued, during the thirty-seventh session of the Assembly, its consideration of the draft declaration and provisionally adopted articles 6 to 10 of the draft declaration, as well as a new article which was not given a number.

By its resolution 37/169 adopted on 17 December 1982, the General Assembly took note of the report of the Working Group,[117] requested the Secretary-General to transmit to Governments, competent organs of the United Nations system and international organizations concerned the reports of the Working Groups established at the thirty-fifth, thirty-sixth and thirty-seventh sessions of the General Assembly and to invite them to bring up to date the comments they submitted or to submit new comments on the basis of the above-mentioned reports. The Assembly decided to establish, at its thirty-eighth session, a working group for the purpose of concluding the elaboration of the draft declaration.

### Q. Indigenous populations

At its thirty-eighth session, the Commission on Human Rights in its resolution 1982/19 of 10 March 1982,[118] recommended to the Economic and Social Council for adoption its draft resolution I,[119] upon which the Council would decide to authorize the Sub-Commission on Prevention of Discrimination and Protection of Minorities to establish annually a working group on indigenous populations to review developments pertaining to the protection and promotion of the human rights and fundamental freedoms of indigenous populations; and further decide that the Working Group should give special attention to the evolution of standards concerning the rights of indigenous populations, taking into account both the similarities and the differences in the situations and aspirations of indigenous populations throughout the world.

---

[117] A/C.3/37/8.

[118] E/1982/12, chap. XXVI A.

[119] *Ibid.*, chap. I A.

The Economic and Social Council endorsed this draft by its resolution 1982/34 of 7 May 1982.

The Working Group on Indigenous Populations held its first meeting from 9 to 13 August 1982 in Geneva. By its resolution 1982/31 of 10 September 1982[120] the Sub-Commission on Prevention of Discrimination and Protection of Minorities, having examined the report of the Working Group at its first session,[121] agreed with the Working Group in its preliminary identification of the main areas of concern; it also decided to request that the Commission on Human Rights and the Economic and Social Council establish a fund for the purpose of allowing representatives of indigenous populations to come to Geneva to participate in the work of the Working Group.

By its resolution 1982/29 adopted on the same day,[122] the Sub-Commission, having examined the report submitted by the Special Rapporteur containing the Supplementary Part of the Final Report relating to the Study of the Problem of Discrimination against Indigenous Populations,[123] requested the Special Rapporteur to continue his work and to submit to the Sub-Commission, at its next session, the last part of the final report, including the conclusions, proposals and recommendations of the study.

### R. Human rights of migrant workers

At its thirty-eighth session the Commission on Human Rights, by its resolution 1982/35 of 11 March 1982,[124] *inter alia*, welcomed the progress made so far by the Working Group established by the General Assembly to elaborate an international convention on the protection of the rights of all migrant workers and their families, and expressed the hope that the General Assembly will complete the elaboration of the convention as soon as possible.

The Working Group held an intersessional meeting from 10 to 21 May 1982, and a session during the thirty-seventh session of the General Assembly, from 18 October to 16 November 1982.

By its resolution 37/170 of 17 December 1982, the General Assembly took note of the report of the Working Group[125] and expressed its satisfaction with the substantial progress made so far by the Group; it decided that the Group should hold an intersessional meeting in the spring of 1983 in order to complete its task; it invited the Secretary-General to transmit the report of the Working Group to Governments; it further decided that the Group should meet during the thirty-eighth session of the Assembly in order to continue and, if possible, to complete the elaboration of the international convention.

---

[120] E/CN.4/1983/4, E/CN.4/Sub.2/1982/43, chap. XXI A.

[121] E/CN.4/Sub.2/1982/33 and E/CN.4/Sub.2/AC.4/1982/R.1.

[122] E/CN.4/1983/4, E/CN.4/Sub.2/1982/43, chap. XXI A.

[123] E/CN.4/Sub.2/1982/2 and Add.1-7.

[124] E/1982/12, chap. XXVI A.

[125] A/C.3/37/7 and Corr.1 and 2.

## S.  The role of youth in the promotion and protection of human rights

At its thirty-eighth session, the Commission on Human Rights, in its resolution 1982/36 adopted on 11 March 1982,[126] emphasized the important role of young people in the promotion of their country's political, economic and social development; called upon all States to take appropriate action for the exercise by youth of all their human rights and fundamental freedoms; requested the Secretary-General to submit to the Commission a progress report on the implementation of the Programme of Measures and Activities in connection with International Youth Year; it also decided to examine at its fortieth session the question of the exercise by youth of all their human rights and fundamental freedoms, including the right to education and to work.

The Sub-Commission on Prevention of Discrimination and Protection of Minorities had before it, at its thirty-fifth session, a preliminary report[127] by two of its members on conscientious objection to military service. By its resolution 1982/30 of 10 September 1982,[128] the Sub-Commission requested the Special Rapporteurs to prepare a final report based on comments received on their preliminary report, and to develop principles related to (*a*) recognizing the right to refuse service in military or police forces used to enforce *apartheid*, to pursue wars of aggression, or to engage in any other illegal warfare; (*b*) recognizing the possibility of the right of all persons to refuse service in military or police forces on grounds of conscience or deeply held personal conviction, and their responsibility to offer instead of military service any other service in the social or economic field; (*c*) urging Member States to grant asylum or safe transit to another State to persons compelled to leave their country of nationality solely because of conscientious objection to service in the military forces.

At its thirty-seventh session the General Assembly adopted three resolutions on youth and human rights. In its resolution 37/48 of 3 December 1982 the Assembly, *inter alia*, endorsed the recommendations made by the Advisory Committee for the International Youth Year for the further implementation of the Specific Programme of Measures and Activities to be undertaken prior to and during the International Youth Year; in its resolution 37/49 adopted on the same day, the Assembly called upon all States, all governmental and non-governmental organizations and the interested bodies of the United Nations and specialized agencies to pay continuous attention to the implementation of Assembly resolution 36/29 relating to efforts aimed at the promotion of human rights and their enjoyment by youth, particularly the right to education and vocational training and to work, with a view to resolving the problem of youth unemployment; in its resolution 37/50 also adopted on the same day, the Assembly, *inter alia*, invited Member States, specialized agencies, regional commissions, intergovernmental organizations and non-governmental youth organizations to communicate and further promote the guidelines and additional guidelines for the improvement of channels of communication between the United Nations and youth and youth organizations and to offer additional suggestions for their further development.

---

[126] E/1982/12, chap. XXVI A.

[127] E/CN.4/Sub.2/1982/24.

[128] E/CN.4/1983/4, E/CN.4/Sub.2/1982/43, chap. XXI A.

## T.   Human rights and scientific and technological developments

At its thirty-eighth session the Commission on Human Rights adopted a number of resolutions relating to the question of human rights and scientific and technological developments.

By its resolution 1982/4 of 19 February 1982,[129] the Commission stressed the importance of the implementation by all States of the provisions and principles contained in the Declaration on the Use of Scientific and Technological Progress in the Interests of Peace and for the Benefit of Mankind in order to promote human rights and fundamental freedoms under conditions of scientific and technological progress; it also reiterated its request to the Sub-Commission on Prevention of Discrimination and Protection of Minorities to undertake, as a matter of priority, a study on the use of the achievements of scientific and technological progress to ensure the right to work and development.

By its resolution 1982/5 of the same date,[130] the Commission strongly condemned Israel for its act of aggression against the Iraqi nuclear installation which constitutes a dangerous escalation of Israeli violations of the sovereign rights of States to scientific and technological development.

As regards the question of persons detained on the grounds of mental ill-health, the Commission noted with appreciation the preliminary report of the Special Rapporteur[131] and decided to consider the final report at its thirty-ninth session (resolution 1982/6 of 19 February 1982).[132]

Finally, the Commission adopted, on the same day, resolution 1982/7,[133] by which it requested the Sub-Commission to carry out a study on the negative consequences of the arms race, particularly the nuclear arms race in all its aspects, for the implementation of economic, social, cultural as well as civil and political rights, the establishment of a new international economic order and, above all, of the inherent right to life, and to submit that study to the Commission at its fortieth session. It also requested the Secretary-General to bring this resolution to the attention of the Economic and Social Council, the General Assembly and other United Nations bodies concerned with disarmament matters.

At its thirty-fifth session the Sub-Commission had before it the report of its Special Rapporteur on the question of persons detained on grounds of mental ill-health.[134] During that session, a Working Group was established to consider the draft body of guidelines, principles and guarantees for the protection of the mentally ill or persons suffering from mental disorder. By its resolution 1982/34 of 10 September 1982[135] the Sub-Commission, having considered the report by the Special

---

[129] E/1982/12, chap. XXVI A.

[130] *Ibid.*

[131] E/CN.4/Sub.2/474.

[132] E/1982/12, chap. XXVI A.

[133] *Ibid.*

[134] E/CN.4/Sub.2/1982/16.

[135] E/CN.4/1983/4, E/CN.4/Sub.2/1982/43, chap. XXI A.

Rapporteur as well as the report of the Sessional Working Group,[136] recommended to the Commission for adoption draft resolution IX,[137] which contained recommendations to the Economic and Social Council to request the Special Rapporteur to supplement expeditiously her final report, taking into account the basic views expressed in the Sub-Commission and the Commission; and to request the Sub-Commission to establish at its next session a Sessional Working Group for a proper examination of the draft body of principles, guidelines, and guarantees, and to submit the revised final report to the Commission at its fortieth session.

The General Assembly also examined the question of human rights and scientific and technological developments at its thirty-seventh session. In its resolution 37/188 of 17 December 1982, it urged the Commission, and through it the Sub-Commission, to continue and expedite their consideration of the question of persons detained on the grounds of mental ill-health, with a view to the Commission's submitting its views and recommendations to the General Assembly at its thirty-ninth session, through the Economic and Social Council.

By its resolution 37/189A of 18 December 1982, the Assembly again called all States, appropriate organs of the United Nations, specialized agencies, and organizations concerned to take the necessary measures to ensure that the results of scientific and technological progress are used exclusively in the interests of international peace, for the benefit of mankind for promoting and encouraging respect for human rights and fundamental freedoms. It requested the Commission in its future activities to stress the need to ensure the right of everyone to life, liberty and security of person, and to live in peace.

By its resolution 37/189B of the same date, the Assembly, noting with satisfaction the report of the Secretary-General on human rights and scientific and technological developments,[138] invited those Member States, specialized agencies and other organizations of the United Nations system that had not yet done so to submit information on the implementation of the Declaration on the Use of Scientific and Technological Progress in the Interests of Peace and for the Benefit of Mankind.

## U. The realization of economic, social and cultural rights

### 1. RIGHT TO DEVELOPMENT

The Working Group of Governmental Experts on the Right to Development held its third session in Geneva from 18 to 22 January 1982.

By its resolution 1982/17 of 9 March 1982[139] the Commission commended the report of the Working Group[140] and decided to reconvene the Working Group in order to allow it to elaborate a draft declaration on the right to development; it

---

[136] E/CN.4/Sub.2/1982/17.

[137] E/CN.4/1983/4, E/CN.4/Sub.2/1982/43, chap. I A.

[138] A/37/330 and Add.1.

[139] E/1982/12, chap. XXVI A.

[140] E/CN.4/1489.

requested the Group to hold two meetings of two weeks each in Geneva, the first in June/July 1982, and the second in September/October 1982. The Commission also took note of the second part of the study prepared by the Secretary-General on the regional and national dimensions of the right to development as a human right.[141]

By its decision 1982/141 of 17 May 1982, the Economic and Social Council approved the Commission's request to the Working Group to hold two meetings in Geneva in 1982. Pursuant to this decision, the Working Group held its fourth session from 28 June to 9 July 1982 and its fifth session from 22 November to 3 December 1982 in Geneva.

At its thirty-fifth session, the Sub-Commission on Prevention of Discrimination and Protection of Minorities had before it a report by its Special Rapporteur entitled "Study of the New International Economic Order and the Promotion of Human Rights".[142] By its resolution 1982/8 of 7 September 1982,[143] the Sub-Commission expressed its strong appreciation to the Special Rapporteur and requested him to continue his work with a view to submitting the second and last part of the report to the Sub-Commission at its next session.

By resolution 1982/6 of the same date,[144] the Sub-Commission emphasized the importance of promoting full respect for human rights by accelerating the development process together with measures designed to strengthen respect for the rule of law and to improve knowledge and understanding of the legal system.

By resolution 1982/7 also adopted on 7 September 1982,[145] the Sub-Commission recommended to the Commission for adoption draft resolution II,[146] by which the Commission would recommend to the Economic and Social Council that it authorize the Sub-Commission to entrust one of its members with the preparation of a study on the right to adequate food as a human right.

At its thirty-eighth session the General Assembly, in its resolution 37/199 of 18 December 1982, *inter alia*, requested the Commission on Human Rights to take the necessary measures to promote the right to development, taking into account the results of the Working Group of Governmental Experts on the Right to Development, and welcomed the decision of the Commission that the Group should continue its work with the aim of presenting as soon as possible a draft declaration on the right to development.

By its resolution 37/200 of the same date, the Assembly considered that efforts to promote and protect human rights at the international level should be accompanied by efforts to establish a new international economic order.

By its resolution 37/55 of 3 December 1982, the Assembly requested the Commission on Human Rights to consider at its next session the question of popular participation as an important factor in development and in the realization of human

---

[141] E/CN.4/1421.

[142] E/CN.4/Sub.2/1982/19/Rev.1 and Add.1.

[143] E/CN.4/1983/4, E/CN.4/Sub.2/1982/43, chap. XXI A.

[144] E/CN.4/Sub.2/1982/43, chap. XXI A.

[145] *Ibid.*

[146] *Ibid.*, chap. I A.

rights, and to submit to the Assembly, through the Economic and Social Council, appropriate suggestions for a more complete realization of human rights.

## 2. RIGHT TO EDUCATION

At its thirty-seventh session, the General Assembly had before it a report of the Director-General of the United Nations Educational, Scientific and Cultural Organization on the right to education.[147]

By its resolution 37/178 of 17 December 1982 the General Assembly, *inter alia*, again invited all States to consider the adoption of appropriate measures in order to ensure full implementation of the right to universal education; invited all specialized agencies to co-operate with UNESCO to ensure education a high priority in the implementation of various programmes and projects within the framework of the International Development Strategy for the Third United Nations Development Decade; invited UNESCO to continue its intensive efforts for the promotion at the universal level of the right to education and to inform the Assembly of the progress achieved in this field.

## V. Further promotion and encouragement of human rights and fundamental freedoms

### 1. PROGRAMME AND METHODS OF WORK OF THE COMMISSION AND ITS SUB-COMMISSION

At its thirty-eighth session, the Commission on Human Rights established an informal open-ended Working Group to continue the overall analysis on the further promotion and encouragement of human rights and fundamental freedoms. The Working Group concentrated its discussions on the functioning and work methods of the Commission and submitted, in its report to the Commission,[148] a number of proposals.

In its resolution 1982/40 of 11 March 1982,[149] the Commission took note with satisfaction of the report of the Working Group and decided, *inter alia*, to recommend to the Economic and Social Council to consider the possibility of rescheduling the annual session of the Commission and the Sub-Commission; to establish at its next session an informal group of ten to consider the possibility of rationalizing its agenda for the fortieth session; to consider at its next session the elaboration of its programme and methods of work; to establish at that session an open-ended Working Group to continue the ongoing work on overall analysis.

By its decision 1982/145 of 7 May 1982, the Economic and Social Council decided to consider the question of possible rescheduling of the Commission's annual session at its second regular session of 1982.

---

[147] A/37/521.

[148] E/1982/12/Add.1, E/CN.4/1982/30/Add.1 B.

[149] E/1982/12, chap. XXVI A.

During its thirty-eighth session, the Commission also discussed the question of the terms of reference and activities of the Sub-Commission on Prevention of Discrimination and Protection of Minorities. By resolution 1982/23 adopted on 10 March 1982,[150] the Commission called upon the Sub-Commission to be guided in the fulfilment of its functions and duties by the relevant documents and resolutions of the Commission, the Economic and Social Council, and the Assembly, defining the terms of reference of the Sub-Commission; to take into account the comments and suggestions made during the consideration of its report by the Commission and to attach in the future a complete list of the studies under preparation; the Commission further considered that due attention must be paid to the necessity of choosing as an alternate a person with the requisite expertise and qualifications and that it must be kept in mind that the appointment of a Government official as an alternate may sometimes not be in keeping with the character of the Sub-Commission, as a body composed of experts.

## 2. CREATION OF A POST OF HIGH COMMISSIONER FOR HUMAN RIGHTS

By its resolution 1982/22 of 10 March 1982,[151] the Commission requested the Sub-Commission to formulate a first study on possible terms of reference for the mandate of a High Commissioner for Human Rights and to submit its proposals to the Commission at its next session. By its resolution 1982/40 of 11 March 1982,[152] it decided to inform the Assembly, through the Economic and Social Council, that it intended to keep under continued consideration the proposal for the creation of a post of a United Nations High Commissioner for Human Rights.

At its thirty-fifth session, the Sub-Commission, upon its decision 1982/5 of 23 August 1982,[153] set up an informal Working Group to prepare a report on the question of possible terms of reference for the mandate of a High Commissioner for Human Rights. The Group submitted its report[154] to the Sub-Commission. By its resolution 1982/27 of 10 September 1982,[155] the Sub-Commission submitted to the Commission on Human Rights a number of proposals concerning the possible terms of reference for the mandate of a High Commissioner for Human Rights.

At its thirty-seventh session the General Assembly, in its resolution 37/200 of 18 December 1982, *inter alia*, requested the Commission at its thirty-ninth session to continue its efforts to improve the capacity of the United Nations system to take urgent action in cases of serious violations of human rights, bearing in mind the proposals submitted by the Sub-Commission on possible terms of reference for the draft mandate of a High Commissioner for Human Rights.

---

[150] *Ibid.*

[151] *Ibid.*

[152] *Ibid.*

[153] E/CN.4/1983/4, E/CN.4/Sub.2/1982/43, chap. XXI B.

[154] E/CN.4/Sub.2/1982/36.

[155] E/CN.4/1983/4, E/CN.4/Sub.2/1982/43, chap. XXI A.

### 3. PUBLIC INFORMATION ACTIVITIES IN THE FIELD OF HUMAN RIGHTS

At its thirty-eighth session, the Commission on Human Rights had before it a report by the Secretary-General concerning stimulation of public interest in the promotion and protection of human rights.[156]

In its resolution 1982/42 of 11 March 1982,[157] the Commission, *inter alia*, invited the Secretary-General to give increased attention to the stimulation of public interest in the promotion and protection of human rights, particularly in the light of the commemoration in 1983 of the thirty-fifth anniversary of the Universal Declaration of Human Rights; welcomed the launching in the 1982-1983 biennium of the proposed dissemination programme covering international instruments on human rights; requested the Secretary-General to consider establishing, particularly in developing countries, small reference libraries containing material of scholarly and public interest in the field of human rights.

### 4. REGIONAL ARRANGEMENTS FOR THE PROMOTION OF HUMAN RIGHTS

In accordance with General Assembly resolution 36/154 of 16 December 1981, a Seminar on National, Local and Regional Arrangements for the Promotion and Protection of Human Rights in the Asian Region[158] was held at Colombo, Sri Lanka, from 21 June to 2 July 1982.

Among its various conclusions and recommendations, the seminar recommended that the United Nations be requested to contribute to the promotion of human rights through, *inter alia*, the carrying out of studies and research, the organization of seminars, symposia and conferences and the dissemination of information on human rights; that a programme for teaching, seminars, training and education in the field of human rights be developed for the Asian and Pacific region; that periodic meetings of representatives of Governments and national institutions in the field of human rights be held in the region; that a number of studies be undertaken.

In its resolution 37/171 of 17 December 1982, the General Assembly took note of the report of the seminar and requested the Secretary-General to transmit it to States Members of the Economic and Social Commission for Asia and the Pacific (ESCAP), to invite them to comment thereon and to submit the report of the seminar together with comments received thereon to the Commission at its fortieth session and to report through the Economic and Social Council to the General Assembly at its thirty-ninth session.

By its resolution 37/172 adopted on the same day, the Assembly noted with satisfaction the progress achieved so far in the promotion and protection of human rights at the regional level; it further commended the Organization of African Unity for its continuing efforts to promote respect for the guarantees and norms of human

---

[156] E/CN.4/1496.

[157] E/1982/12, chap. XXVI A.

[158] ST/HR/SER.A/12.

rights and fundamental freedoms and noted with interest the African Charter on Human and Peoples' Rights and the efforts to obtain its early entry into force; it also requested the Secretary-General to compile and update his reports on regional arrangements for the promotion and protection of human rights and to report to the General Assembly at its thirty-eighth session.

### 5. OTHER MEASURES FOR THE PROMOTION AND PROTECTION OF HUMAN RIGHTS

#### Equatorial Guinea

At its thirty-eighth session, the Commission on Human Rights had before it a report by the Secretary-General[159] in which the Commission was informed that on 19 August 1981 a copy of a draft plan of action for the restoration of human rights and fundamental freedoms in Equatorial Guinea had been submitted to the Government of Equatorial Guinea for its consideration and comments. By its resolution 1982/34 of 11 March 1982[160] the Commission took note of the report of the Secretary-General and recommended its draft resolution III[161] to the Economic and Social Council for adoption.

Upon this draft, further endorsed by Economic and Social Council resolution 1982/36 of 7 May 1982, the Council took note of the plan of action proposed by the Secretary-General; it requested the Secretary-General to discuss with the Government of Equatorial Guinea the role that the United Nations could play in the implementation of the plan of action, and to inform the Council at its second regular session of 1982 of the steps taken to implement the present resolution and to report further to the Commission on Human Rights at its thirty-ninth session.

On 27 July 1982 the representative of the Secretary-General informed the Council at its second regular session of steps taken in compliance with Council resolution 1982/36. He further mentioned the request of the President of Equatorial Guinea to the United Nations to provide the Government with two qualified international experts to assist the Equatorial Guinea National Commission in drafting a new Constitution; this request had been welcomed by the Secretary-General and two experts had been recruited. By its decision 1982/150, the Council took note of the oral report made by the representative of the Secretary-General.

#### Uganda

By its resolution 1982/37, adopted on 11 March 1982,[162] the Commission on Human Rights requested the Secretary-General rapidly to establish contacts with the Government of Uganda in order to provide, within the framework of the Programme of Advisory Services, all appropriate assistance to help the Government of Uganda to take measures to continue guaranteeing the enjoyment of human rights and fundamental freedoms; it also invited all States, specialized agencies and United Nations organs, as well as humanitarian and non-governmental organizations, to

---

[159] E/CN.4/1495.
[160] E/1982/12, chap. XXVI A.
[161] *Ibid.*, chap. I A.
[162] E/1982/12, chap. XXVI A.

lend their support and assistance to the Government of Uganda in its efforts to guarantee the enjoyment of human rights and fundamental freedoms. The Commission also recommended its draft decision 14[163] for adoption to the Economic and Social Council. This draft was further endorsed as Council decision 1982/132 of 7 May 1982, upon which the Council approved the Commission's decision to request the Secretary-General, in response to the interest expressed by the Government of Uganda, to provide consultative advisory services and other forms of appropriate assistance to help the Government of Uganda to take measures to continue guaranteeing the enjoyment of human rights and fundamental freedoms.

## W. Advisory services in the field of human rights

During 1982, a regional seminar was organized under the Advisory Services Programme in the field of human rights on "National, Local and Regional Arrangements for the Promotion and Protection of Human Rights in the Asian Region", and was held, at the invitation of the Government of Sri Lanka, at Colombo, from 21 June to 2 July 1982. The report of the seminar[164] was submitted to the General Assembly at its thirty-seventh session.[165]

In 1982, under the Programme of Advisory Services, 32 individual fellowships in the field of human rights were granted to nationals of various countries.

---

[163] *Ibid.*, chap. I B.
[164] ST/HR/SER.1/12.
[165] A/37/422.

# Section B. Specialized agencies

## A. Food and Agriculture Organization of the United Nations (FAO)

Since the submission in 1981 of document E/1981/22 to the Economic and Social Council under the International Covenant on Economic, Social and Cultural Rights, the main developments in FAO in the field of human rights have been in the area of rural women's rights.

As part of its mandate and as a follow-up to the World Conference on Agrarian Reform and Rural Development (WCARRD), FAO continues to give importance to the dignity and human rights of the rural population. The WCARRD Programme of Action adopted at the July 1979 Conference stressed that:

"National progress based on growth with equity and participation requires a redistribution of economic and political power, fuller integration of rural areas into national development efforts, with expanded opportunities of employment and income for rural people."

Within this context, Member Governments adopted the principle of women's participation and contribution on an equal basis with men and of sharing fully in improved conditions. The section on "The Integration of Women in Rural Development" of WCARRD Programme of Action emphasized that women should have equitable access to land, water, other natural resources, inputs and services and equal opportunity to develop and employ their skills. Particular emphasis was given to women's equal legal status and a request that Governments should "repeal those laws which discriminate against women in respect of rights of inheritance, ownership and control of property" and to "repeal laws and regulations which inhibit effective participation by women in economic transactions and in the planning, implementation and evaluation of rural development programmes".

FAO has been a supporter of the Convention on the Elimination of Discrimination against Women and originally requested a separate article related to rural women, which now stands as article 14 of the Convention. This Convention has an important link with human rights issues as it lays the foundation for Governments to review and revise legislation to advance the position and status of women.

## B. International Labour Organisation (ILO)

The following developments in the field of human rights can be mentioned as regards activities of the International Labour Organisation during 1982:

1. *General.* Most of the activities of the International Labour Organisation have a bearing on the recognition and promotion of human rights, as defined in the Universal Declaration of Human Rights.

2. *Adoption of international standards.*  At its 68th Session, 1982, the International Labour Conference adopted the following instruments:

Maintenance of Social Security Rights Convention, 1982 (No. 157);

Termination of Employment Convention, 1982 (No. 158);

Termination of Employment Recommendation, 1982 (No. 166).

The Conference also adopted a Protocol to the Plantations Convention, 1958 (No. 110).

3. *Ratification of conventions.*  During 1982, 66 ratifications of international labour conventions were registered bringing the total to 4,999 at 31 December 1982. At that date the numbers of ratifications of certain key conventions dealing with trade union rights, forced labour, equality and employment were as follows:

| Convention | Number of ratifications |
|---|---|
| Freedom of Association and Protection of the Right to Organise Convention, 1948 (No. 87) | 94 |
| Right to Organise and Collective Bargaining Convention, 1949 (No. 98) | 110 |
| Workers' Representatives Convention, 1971 (No. 135) | 38 |
| Rural Workers' Organisations Convention, 1975 (No. 141) | 22 |
| Labour Relations (Public Service) Convention, 1978 (No. 151) | 14 |
| Forced Labour Convention, 1930 (No. 29) | 125 |
| Abolition of Forced Labour Convention, 1957 (No. 105) | 107 |
| Equal Remuneration Convention, 1951 (No. 100) | 102 |
| Discrimination (Employment and Occupation) Convention, 1958 (No. 111) | 102 |
| Employment Policy Convention, 1964 (No. 122) | 69 |

4. *Committee of Experts on the Application of Conventions and Recommendations.*  The Committee of Experts held its 52nd Session in March 1982. Its main report, containing in particular comments arising out of the examination of reports on ratified conventions, was published as Report III (Part 4A) of the International Labour Conference, 68th Session. The Committee also made a general survey (Report III (Part 4B)) concerning the implementation of the Tripartite Consultation (International Labour Standards) Convention, 1976 (No. 144) and the Tripartite Consultation (Activities of the International Labour Organisation) Recommendation, 1976 (No. 152).

5. *Representations and complaints concerning the observance of ratified conventions.*

(*a*) The Governing Body examined a representation presented by the International Organisation of Employers under Article 24 of the ILO Constitution concerning the observance by Nicaragua of the Abolition of Forced Labour Convention, 1957 (No. 105) and approved conclusions on the case in November 1982—see ILO *Official Bulletin*, vol. LXVI, 1983, Series B, No. 1, pp. 153 to 169.

(*b*) The Governing Body received a representation by the Norwegian Federation of Trade Unions concerning the observance by Norway of the Discrimination (Employment and Occupation) Convention, 1958 (No. 111), and in June 1982 established a committee to examine this representation.

(c) A representation by the Norwegian Federation of Trade Unions concerning the observance by Turkey of the Right of Association (Agriculture) Convention, 1921 (No. 11) and the Right to Organise and Collective Bargaining Convention, 1949 (No. 98), received in June 1982, was referred to the Committee on Freedom of Association and has been examined in connection with a series of complaints pending before that Committee.

(d) In March 1982 the Governing Body appointed a Commission of Inquiry to examine complaints filed by several workers' delegates to the International Labour Conference in 1981 concerning the observance by the Dominican Republic and Haiti of several conventions relating to forced labour, freedom of association and collective bargaining in relation to the employment of Haitian workers on the sugar plantations of the Dominican Republic.

(e) During the session of the International Labour Conference, in June 1982, two workers' delegates filed a complaint alleging non-observance by Poland of the Freedom of Association and Protection of the Right to Organise Convention, 1948 (No. 87) and the Right to Organise and Collective Bargaining Convention, 1949 (No. 98). The Governing Body referred this complaint to the Committee on Freedom of Association for examination in the context of the case concerning Poland already before that Committee.

6. *Governing Body Committee on Freedom of Association.* This Committee held three meetings in 1982 and submitted eight reports to the Governing Body containing conclusions in 137 cases—see 214th to 221st reports, ILO *Official Bulletin*, vol. LXV, 1982, Series B, Nos. 1 to 3. A mission to Poland was carried out by a representative of the Director-General in May 1982, just before the Committee's examination of the case concerning that country in the same month. Another mission was carried out to Turkey in July 1982, the report on which was considered by the Committee in November 1982.

7. *Activities concerning* apartheid *and promotion of equality in southern Africa.* A *Special Report on the Application of the Declaration concerning the Policy of* Apartheid *in South Africa*, as updated by the International Labour Conference in 1981, was presented to the Conference at its 68th Session (June 1982). In addition to reviewing developments within South Africa and at the international level, it included information on action against *apartheid* taken by governments and by employers' and workers' organisations. The report was examined by the newly created Conference Committee on *Apartheid*, which adopted conclusions as a basis for further action by the ILO—see ILO *Official Bulletin*, vol. LXV, 1982, Series A, No. 2, pp. 91-92. The Organisation intensified its activities of assistance to front-line States, national liberation movements, and black workers and their trade unions in South Africa. Projects of assistance were approved involving expenditure of nearly $1.5 million, including vocational rehabilitation of war victims and other disabled persons, a training workshop on rural development options for Namibia, workers' education assistance to migrant workers in southern Africa, training in employment and developing planning, and development of informal sector activities in front-line States and other countries neighbouring upon South Africa.

8. *Situation of workers of the Arab territories occupied by Israel.* A further mission by representatives of the Director-General was carried out in February 1982 to examine the situation of workers of the Arab occupied territories. Contacts

were also established with neighbouring countries and Palestinian representatives. The report on these missions was included in the report of the Director-General presented to the International Labour Conference at its 68th Session.

## C.  United Nations Educational, Scientific and Cultural Organization (UNESCO)

As regards UNESCO activities in the field of human rights during the year 1982, mention can be made of the following developments:

### 1. EXAMINATION OF CASES AND QUESTIONS CONCERNING THE EXERCISE OF HUMAN RIGHTS COMING WITHIN UNESCO'S COMPETENCE

The Committee on Conventions and Recommendations met in private sessions at UNESCO Headquarters from 21 April to 3 May and 30 August to 7 September 1982 in order to examine communications which had been transmitted to it in accordance with decision 104 EX/3.3 of the Executive Board.

At its spring session, the Committee was seized with 58 communications of which 54 were examined from the standpoint of their admissibility and 4 were examined as to their substance. Of the 54 communications in the first category, six were declared admissible, 13 were declared inadmissible, six were struck out from the list since they were considered by the Committee as having been settled and one was forwarded to another UN organization for appropriate action. The examination of 32 communications was suspended. The Committee presented its report to the Executive Board at its 114th session.

At its autum session, the Committee had before it 55 communications of which 45 were examined as to their admissibility. Out of these 55 communications, one was declared admissible, 12 were declared inadmissible, the examination of 37 communications was suspended, 4 communications were struck out from the list since they were considered as having been settled, and 1 communication concerning a missing person was transmitted to the Working Group on Enforced or Involuntary Disappearances, set up by the United Nations Commission on Human Rights. The Committee presented its report on its examination of these communications to the Executive Board at its 115th session. Due to the urgent nature of one communication, the Committee examined it at an extraordinary session held on 3 December 1982.

### 2. RESPECT FOR HUMAN RIGHTS: RESEARCH INTO THE CAUSES OF HUMAN RIGHTS VIOLATIONS

#### (a) *Implementation of the Declaration on Race and Racial Prejudice*

The purpose of the advisory meeting on the preparation of the report by the Director-General on the world situation in the fields covered by the Declaration on Race and Racial Prejudice (Lisbon, 14-17 June 1982) was to consider the best methods to be followed in preparing the report requested of the Director-General by the General Conference in paragraph 2 of the resolution on the implementation of the Declaration on Race and Racial Prejudice, adopted in 1978. It was attended by 12 participants, 23 observers from Member States and 19 observers from nongovernmental organizations, and enabled a reference framework to be drawn up for the preparation of the report which the Director-General is to submit to the General Conference at its twenty-second session. The Director-General transmitted this reference framework to the 158 Member States of UNESCO as an annex to a circular letter dated 12 October 1982, inviting them to forward their replies to him not later than 1 March 1983. On the basis of the information received, the Director-General drew up his second "Report on the world situation in the fields covered by the Declaration on Race and Racial Prejudice and recommendations designed to promote the implementation of the Declaration" (document 22 C/86 and 22 C/86 Add.).

(b) *Studies on the various forms of human rights violations*

On the basis of historical, legal, economic and sociological studies, the 14 participants and 16 representatives or observers of intergovernmental organizations and non-governmental organizations who attended the Meeting of Experts on the Role of Private Authorities as Limiting Factors for Human Rights (Algiers, 5-8 December 1982) concluded, *inter alia*, that certain private authorities, and particularly transnational companies, could contribute to a limitation of the rights of the individual and of peoples in both their national and their international dimensions. The meeting's working documents and final report were reproduced and distributed to interested institutions.

### 3. TRAINING AND TEACHING IN THE FIELD OF HUMAN RIGHTS

(a) *Implementation of the Plan for the Development of Human Rights Teaching*

(i) *Development of national, regional and international institutions for teaching and research relating to human rights*

To encourage the establishment of institutions capable of sustained teaching and research activities relating to human rights, UNESCO has provided assistance for several international or regional meetings of human rights experts, to prepare for the establishment of institutional networks.

In March 1982, a regional Seminar on Human Rights in African Cultural Traditions was organized with the assistance of UNESCO, in conjunction with the Institute of Human Rights and Peace in Dakar, Senegal. This seminar was particularly important in that it helped identify priorities in human rights teaching and research in Africa. In October 1982, UNESCO, under contract with the Association of Young African Lawyers, organized in Lomé (Togo) a regional meeting on human rights within the African tradition.

In October 1982, in conjunction with the United Nations University and the Indian Centre for Human Rights Education and Research, UNESCO organized a regional seminar in New Delhi on human rights in Asia. While emphasizing the universal nature of human rights, the seminar sought to establish research programmes which would meet the particular needs of the region, and to encourage co-operation in the circulation and exchange of information.

UNESCO contributed to the meeting on the co-ordination of information in Latin America, held in Quito, Ecuador, from 17 to 20 June 1982, organized by the Human Rights International Documentation System (HURIDOCS) and the Latin American Association for Human Rights (ALDHU). This meeting was attended by representatives from 50 organizations that specialize in the protection and promotion of human rights. It outlined the methods and basis for a common information and documentation system and for the development of a network of specialized institutions in this field in Latin America.

Since the Plan for the Development of Human Rights Teaching was drawn up, regular exchanges of information have taken place at periodic meetings between the non-governmental organizations and the Secretariat. In March 1982, the Director-General approved the establishment of a joint UNESCO/NGO Committee for the promotion of human rights teaching. The aim of this Committee is to ensure better co-ordination of the activities of NGO's in this field and to provide for regular exchanges of information between the Secretariat and the NGOs in their respective fields of competence in order to achieve effective implementation of the Plan.

(ii) *Meeting of Experts on the Teaching of Human Rights*

A meeting was held in Strasbourg (France), from 26 to 30 July 1982, on the teaching of human rights. It was called by UNESCO and organized in conjunction with the International Institute of Human Rights, Strasbourg:

To consider ways and means of strengthening national, regional and international infrastructures for the development of human rights teaching and research;

To study various approaches to human rights teaching and research in different regions of the world;

To examine the advisability of establishing an association of human rights teachers.

Those attending the meeting included university teachers, researchers and professionals specializing in human rights, representatives and observers from international, governmental and non-governmental organizations concerned with the promotion of human rights, and observers from UNESCO Member States.

The main recommendations of the Strasbourg meeting were that:

Human rights teaching should be based on and supported by research. Such research should be multidisciplinary. It should be conducive to a better understanding of the factors that lead to the violation of human rights, and conducive to the definition of the institutional policies and procedures that are needed to ensure those rights;

Research and teaching on matters of crucial importance for human rights should be encouraged throughout the international community, particularly on the following subjects: *apartheid* and the consequences of colonialism, neo-colonialism and racism of all kinds; International and internal armed conflict and the arms race, which have massive socio-economic repercussions and threaten the survival of humanity; torture, disappearances, State and all other terrorism, and executions, particularly of an arbitrary or summary character; poverty or starvation; the continuing flow of refugees; the protection of minorities; the right to liberty and security of the person; the right to fair administration of justice; freedom of thought, conscience and religion.

(b) *Resolution 13.5 adopted by the General Conference at its 22nd session, entitled "Plan for the Development of Human Rights Teaching"*

"*The General Conference,*

"*Recalling* that, under the terms of its Constitution, the purpose of UNESCO is 'to contribute to peace and security by promoting collaboration among the nations through education, science and culture in order to further universal respect for justice, for the rule of law and for the human rights and fundamental freedoms which are affirmed for the peoples of the world, without discrimination of race, sex, language or religion, by the Charter of the United Nations',

"*Considering* that the Plan for the Development of Human Rights Teaching is one of UNESCO's major contributions to the promotion of human rights, in its fields of competence, and that education, teaching and access to information are of particular importance in the promotion of human rights and the rights of peoples,

"*Recalling* resolutions 3/03 and 3/04 which it adopted at its twenty-first session and resolution 2/13 adopted at its fourth extraordinary session,

"*Recalling* Recommendation No. 5 on the teaching of human rights adopted by the Intergovernmental Conference on Education for International Understanding, Co-operation and Peace and Education relating to Human Rights and Fundamental Freedoms, with a View to Developing a Climate of Opinion Favourable to the Strengthening of Security and Disarmament (Paris 1983),

"*Congratulating* the Director-General on the effectiveness with which he has so far implemented the Plan for the Development of Human Rights Teaching,

"1. *Invites* Member States to increase their efforts to implement teaching, research and information and exchanges of experience and documentation in the field of human rights, at the national, regional and interregional levels;

"2. *Further invites* Member States to assist in the implementation of the Plan through increased contributions to the Voluntary Fund for the Development of Knowledge of Human Rights through Teaching and Information;

"3. *Invites* the Director-General to intensify his efforts to achieve the implementation of the Plan through effective co-operation and co-ordination with scientific institutions and with international governmental and non-governmental organizations and through increased research relating to human rights, both within individual disciplines and at the multidisciplinary level, taking into account the need to co-ordinate effectively the various efforts being made by scientific institutions in connection with training, research and publications regarding human rights;

"4. *Further invites* the Director-General to give particular attention, within the framework of the Programme and Budget for 1984-1985, to the following activities, with a view to the effective implementation of the Plan for the Development of Human Rights Teaching:

"(*a*)   The intensification of co-operation with a view to strengthening regional and national institutions which contribute to human rights training and research;

"(*b*)   The strengthening of co-operation with non-governmental organizations and professional associations in order to promote training activities and the spread of information in the field of human rights, in particular by fostering the establishment of networks for exchanges of information and documentation in that field;

"(*c*)   The extension of interdisciplinary research on the causes and consequences of violations of human rights, fundamental freedoms and the rights of peoples;

"(*d*)   Continued publication and distribution of UNESCO's bulletin entitled Human Rights Teaching, in order to encourage research, teaching and co-ordination by better circulation of the findings of research into human rights, fundamental freedoms and the rights of peoples;

"5.   *Invites* the Director-General, lastly:

"(*a*)   To devote, in the preparation of the Draft Programme and Budget for 1986-1987, particular attention to the implementation of the Plan and to UNESCO's activities in the field of human rights teaching;

"(*b*)   To organize, within the limits of existing budgetary resources and if possible in 1984, a meeting to examine the Plan for the Development of Human Rights Teaching and the progress made in implementing it."

In application of the above resolution concerning the Plan for the Development of Human Rights Teaching, the implementation of the Plan will continue. In this connection, encouragement will be given to the activities of Member States, national commissions, and non-governmental organizations for the establishment and extension of international, regional or national documentation services and networks for the exchange of information and experience. Encouragement will also be given to the establishment and development of research and training institutions particularly as regards the organization of training courses and seminars and production of teaching materials.

## 4.   TEACHING OF HUMAN RIGHTS AT PRIMARY AND SECONDARY SCHOOL LEVEL

### Associated Schools Project in Education for International Co-operation and Peace

Ever since it was set up in 1953, the subject of human rights has been one of the main themes of study for institutions taking part in the Associated Schools Project. At the close of 1982, there were over 1,629 schools at different levels of education affiliated to the Project in 80 Member States. The type of teaching methods and techniques utilized to ensure the inclusion of human rights in the curriculum vary according to the various levels of education. For example, at the pre-school and primary levels of education, a wide range of socio-effective methods are introduced with a view to promoting respect for others, and notions of duties and responsibilities. At the secondary school level, a more cognitive approach is often used in learning about human rights issues, international instruments such as the Universal Declaration of Human Rights, the UNESCO Recommendation concerning Education for International Understanding, Co-operation and Peace and Education relating to Human Rights and Fundamental Freedoms, etc. Associated Schools often undertake specific human rights activities in connection with Human Rights Day (10 December), United Nations Day (24 October), as well as other international days.

The importance of teaching human rights was underlined at two major regional seminars of Associated School national co-ordinators in Latin America (Bucaramanga, Colombia, 27 to 30 September 1982) and in Europe (Mauerbach, Austria, 10 to 13 May 1982).

At the close of 1981, an experimental interregional project on the study of contemporary world problems at the secondary school level of education was launched, of which human rights was one of the three issues retained. Throughout 1982, Associated Schools in nine Member States (Asia: India, Philippines and Thailand; Europe; Czechoslovakia, Germany, Federal Republic of, and United Kingdom; and Latin America: Argentina, Chile and Colombia) undertook experimental activities on human rights.

With a view to examine the role of pre-school education in furthering international understanding, peace and human rights an international consultation was held in co-operation with the World Organization for Early Childhood Education in Sèvres, France, in May 1982.

At the close of the year there were 1,734 institutions taking part in the Associated Schools Project in 85 Member States. One of the four main areas of study for Associated Schools is human rights and throughout the year, a wide range of activities were carried out in different parts of the world.

## 5. UNESCO's Programme for the Struggle against *Apartheid*

At its Fourth Extraordinary Session in 1982, the General Conference of UNESCO adopted the Second Medium Term Plan 1984 to 1989. Within the Second Medium Term Plan, one major programme is devoted to the Elimination of Prejudice, Intolerance, Racism and *Apartheid* and includes a specific programme on the Struggle against *Apartheid*. Within the framework of this programme, UNESCO is continuing its programme of scientific research on the causes and manifestations of *apartheid* and on the social and economic history of southern Africa, including focus on pre-colonial State formation.

## 6. Public information activities

In 1982, the "Youth Day for Human Rights" organized by UNESCO at its Paris Headquarters, was devoted to the problems of the aging and the rights of the elderly. It was attended by more than 400 young people aged from 12 to 18, from several French and international educational establishments.

## D. World Health Organization (WHO)

The question of child labour and health continues to be of concern to WHO. Studies have been undertaken in 1982 in two countries and two national seminars have been organized. WHO is also collaborating actively with the International Society for the Prevention of Child Abuse and Neglect (ISPCAN).

Following a recommendation of the International Conference on *Apartheid* and Health organized by WHO in 1981, a joint WHO/National Liberation Movement's Action Group studied ways and means of helping the national liberation movements and the refugee victims of *apartheid*.

In resolution A/RES/37/194 the thirty-seventh session of the General Assembly in 1982 adopted the Principles of Medical Ethics relevant to the role of health personnel, particularly physicians, in the protection of prisoners and detainees against torture and other cruel, inhuman or degrading treatment or punishment. These principles had been prepared by WHO in collaboration with the Council for International Organizations of Medical Sciences. They were brought to the attention of all Member Governments, as well as all non-governmental organizations concerned.

WHO is showing great and increasing concern about migrants' health and pays great attention to the programme of workers' health. Several resolutions of the World Health Assembly highlight the need for comprehensive health programmes for workers, and for special attention to vulnerable groups of workers or to those to whom health services are not available. Studies of health problems of migrant workers have been included in the global medium-term programme for workers' health developed according to the Seventh General Programme of Work covering the period 1984-1989.

# ANNEX

# Additional guidelines for the implementation of article 7 of the International Convention on the Elimination of All Forms of Racial Discrimination,
## as contained in decision 2 (XXV) adopted by the Committee on the Elimination of Racial Discrimination at its 571st meeting of 17 March 1982

*The Committee on the Elimination of Racial Discrimination,*

*Recalling* its revised general guidelines concerning the form and contents of reports relating to article 7 of the Convention (CERD/C/70) as well as its General Recommendation V adopted on 13 April 1977,

*Having considered* the various proposals, particularly those submitted by the United Nations Educational, Scientific and Cultural Organization in document CERD/C/69/Add.1,

*Wishes* to draw the attention of the States parties to the following suggestions:

1. The reports should provide as much information as possible on each of the main subjects mentioned in article 7 under the following separate headings:

(1) Education and teaching,

(2) Culture,

(3) Information.

2. Within these broad parameters, the information provided should reflect the measures taken by the States parties:

(*a*) To combat prejudices which lead to racial discrimination,

(*b*) To promote understanding, tolerance and friendship among nations and racial or ethnic groups.

## I. *Education and teaching*

3. This part should describe legislative and administrative measures, including some general information on the educational system, taken in the field of education and teaching to combat racial prejudices which lead to racial discrimination.

4. It should indicate whether any steps have been taken to include in school curricula and in the training of teachers and other professionals, programmes and subjects to help promote human rights issues which would lead to better understanding, tolerance and friendship among nations and racial or ethnic groups.

5.   It should also provide information on whether the purposes and principles of the instruments mentioned in the Committee's general guidelines (CERD/C/70, art. 7, letter C) are included in education and teaching.

## II. *Culture*

6.   Information should be provided in this part of the report on the role of institutions or associations working to develop national culture and traditions, to combat racial prejudices and to promote intra-national and intra-cultural understanding, tolerance and friendship among nations and racial or ethnic groups.

7.   Information should also be included on the work of solidarity committees or United Nations associations to combat racism and racial discrimination and the observance by States parties of Human Rights Days or campaigns against racism and *apartheid*.

## III. *Information*

8.   This part should provide information:

(*a*)   On the role of State media in the dissemination of information to combat racial prejudices which lead to racial discrimination and to inculcate better understanding of the purposes and principles of the above-mentioned instruments;

(*b*)   On the role of the mass information media, i.e. the press, radio and television, in the publicizing of human rights and disseminating information on the purposes and principles of the above-mentioned human rights instruments.

Printed at United Nations, Geneva     03000P     United Nations publication
GE.88-17790     Sales No. E.88.XIV.6
October 1989–3,795

ISBN 92-1-154071-2
ISSN 0251-6519